Théophile Gautier
A Romantic Critic of the Visual Arts

THÉOPHILE GAUTIER

A Romantic Critic
of the Visual Arts

ROBERT SNELL

CLARENDON PRESS · OXFORD

1982

Oxford University Press, Walton Street, Oxford OX2 6DP
London Glasgow New York Toronto
Delhi Bombay Calcutta Madras Karachi
Kuala Lumpur Singapore Hong Kong Tokyo
Nairobi Dar es Salaam Cape Town
Melbourne Auckland
and associate companies in
Beirut Berlin Ibadan Mexico City

Published in the United States by
Oxford University Press, New York

British Library Cataloguing in Publication Data

Snell, Robert
  Théophile Gautier.
  1. Art, French
  709'.44   N6847   80-42257

  ISBN 0-19-815768-1

Typeset by Macmillan India Ltd., Bangalore
Printed in Hong Kong

TO MY PARENTS

Preface

The poet and novelist Théophile Gautier remains only imperfectly known as an art critic. Yet his criticism is of undeniable importance and value. It spans a period from around 1830 to 1872, a period of extraordinary and unprecedented artistic activity in France, and it covers this period almost week by week; it is the work of a highly accomplished man of letters who displayed an intense and enlightened sympathy for visual artists, and who for most of his career stood at the very centre of Parisian artistic and literary life. As such, it constitutes a unique document; it deserves closer attention for its own sake and a more generous treatment, and its qualities wider recognition than they have up to now received.

Gautier was a towering representative of a particularly Romantic state of mind and sensibility, and in order to explore and to come to some realistic understanding of this, a dual effort is necessary: to try to arrive at an inside view of the man, to maintain a sympathetic alertness to his aims and paint a coherent picture of his world-view; at the same time, to achieve a degree of historical perspective, an awareness, from the outside, of the influences and tensions which were to direct and find themselves reflected in his vision. The relationship between his quintessentially Romantic viewpoint, and the changeable cultural climate of his age, is the key to the narrative of Gautier's career.

His observations and reactions can sometimes seem contradictory, disingenuous, or, in the light of hindsight, simply off the mark; but if we occasionally find ourselves unresponsive to Gautier's critical prose, the phenomenon of his massive success with a nineteenth-century public cannot be ignored. It is easy to condemn him, for example, for his failure to react favourably to Manet; but a fuller awareness of Gautier's standpoint, as he lived it, and of the particular

expectations which his background and circumstances in-
stilled in him and others of his generation, might help us,
indirectly, to more complete perceptions of Manet's impact,
and provide us with first-hand insights into aspects of
nineteenth-century taste itself – such, ultimately, should be
the value of a study which is specifically on Gautier to other
students of the nineteenth century. Without this emphasis, a
study of this kind is in danger of ending merely as an
unquestioning reiteration of views which have proved acceptable to the twentieth century.

An effort of the imagination, and a willingness temporarily
to suspend judgement, constitute an approach which, after
all, Gautier would have recommended himself; we might
even, in the process of assessing Gautier, be led to a
recognition of the relativity of some of our own habitual
responses and inherited preferences, and to a healthy ques-
tioning or to a more informed, more convinced affirmation of
them – for this, surely, should be much of the value of reading
a critic of the past at all.

The translations are, with a few acknowledged exceptions,
my own, and I must assume sole responsibility for them; the
punctuation of the original quotations has been altered here
and there for the sake of clarity. In order to retain an idea of
the flavour of the French prose, some selected passages have
been reprinted in an appendix; an asterix in the text refers to a
passage which is to be found in the original in the appendix.
Apart from the translation of quotations, and some essential
editing and rewriting, the form of the present work is that in
which it was submitted, in 1978, as a Ph.D thesis for the
University of London. I am indebted to the University's
Central Research Fund and to the Graves Fund of the
Courtauld Institute for financial assistance, and to the
Department of Education and Science, and acknowledge
the help of these bodies. Thanks are also due to numerous
members of staff at the British Museum, the British Library
Newspaper Library in Colindale, the University of London
Library, and the Bibliothèque Nationale; among friends who
have helped with all kinds of encouragement and stimulus
Kevin Mangan, Christopher Newall, Dr Sandra Freeman,
Terry Wood, and Linda King deserve special thanks. I am

particularly grateful to Helen Cavanagh, Mrs Henry Rockwell, and Mary Barnes for their care and concern in preparing successive typescripts, to Professor John Weightman of Westfield College, University of London, for kindly and invaluable criticism, and to the late Keith Roberts, for what I have since learned was characteristic of him: real help and encouragement offered with infectious enthusiasm.

Finally I owe a great debt of gratitude and affection to Nona Shepphard, for much wise advice and for all her constructive interest and good humour. But my largest debt of all is to my supervisor at the Courtauld Institute, Dr Anita Brookner, the vitality of whose teaching has been of inestimable value, and whose ever generous help it is a pleasure to acknowledge here.

Contents

List of Plates

(*between pages 144 and 145*)

Abbreviations

ABC du Salon de 1861	Gautier, *Abécédaire du Salon de 1861*
BA en E	Gautier, *Les Beaux-Arts en Europe*
H du r	Gautier, *Histoire du romantisme. Notices romantiques . . .*
J des G	*Journal des Goncourt*
J off	*Le Journal officiel*
Mon	*Le Moniteur universel*

Introduction

'Gautier, all his features sunken and heavy, the lines buried in flesh, a slumber of the physiognomy, an intelligence stranded in a barrel of matter, the lassitude of a hippopotamus, intermittent comprehension: deaf to ideas, suffering from aural hallucinations, listening to something behind him when you address him to his face.'[1] (*plate 1*)

Caught by the Goncourt brothers at the offices of *L'Artiste* and impaled in their collection on January 3 1857, this unlikely butterfly is not immediately recognizable as the kin of Whistler's delicate creature in yellow and white. Is this the 'parfait magicien ès lettres françaises', the 'poète impeccable' to whom Baudelaire dedicated *Les Fleurs du mal* in the same year? The Goncourts' description hardly corresponds to our image of Théophile Gautier the ardent partisan of Romanticism, with his long flowing locks, flamboyantly flared jacket, and red doublet; nor does it sound like the serene poet of Art for Art's Sake, whose spirit floats on winged verse towards the Ideal.

If Gautier is remembered by posterity as a fashionable butterfly flitting from phrase to perfumed phrase, he occupied most of his writing life in the more mundane role of professional journalist. He was no doubt preparing an article to appear in the next day's edition of *L'Artiste* when the Goncourts walked into the editorial offices. For nearly forty years Gautier wrote regular art criticism, as well as literary, theatre, opera, and music criticism, not, finally, for his personal satisfaction as a poet or as an amusing literary sideline, but in order to provide a steady income for himself and his family. In 1857 he was one of *L'Artiste*'s editors; his career as a journalist had started seriously twenty-one years earlier, in 1836, when he had entered the newspaper world through the columns of *La Presse*. It was to continue for another fifteen years, until a few months before his death in

1872 at the age of sixty-one. A glance through the Vicomte Spoelberch de Lovenjoul's massive *Histoire des œuvres de Théophile Gautier* will show that a very large part of his literary output is accounted for by journalism; most of his criticism is still only to be read in newspaper libraries, in the original newspapers, numerous periodicals, and reviews to which he contributed.

Gautier would have preferred to be remembered for a few immaculate lines of verse or for his red waistcoat, rather than for his features, 'sunken and heavy', at the age of forty-six. He would readily have blamed journalism for the face the Goncourts described; their diary in the 1850s and '60s contains frequent transcriptions of Gautier's weary laments about his profession. Writing bores him, and always has done, he complains, and in an outburst of frustration for the eager brothers to relish, refers to his writing desk as a torturer's rack. His conversation, as the Goncourts recorded it, was rich in irony and hyperbole; yet he was not exaggerating much when he told them, in his office at *L'Artiste*, that he wrote as steadily as a public scribe.[2]

The experience of reading Gautier's immense output as an art critic can well be described in similar terms to those used by the Goncourts in their sketch of his physical presence. A heavy weariness underlies much of his later writing, the 'hippopotamus's lassitude' that the Goncourts read in his posture. It is partly concealed by the ironical turn of mind he displayed in his conversation, although in his day-to-day writing his sense of irony is necessarily less monstrous than monotonous. One must expect to read the same witty paradox or fine, highly coloured descriptive phrase several times over, and suffer consequent disillusionment; by its very nature, the text is repetitive, and often inconsistent. It is a 'barrel of matter' like an extension of its author's person, in which intelligence must somewhere be hidden: within its bulk it must contain real insights into Gautier's most cherished feelings about art, or offer glimpses of the precise workings of a critical and creative mind. Yet reading his criticism sometimes produces the uncomfortable feeling that Gautier was away doing something else when it was written, that his articles regularly and dutifully wrote themselves in time for going to press. The Goncourts were struck by the intermittence of his comprehension and his 'aural hallucinations'; if he seemed partly absent from his own earth-bound body, he is certainly elusive in his prose. Was this facility for making himself disappear part of what Baudelaire meant when he called him a 'perfect magician'? In his conversation with the Goncourts in January 1857, Gautier chose to liken himself to another figure from the world of popular entertainment: 'I am a man of letters, I ought to know my job. With a sheet of paper in front of me, I am like a clown on the springboard . . .'[3] He knew his job so well that he could do it with his eyes shut. 'I don't go fast . . . but I keep going, because, you see, I'm not after the best. An article, a page, is something you get right first time. It's like a baby: either it's made or it's not. I never think about what I'm going to write. I just pick up my pen and write . . .' Writing copy year after year evolved into a semi-automatic procedure: 'I've also got a very well-ordered syntax in my head. I throw my sentences in the air, like cats; I know that they will fall on their feet. It's very simple: all you need is good syntax. I could teach anyone to write . . .'

Gautier's tremendous verbal facility is one of his most striking characteristics, and one which enabled him to go on turning out articles on subjects that had long ceased to hold any interest for him. With his syntax in order he could write on almost anything, and was indeed called upon to do so. If there is any subject faced with which a writer is stuck for words, he maintained, then he is not a writer.[4] Gautier was a true professional, and the very model of a nineteenth-century eclectic; the range of his knowledge was immense. *Souvenirs de théâtre, d'art et de critique*, a collection of his articles reprinted in 1883, contains pieces variously entitled 'Industrial Statistics of the Ain', 'Beauties of the Opera', 'Marionettes', 'The Bonapartes', 'The Gladiators' (a review of a new English novel), and 'The Excavations on the Palatine Mount', which includes an account of Roman wall-painting. His art criticism familiarly embraces the techniques of oil-painting, fresco, water-colour, etching, engraving, lithography, glass-painting, ceramics, restoration, and casting in bronze; he speaks with authority on stained glass, porcelain, and tapestry, helps us to sympathize with the problems of a decorator of clocks and a painter of cupolas, and introduces us to the mechanics of photo-sculpture. He convinces us that the devotional objects made by the archaeologist Didron 'satisfy both dogma and science'; he sketches feasible schemes for the state patronage of impoverished artists, for the interior decoration of large town houses, and for the sculpting of façades for model working-class dwellings.

Gautier lived in an age whose eclectic tastes were reflected in its art. Together with his familiarity with craft and technique, he brought to bear on this art his verbal erudition as art historian, anthropologist, and traveller. Whether he was describing an oriental café scene by Decamps or the gladiators' armour in Gérôme's '*Ave, Caesar, morituri te salutant!*', he always got the words right, echoing the mid-nineteenth century's craving for local colour, however esoteric its sources. If Stendhal favoured the Civil Code as reading beneficial to his style, Gautier advised the dictionary. No vocabulary could be large enough to encompass the world of art, which in turn reflected the infinity of Creation; this was demonstrated at the Exposition Universelle of 1855, where the critic found himself confronted, among other things, with 'ethnographical water-colours' depicting the vanishing races of the Hungarian plains. The Middle East, Gautier's readers learnt, in case they did not know already from Gérôme's travel sketch-books, was inhabited by ' . . . the fierce Wahabi . . . the Arnaut with his eagle's eye and nose . . . the placid fellah' who combined to make up a crowd 'which parts under the kourbash before the horse of the Bey, who is accompanied by his sais . . . in his domino-like habbarah . . .'[5] He believed in calling a 'pschent' a 'pschent' if it was the only word to describe what he wanted to describe: it is up to the reader to know what words mean, he told the Goncourts in 1857.[6]

Priding himself on being able to write about anything, he was, it is true, able to adapt his prose style to produce splendidly evocative descriptions of very different kinds of art: he is equally at home with Meissonier or Veronese, with a

Pradier bust or a Victor Hugo sketch. Yet his most thorough visual evocations tend to be long; his Salons are usually organized under conventional headings such as history, genre, or landscape, and individual articles, dealing with groups of artists working in similar styles and on similar motifs, can read like relentless exercises in pursuit of the same unrelieved verbal effects.

The often monotonous texture of his prose is also a result of his highly developed faculty for empathy. He had so well trained himself to identify with the artist, his aims and his problems, that he almost reduced his task as a critic to that of simply reflecting the artist's work in prose transcriptions. This empathy is at the same time his greatest strength and his greatest weakness as a critic, the source of the greatest pleasures and irritations to be found in his writing. When he took over the editorship of *L'Artiste* in 1856, his published intention was to admire as much as he could, as admiration was a critic's greatest joy, and he was in fact almost always sympathetic and indulgent to working artists, even towards those whose aims were most alien to him, like Courbet, and even, in the end, to his number one *bête noire*, Paul Delaroche. Where he felt a genuine kinship with an artist, where that artist's vision somehow coincided with his own, his writing is richly illuminating, and enhances the experience of confronting the artist's work; this can be felt in the case of Delacroix, for example. Just as often, Gautier's evocations are a pleasure in their own right; they can be read as almost independent works of art in prose. Delacroix in particular inspired such prose improvisations. But most often Gautier was obliged to lavish his indulgence as a matter of routine on the hundreds of other artists who exhibited in the Salons, and here his criticism is mainly interesting as an art-historical record, to be referred to in a detailed account of nineteenth-century Salon art. His indulgence, as we shall see, was partly the result of a journalist's diplomatic policy, for even Gautier at the height of his reputation as a critic felt he could not afford to risk treading on people's toes in the relatively small Parisian art world. It is where indulgence looks like a necessary attribute of his job, where we feel that he is simply being indiscriminating, that the 'public scribe' seems to come into his own, and the poet to withdraw behind an impenetrable barrier of prose.

Paradoxically, it is through this impression that Gautier is absent, that is, when his prose is at its most opaque and his criticism most tedious, that we are able to link the unlikely butterfly, the hippopotamic journalist, with the impeccable poet and perfect magician: in all his work, he wants to be somewhere, or something, else. A truly successful work of art for Gautier is one that will transport him somewhere else, in time, in space, or in both. It is a world to itself, into which he can wholly enter and allow himself to be absorbed. It must be *vraisemblable* from the points of view of local colour, historical accuracy, atmosphere, anatomy, and psychology, it must have dramatic unity, but where it is situated in time or space is largely a matter of indifference: anywhere will do, as long as it is not here. The aesthetic experience for Gautier can be described as a transcendental one. It approaches the spheres of mysticism: the self is transcended through contemplation of exterior form, and mental absorption in it. Dream of escape to an ideal place is not an unusual Romantic phenomenon;[7] Gautier, by linking it thus to form in art, particularly in painting, gave it a less literary and more mystical emphasis. It is perhaps in this area that we shall be able to discern more clearly his contribution as a critic to nineteenth-century sensibility. When he is absent from his prose, it is thus because his subject-matter does not provide a solid enough platform for escape, for verbal reverie in which he can actively collaborate with his syntax and ever productive mental dictionary.

Gautier frequently enlisted ghost-writers, most notably his son, Toto, Théophile the younger, born in 1836 and familiar from an early age with his father's style. Gautier père's routine of almost annual Salons to inspect and review, Prix de Rome exhibitions, visits to artists' studios, first nights, did nothing to alleviate his nearly pathological restlessness; he effected physical escape as frequently as he could on commissions abroad. When these were not forthcoming, his desire to be transplanted expressed itself in a passion for exotic costume and accoutrements, for importing foreign customs into the home. We can picture him sitting cross-legged on his oriental divan, surrounded by a harem of cats and the smoke from his hookah, indulging in the inscrutable dreams of a hashisheen. He would wear a fur coat in warm weather, explaining that he never could get used to France's nordic climate; he kept his long hair well after that Romantic fashion had died out, and he treated his guests to risotto.

Where the Orientalists and ethnographic painters helped satisfy his travel lust, the nineteenth century's passion for historical reconstruction in painting served him well for excursions into time past. The periods into which he transported himself in his own work were always highly picturesque; the pattern is set in his youthful ode to the sculptor Jean-Bernard Duseigneur, which was written in 1831 at the height of Romantic fervour. Here the ideal was the Roman Renaissance: 'There, Duseigneur, can one live and love . . .' among '. . . Those Greek, Roman, Gothic, or Moresque edifices . . .' and the colourful crowd, '. . . The bandit from the Abruzzi . . . The monk with his three chins . . . The old beggar-woman . . .'[8] Nineteenth-century Paris was to remain inhospitable to a 'worshipper of art', to 'a man for whom the visible world exists';[9] the reality of 'the fog of this teeming Paris' with its 'wan façades' was always to be unacceptable. Above all Gautier cherished a vision of himself as a Greek from the time of Homer, serene and magnificent in his potent barbarism; the eighteenth century was also a sympathetic milieu, and was evoked in early poems such as 'Rocaille' and 'Watteau',[10] and, in a vaguer, more abstract fashion, in *Mademoiselle de Maupin*. *Le Capitaine Fracasse* is a novel set in a boisterously imaginative French Renaissance, while *Le Roman de la momie* is a more scientific reconstruction of ancient Egypt.

In this last novel, Gautier's fascination with trips through time becomes macabre, fetishistic eroticism. A young English Lord witnesses the unravelling of a mummy, and falls in love with the beautiful princess thus revealed intact three thousand five hundred years after her death. He experiences such 'retrospective desire' for 'the virginal nudity of her beautiful forms, which retain, in spite of the passing of so many centuries, all the roundness of their contours'[11] that he spends the rest of his days in the ancient Egypt of his imagination. The hero of the story *Arria Marcella* falls in love with a girl whose sculptural outline is perfectly preserved in the lava of Vesuvius; he wakes up one day to find himself strolling through the busy streets of Pompeii before the eruption, in search of his Ideal made flesh.

Seen in this light, Gautier's massive nostalgia for picturesque, idealized past epochs is a yearning to embrace all sensual experience; it is an extension of his claim that it was possible to describe anything. This nostalgia is finally directed towards his own red-waistcoated youth, when his powers of grasping sensual experience were at their height; nostalgia for the passions that moved him and which he shared with the painter and poet comrades of his Romantic youth is the keynote of the last years of his art criticism. *L'Histoire du romantisme*, written within a year of his death in 1872, is a final grand attempt to gather the strands of his personal nostalgia and fix them permanently, a last reverie. He banishes the unpicturesque spectacle of Paris's recovery from the Commune, and relives the glorious first night of *Hernani*, thus providing us with a glowing, first-hand account of the forces that were to guide and colour the whole of his writing life.

I Biography

I Self-image

Gautier left no full autobiography. Nineteenth-century lives, he commented, offer little biographical interest; there is no longer any place for men of action in a modern civilized society whose achievements are intellectual, scientific, and peaceful. The lives of artists and thinkers, unpunctuated by dramatic incident, do not call for picturesque description or colourful narrative. '. . . the individual disappears, only ideas remain'[1] he wrote in 1857 in an obituary for the sculptor Simart. 'To recount the life of an artist nowadays, you need do no more than analyse his ideas, note his intellectual place *vis-à-vis* his contemporaries and give a catalogue of his work.' This sober pattern is the same for even the most passionate and exalted talents. It was to Delacroix's credit that 'he was infected with the fevers of his age and represented its troubled ideal';[2] yet in everyday life Delacroix fastidiously kept contemporary fevers and troubles at arm's length. 'In him, intellectual strength took the place of physical strength.' Outwardly, the life of Gautier's modern artist was becoming less and less distinguishable from the monotonous, conformist life of the frock-coated crowd; even the obituaries of an Ingres or a Delacroix are not spiced with anecdote or adventure. It is on their inner lives that Gautier lavishes his admiration, and his poetic evocations of their artistic personalities do not need to draw on a wealth of prosaic biographical detail for support.

Gautier's own personal reminiscences are fragmentary and far from dispassionate; they show little of an ageing citizen or sober critic's concern to make a painstaking record of his life and times. It was only in the last year of his life that he felt a need, or was able, fully to organize memories of his youthful awakening to the Romantic movement into a series of articles, published after his death as *L'Histoire du romantisme*. In this book, Gautier escapes into a past in which he himself is a colourful, central figure, a past in which he can thus be wholly absorbed. He turns his back on old age, routine, and drab surroundings and recalls life as he would have liked it always to have been. But in order to recapture the ideas and sensations that carried him away in his youth, and lose himself in them, he must first efface himself from the present of 1872; it is almost as if his mnemonic perceptions could not be wholly engaged until he had achieved anonymity, like Baudelaire's unobserved observer of modern life. Thus the sixty-year-old Gautier makes a final statement of his wish to be absent from his writing: 'if we knew of a means of disappearing completely from our work, we would use it. The "I" repels us so much that our expressive formula is "we", the vague plural of which immediately obliterates the personality and makes you one of the crowd again.'[3] On occasions when he was obliged to give an account of himself, his desire for self-effacement and absorption in distant and preferable worlds transformed itself into monstrous, self-conscious flamboyance. There was little room for any in-between approach, as this might lead him into an account of the largely regular existence which he shared with the undifferentiated bourgeois thousands. His fullest autobiographical sketch was published by *L'Illustration* in 1867,[4] to accompany an engraving of his photograph, a distinction afforded him not only as a working critic of considerable influence, but also as one of the grand old men of the Romantic school; this was a reputation he clearly relished living up to. This article, snippets of reported conversation, and the subsequent elaborations of admiring contemporary memoir writers (who seem to have felt an irresistible attraction to the playful, satirical tone of the veteran Romantic's autobiographical comments), combine to provide us with an introductory biographical sketch which Gautier would wholeheartedly have submitted for public approval. It mixes fact with rather more dubious and unverifiable information; it is colourful, anecdotal, and mythic.

Alleged to be of Oriental ancestry,[5] Gautier was conceived at the château d'Artagnan, hereditary seat of the hero of *The Three Musketeers*, where his parents had spent the early part of their marriage. They later moved to Tarbes, on the French side of the Pyrenees, and rented shabby rooms previously tenanted by a troupe of itinerant actors, who had left behind some props; according to legend, Mme Gautier gave birth to Théophile clinging to Cinderella's throne.[6] When he was three, his parents settled in Paris, where he was afflicted with such overwhelming nostalgia for Gascony that he attempted suicide. His appearance at this time was strongly suggestive of his Southern provenance: 'I was a meek, sad, and sickly child, with a strangely sallow complexion that astonished my young pink and white fellows. I was like some little Spaniard from Cuba, homesick and shivering from the cold, sent to France to be educated.' He was desperately unhappy at school, 'like a caged swallow that refuses to eat and dies'. Yet he had outstanding potential: 'I showed all the promise of a brilliant pupil, if I lived.'[7] At the Lycée Louis-le-Grand his chief tormentor was a savage dog, of which he wrote some fifty years later, 'if I could still recognize him after such a long time, I would leap at his throat and strangle him.'[8] At the Collège Charlemagne he produced verse, and at the same time attended the studio of the painter Rioult, where he was disappointed by the sight of his first female model, 'so much does art add even to the most perfect natural creation'. From this moment, he said, 'I have always preferred statues to women, and marble to flesh'.[9] Finding himself too fashionably sickly, he resolved to cultivate his physique. He admired boxers and athletes above all other mortals, and scored a record 532 pounds with a blow from his fist on a test-your-strength machine, a feat 'that has gone down in history, the proudest act of my life.'[10] Many years later, he summed up his life thus: 'As for myself, I'm strong, I can score 357 on the test-your-strength machine and coin metaphors that are unmixed: what more could you ask?'[11] He concluded his list of achievements as a literary man: 'Altogether, something like three hundred volumes, for which everyone calls me lazy and asks me what I do with myself. That really is all I know about myself.'[12]

This blown-out Rabelaisian skeleton for an autobiography contains much that is implicit in Gautier's writing, salient aspects of his image of himself that he particularly cherished. At the same time, there is weariness behind his teasingly ironical statements; it is as if this is a story that has been rehearsed, to be trotted out under interrogation. Gautier is a displaced and misunderstood Southerner, a repressed exotic suffering from a nameless nostalgia for simpler, more direct living; his direct, boastful, and deliberately boorish comments upon himself constitute a challenge to the complexity of nineteenth-century urban life and to its tedious sophistication. He would like to be able to offer clean solutions to life's daily tribulations; he would not hesitate to strangle the dog that had first singled him out as a special victim for persecution. He is sure of his strength and capable of anything; he has the magic of infinite metaphors at his fingertips. As a spiritual descendant of d'Artagnan, as an inheritor of the instincts of an itinerant player, as a powerful athlete with Oriental blood in his veins, he wishes to be free of preoccupation with the everyday and ordinary, in order to be able to look down upon the world with serene detachment. He concerns himself with ideals, with an art which can improve upon real life. His comment from the 1867 article in *L'Illustration*, 'I have always preferred statues to women', may be a boisterous, ironical dig at his own reputation as a womanizer and a writer of pornographic verses;[13] it is also an uncomfortable example of how thinly his irony, if this is irony, sometimes veils bleaker insights. Paying his respects to Gautier's corpse, Edmond de Goncourt was struck by the dead poet's 'wild serenity of a barbarian slumbering in the void';[14] Gautier also resembles the Sun King of his early poem 'Versailles',[15] his soul wandering forever among a population of unblemished but lifeless statues.

It is hard to avoid constantly being confronted by such ideas, in one form or another, throughout Gautier's criticism. He returns again and again to the same preoccupations, and in particular to an obsession with permanence and death. In *L'Histoire du romantisme* he rereads his old letters to his former schoolfriend Gérard de Nerval, and finds

familiar words, habitual turns of phrase, ideas and pieces of news current then. How distant all that is . . . and yet how close still! How little the heart changes! How the same ideas meander through the convolutions of the brain, crossing each other's paths and exchanging greetings at the usual meeting-places. We could have put most of these sentences in the post yesterday, and thirty years old as they are they would not, on arrival, seem much more out of date than if they had been written that morning. Man does not change as much as he likes to think![16]

He is always sure of coming across familiar ideas given form by familiar words, and can greet them without surprise, as consoling friends. The consistency with which the same truisms find the same expression throughout the forty years of his writing is matched by his capacity for detachment from them, and by an equal capacity for self-contradiction. He even sees his mind from the outside, as a closed structure of convolutions built for the endless circulation of the same thoughts. It is as if he had been born with the intuition of certain key truths with which he could feel satisfied, and thus relieved of the necessity of finding out new ones, could put judgement aside and get on with the disinterested observation of particularities. He dreamt of alternative existences and of an ideal universe; yet at any single moment the real world was not, for Gautier, a world of imminent future possibilities, but a static creation in its definitive form.

Behind the prose with which he could describe anything, and in which equal weight was often given to whatever he described, there was thus a huge diffidence. His unselective, formal view of the world offers two edges. At its most disquieting, it reveals forms devoid of life and meaning, a world of lurking existential threat. Here Gautier seems to anticipate a particularly modern artistic dilemma, the dilemma of the artist for whom the object or the visible form becomes an end in itself. Harold Rosenberg, writing on 'The American Action Painters' in 1952, pointed to the dangers facing artists of his own generation: 'The artist works in a condition of open possibility, risking, to follow Kierkegaard, the anguish of the aesthetic, which accompanies possibility lacking in reality. To maintain the force to refrain from accepting anything, he must exercise in himself a constant NO!'[17] Gautier's world was less one of 'possibility lacking in reality' than a world whose constituent elements lacked any possibility for change and growth. When Gautier failed to say 'no' to his formal and descriptive instincts, to select from all that he perceived, he risked producing a static, inorganic, and chilling universe. As an idealist who sought an attitude of god-like indifference to real life in order to recreate it in an improved, less problematic, and more picturesque form, he became the poet of abandoned statues and empty suits of armour, from which any life was absent.

On the other hand, this formal view can also have a refreshing and purgative effect. What Gautier loses through his failure to select and to make critical judgements, he gains in freshness and immediacy. His descriptions, with their myopic attention to detail, can enable his readers to see works of art or the landscapes he visited as it were for the first time; the corollary of his diffident and lethargic assimilation of whatever was placed before him is thus an attitude of healthy open-mindedness, which enables him to present his readers with objects-in-themselves, rather than with his own pre-conceptions about these objects. He will frequently describe things, it is true, in terms of the feelings and associations they provoke in him; he is almost never to be heard dismissing what is before him as typical or all too familiar, as might a blasé *cognoscente*. This open-minded attitude finds wide application in his travel books, and is possibly best vindicated in *Tableaux de siège*, his account of Paris during 1870–71. *Tableaux de siège* contains passages of manifest tenderness and meditations on the futility of war which might, to a twentieth-century reader, appear commonplace; its power, however, lies in its careful descriptions of the desolate Parisian landscape. To an inescapable reality of indiscriminate destruction, these descriptions offer the only life-enhancing reaction that is perhaps possible: they express the simple joy of perception, even when all else has failed. '. . . man is a matter of perfect indifference to me', Gautier confided to the Goncourts.[18] 'In plays, when the father presses his long-lost daughter against the buttons of his waistcoat, it's of absolutely no consequence to me; I only see the fold in the girl's dress. I am a *subjective* being.' Gautier's primary function, it might be said, was as a monitor of inarticulate visual form. He lived through his visual sensations, and as a 'subjective being', a *nature subjective*, was often unable to reject what he received, seeming almost to lack the mental equipment for selectivity. It is as if he could not relate items of visual data, such as the fold in an actress's costume, to the rest of his experience, as if this visual sensation were experienced in isolation, so that he could not refer it to a larger whole or assimilate it relatively to other sensations. The sensation was a whole in itself, and seems disproportionately important taken out of a rationalized structure of perceptions. Gautier thus excluded or transcended the whole context surrounding the object perceived; and this context included himself and his own self-image. His version of himself, seen in this light, looks more and more like a false front. It is super-real. If Gautier was an uncharacterized perceiving organism inside, his public exterior was exaggeratedly physical and picturesque, in compensation for what he perhaps experienced as a hollow lack of substance, or a premonition and terror of physical transience and death.

Gautier leaves the impression of an invisible man who has decked himself out in exotic, larger-than-life clothes; after all, it is said that he was born on a stage prop. The articles in the wardrobe which allowed him to pass into the outside world were largely collected in the Paris of the 1830s during the years that he recalled in *L'Histoire du romantisme*. 'We had the honour', he proclaims, 'to belong in the ranks of those youthful cohorts which were fighting for the ideal, for poetry and the liberty of art, with an enthusiasm, a bravery and devotion no longer known today.'[19] Such are the sonorous phrases that announce the roll of honour of the 'grande armée littéraire' and its forgotten exploits. Gautier recalls his years of greatest happiness and highest aspiration with the pride and bravado of a Napoleonic hero reliving his campaigns; he belonged to the youth that would conquer the world. 'In the Romantic army as in the army of Italy, everyone was young';[20] Victor Hugo, the Romantic general, was twenty-nine, the same age, Gautier points out, as Napoleon when he set foot in Italy. Also like Bonaparte, Hugo was exiled from France; Gautier was left to become a hero who had lived to see the days of heroism fade away. '. . . we should have been very surprised if anyone had told us we would be a journalist. Certainly, the prospect of such a future would have hardly enthralled us . . .'[21]

2 Youth

Nineteen in 1830, Gautier was an ideal recruit for the Romantic battle. He had indeed been born in Tarbes, on August 30 1811, and christened Pierre-Jules-Théophile. His father was a minor tax official of strong Royalist affiliations who had obtained a post in Paris when the Bourbons returned to power; Théophile was thus a Parisian from the age of three. Jean-Pierre Gautier was well read, and well connected through the interest taken in his family by an abbé de Montesquiou, who became a minister under Charles X. Jean-Pierre showed an enlightened sympathy for his son's artistic aspirations, and financed the publication of Théophile's first *Poésies*: '. . . he was really my only teacher',[22] Théophile wrote in 1867. Although the Gautier family suffered virtual financial ruin in 1830, it was still several years before he was obliged to earn his own living.

He was brought up with two younger sisters in an unconstrained atmosphere that encouraged him to cultivate his talents and to follow them wherever they might lead him. His early tastes hint at much that is to characterize his critic's vision. His aptitude for drawing and his love of Latin verse, for example, were to subsist in a strongly classical vein in his thinking. His father was an enthusiastic Latinist and gave special encouragement to Théophile's penchant at school for Latin verse composition, and it was out of this early talent, perhaps, that there emerged his later tendency to view the world as a dictionary of forms, even more to refer his experience of the world to art he had seen. Classical composition, in the visual arts as in verse, can be conceived as the reordering of already existing forms or phrases, requiring less pure invention than a capacity for the intelligent assimilation of definitive idioms. Hence the French syntax that Gautier had so well in order, the prefabricated sentences that always fell on their feet; hence perhaps the basic structural principle of his whole outlook, which René Jasinski, in *Les*

Années romantiques de Théophile Gautier, encapsulates thus: 'He referred his emotional experience first and foremost to works of art he knew' ('L' émotion chez lui rappelait d'abord les œuvres connues').[23]

His adolescent tastes were conspicuously *recherché*; his chosen Latin models were the poets of the decadence, and he studied then quite extra-curricular authors of the early French Renaissance, particularly Villon and Rabelais—a sign of his literary precocity. His poetic experiments were further encouraged by his friendship at the Collège Charlemagne with Gérard Labrunie, who was three years older and who, as Gérard de Nerval, had had a volume of *Élégies nationales* published while he was still a schoolboy. Nerval's widely read and influential translation of Goethe's *Faust* appeared as early as 1827.

Yet Gautier's first ambition had always been to be a painter; it was with sneaking regret that he would recall his failure to follow this early inclination. Thus in 1829, during his final year at school, he enrolled in the nearby studio of Édouard Rioult, a pupil of David and Regnault, second-prize winner in 1814 and subsequent painter of elegiac nymph and bather scenes as well as of *grandes machines*. Gautier never rejected his classical master; according to Émile Bergerat, there were two small paintings by Rioult in his bedroom in 1872.[24] His admiration for the spirit of 'grâce' and 'naïveté' of Rioult's bathers was evinced in the poem 'A Mon ami Eugène de N***' which appeared in the 1830 *Poésies*.[25] But it was through this studio life, paradoxically and more importantly, that he first came into contact with that 'movement similar to the Renaissance'[26] and was carried away by its energy. His ambitions as a painter were frustrated; short sight handicapped him in his studies of the live model, and the endless reproduction of Germanicus's torso and Jupiter's nose seemed a particularly menial exercise to a young man who in his own eyes and those of admiring relatives had already acquired graphic fluency, superficial as it might have been[27] (*plate 4*). If his adolescent hopes were not fulfilled, he underwent a fuller awakening in compensation, an awakening to Art as a cause, as an independent life-force, no less, to be lived and sustained like life itself.

He recalls the moment of awakening to this new Renaissance in terms which indeed suggest a miraculous rebirth:
'The sap of new life was pulsing vigorously. Everything was
germinating and budding, everything was bursting into life at
the same time. Flowers gave off heady perfumes; the air was
intoxicating. We were beside ourselves with lyricism and
art.'[28] The promise of a magical synthesis of the arts was in
the air, and Gautier's youthful facility with both pen and
brush made him particularly sensitive to its echoes. 'A great
deal of reading went on in the studios at that time. The *rapins*
[an untranslatable slang term meaning art student or dauber]
loved literature, and their specialist education, which
brought them into intimate contact with nature, made them
more receptive to the colours and images of the new poetry.
They were not in the least put off by those precise
and graphic details which were so offensive to the
Classics . . . the *mot propre* held no shocks for them.'
Gautier's reaction to this explosive liberation of the *mot
propre* and to the new world of images and colours that it
revealed was sharpened by the presence of an identifiable
enemy.

We speak of young *rapins*, for there were also well-behaved pupils
who were faithful to Chompré's dictionary and Achilles's tendon,
who were high in the teacher's esteem and held up by him as
examples. But they enjoyed no popularity, and their sober palettes,
on which gleamed neither Veronese green, nor Indian yellow, nor
Smyrna lake, nor any of the seditious colours proscribed by the
Academy, were looked upon with pity.[29]

Outside the studio, the conflict was public, and while the
'jeune rapin' dutifully continued to trace the contours of his
academic plaster cast, it was with the 'Pas d'armes du roi
Jean' or the 'Chasse du Burgrave' on his lips, and
Chateaubriand, Scott, Goethe, Shakespeare, and Byron in
his heart. Towering above all inspirations, the great focus and
rallying point for his untried energies was the figure of Victor
Hugo himself.

Although we were not yet a member of the Romantic group, we

belonged to it in spirit! The preface to *Cromwell* was radiant in our eyes, like the tablets of the law on Sinaï, and its arguments seemed irrefutable. The abuse hurled by the petty little Classic newspapers at the young Master, whom we considered from that time onwards, and with reason, to be France's greatest poet, would throw us into fits of ferocious anger. Thus we were burning to go and fight the hydra of *perruquinisme*.[30]

Théophile's opportunity to prove his allegiance came on February 25 1830, with the eagerly awaited set battle of *Hernani*. He had been presented to Hugo, who was keen to patronize youthful support, by Gérard de Nerval and Petrus Borel in mid-1829; having overcome his initial tongue-tied trepidation, he was received into the Master's house in the rue Notre-Dame-des-Champs. On the first night of *Hernani*, he distinguished himself as Hugo's most ardent partisan, spectacularly long-haired and red-waistcoated. 'Vive Victor Hugo' he recalled writing on walls after the performance.[31]

The famous red waistcoat was a symbol of revolt, conceived in a certain 'mauvais goût de rapin',[32] that remained attached to Gautier's name throughout his life and afterwards. 'Our poetry, our books, our articles, our travels will be forgotten; but people will remember our red waistcoat.' The idea did not displease him; the waistcoat received a chapter to itself in *L'Histoire du romantisme*.[33] But like some of Gautier's other public attributes, this literal article from his wardrobe was more than the simple expression of an exuberant state of mind; even in 1830, at this peak of youthful enthusiasm, Théophile seems partly absent from the proceedings, as he recalls them. He describes the rest of his costume in detail ('very pale watery-green trousers, with black velvet seams . . . a black coat with generous velvet lapels . . . an ample grey topcoat with a green satin lining. A moiré ribbon, which served as a tie and a shirt collar, was wrapped around our neck'), and its effects on the enemies of art, and then apologizes to the reader for talking so much about himself ('the "I" repels us so much . . .'). But he goes on to justify this violation of his natural modesty, 'since it was indeed we who were the model for this wondrous doublet'.

Even here, he represents himself as a passive vehicle for scintillating surface effects, a mannequin which brilliantly displays the season's new colours. The 'gilet rouge' is the first and most striking element in Gautier's public mythology; in the terms in which he recalls it at the end of his life, it is outward compensation for the inner knowledge that the experience of the senses and of the passions is fleeting and transient. As 'the notion of ourselves that we shall leave to the universe', it ensured permanence of a kind, at least.

In February 1830 the red waistcoat was a blunt polemical gesture, a declaration of love for the rich hedonism of art, in favour of the *mot propre* and the diversity of man's capacity for pleasure and experience, and against 'all those larvae of the past and of routine, all those enemies of art, liberty, and poetry, who with their feeble, quivering hands were trying to keep the door to the future closed.'[34] The world as Gautier had discovered it in 1830 was divided into 'flamboyants' and 'grisâtres'; the polarities were clear. Diderot and Rubens qualified as 'flamboyants', Voltaire and Poussin were 'grisâtres'. As a 'flamboyant' *par excellence* and a 'jeune rapin à cœur de lion', Gautier's particular identity was also 'le chevalier du Rouge': 'we loved this noble colour . . . which is purple, blood, life, light, warmth, and which harmonizes so well with gold and marble'.[35] By introducing a note of purple into his chosen hue, Théophile was at pains to avoid any political connotation; but the webs of sympathy, antagonism, and intrigue in Parisian life were not as clearly marked as he might have liked. The struggle that he saw as so sharply defined was to shift emphasis against the background of the July Revolution and its aftermath. René Jasinski thoroughly explores the political and social complexity of the early thirties and the corresponding ideological confusion in which artists found themselves; as he points out, the atmosphere was changing within the stronghold of Hugo's cenacle itself. Hugo and Sainte-Beuve were in private conflict; the older Romantics Nodier, Musset, and Dumas were seeking to reaffirm their own independence, leaving the younger generation to find a new rallying-point for itself amid the chaos. Thus towards the end of 1830, a new grouping emerged at the studio of the young sculptor Duseigneur in the rue de

Vaugirard, styling itself 'Le Petit Cénacle', in order to avoid confusion with Hugo's old circle.[36]

If Hugo's salon had been the nerve-centre, the head-quarters of the young Romantic shock-troops, the Petit Cénacle was a refuge and sanctuary, a world apart like Art itself. With much of Europe beset by political and religious anxiety, by principles and systems in conflict, the Petit Cénacle sought to assert Art as an alternative ideal that was to be taken seriously, an ideal whose timeless value subsisted in spite of contemporary events. Hugo himself was to lay programmatic emphasis on the independent yet permanently relevant force of art in November 1831 in the preface to *Les Feuilles d'automne*; if he was no longer a front-line general, he remained the great intercessor. For Gautier, art was becoming a religion, and 'flamboyant' now stood for more than just the opposite of 'grisâtre', symbolizing, rather, art's supreme self-sufficiency. Although the Petit Cénacle remained as provocative and radical as ever *vis-à-vis* the bourgeois and the academic, it provided Gautier with a broader ideological orientation which was later to enable him to assimilate into his art-world genres other than the colourful, the passionate, and the exotic: Flandrin and Aligny were to have their places in his Salons next to Delacroix and Rousseau, since all shared the same broad ideal. The Petit Cénacle's attempt to set an example of art's emancipation was the germ of the notion of Art for Art's Sake.

The political chaos of 1830 and 1831 was accompanied by the hope of a great renewal, a sense of what Jasinski calls 'l' indéfini du possible',[37] of the infinite possibility of the future, which manifested itself in a flowering of utopist systems and organized ideologies. With Saint-Simonism, Fourierism, Buchez's religion of progress and Leroux's religion of Humanity, the Petit Cénacle shared this broad sense of future. Closed and self-protective like other groupings, it was optimistic and confident in its insistence on the free expansion of the individual, who might find new and unknown resources through the limitless range of art. Its principles were large enough to embrace even the Republicanism of Borel and O'Neddy. I am a republican, Borel wrote in the preface to his *Rhapsodies*, 'because I cannot be a Caribbean; I

need an enormous amount of freedom'; should his republic of
the future fail him, he consoled himself, there remained
Missouri. Borel's republic and his Missouri were the dreams
of an artist: worlds in which unfettered man could realize the
infinite possibilities of his nature.[38]

As a closed world itself, the Petit Cénacle was an attempt to
make dreams come true, one that went beyond the mere
production of works of art. Art was the world with all its
possibilities made available—thus everything was interior to
it, even artists; the Petit Cénacle of *L'Histoire du romantisme*
is a magic land in which artists themselves become works of
art. Appearances told everything, if the carefully restyled
names of some of the group's adherents had not already told
much of the dream worlds to which they aspired: among them
were Jehan du Seigneur, whose medievalized Christian name
suggested 'that he wore Erwin of Steinbach's apron and
was at work on the sculptures of Strasbourg cathedral',[39]
Augustus Mackeat, Philothée O'Neddy, and Napoléon
Tom. These assumed identities were only partly designed to
shock; the circle that met in Duseigneur's studio also looked
upon its interior mythology with guileless sincerity. Medallions depicting each of the friends were modelled by Jehan
and hung conspicuously in the studio window, less in parody
than in unconscious imitation of the venerable and despised
Academy. '. . . when the limitless horizons of youth open
before you, you do not suspect that the present . . . may one
day become history',[40] Gautier wrote, but at the time, the
opposite was probably true: it was future as well as past
history that the Petit Cénacle had its eye on. It was Gautier, in
any case, who later took the trouble to make sure that its
members were fixed and immortalized in their neo-historical
guises, many of the frail medallions having long gone the way
of most of their subjects.

Pétrus Borel, the immediate star around whom the others
orbited at the time, was 'a picture of elegance, born to wear a
wall-coloured cloak through the streets of Seville . . . he was
quite Castilian in his gravity and always looked as if he had
just stepped out of a Velazquez . . . When he put on his hat, it
was like a Spanish grandee covering himself before the

king'.[41] In 1831, of course, Gautier had not yet been to Spain, nor seen many paintings by Velazquez; his memory, with the help of subsequently acquired *mots propres*, has tightened and refined Borel's image, so that it stands out across the years with the precise definition of one of Duseigneur's vanished medallions. Borel has the telling characteristics of a typical Gautier artist: 'Large, bright, and sad eyes, the eyes of an Abencerraje thinking of Granada. The best epithet we could find for those eyes is this: exotic or nostalgic.' They are the eyes of Gautier himself, nostalgic for an ideal or exotic life. 'Pétrus Borel's presence would produce an unaccountable impression, and we finally discovered the reason. He was not contemporary; nothing about him suggested modern man . . . it was hard to believe that he was a Frenchman born in this century. A Spaniard, an Arab, a fifteenth-century Italian—that was more likely.'[42]

Gautier's Borel is essentially picturesque, an impossible figure who does not exist in real time, a two-dimensional motif from painting. His haughty courtesy separates him from others, and he is serenely impassive behind 'the Oriental immobility of his features', as he dreams of higher things. Gautier aspired to impossible states, and so did the friends he admired. The dramatist Joseph Bouchardy also becomes a displaced Oriental, whose mysterious anterior nature is betrayed by features of his appearance. Nineteenth-century dress could not hide the ideal Bouchardy: 'He seemed to be in disguise in his blue coat with its gold buttons . . . like one of those dispossessed princes from British India who can be seen sadly wandering the streets of London.'[43] Like Borel, who by a process of imaginative synthesis becomes a Velazquez, Bouchardy is made to correspond to another picturesque motif Gautier has observed, a real displaced Oriental on the streets of London. The young Romantics, inspired by Romantic literature, largely modelled themselves on its heroes; thus Borel could have played 'the part of the bandit loved by Doña Sol'.[44] Gautier widened the range of references. However affected Gautier's friends were in 1831, in his later account they become truly synthetic creations, made up of pre-existing or prefabricated elements. Their construction follows the principle of reassembly that Jasinski saw at work in Gautier's verse: no formal invention, but the apt rearrangement of already definitive forms.

Eugène Devéria, a slightly older associate of the Petit Cénacle, whose *Naissance de Henri IV* at the Salon of 1827 had given rise to hopes that France had found her Veronese, was a sixteenth-century Venetian. 'He loved satin, damask, and jewels, and would have liked to go about in a robe of gold brocade like one of Titian's magnificos . . . These fantasies of costume would seem strange today, but then we found them quite natural: the word *artist* justified everything.'[45] The most striking example of an artist as an extension of his art is Célestin Nanteuil; as Gautier describes him,[46] he does not even need 'the word *artist*' as an excuse. He is a completely integrated figment of his own imaginary world. He is

the young man from the Middle Ages . . . he was tall and thin, as slender as the spindly columns of a fifteenth-century nave, while his ringlets were a passable imitation of the acanthus leaves on the capitals. His spirit-like figure tapered aloft as if it wished to climb towards heaven with ever intensified ardour, and his head balanced on top like a censer. His complexion was pink and white; the azure of the frescos at Fiesole had been used for the blue of his pupils, and the halo-blond hairs on his head seemed to have been painted in one by one with the gold of medieval miniaturists.

Evocations of the artist and of his work share the same verbal texture in Gautier's prose; Gothic images abound in both, and indeed the entire medieval section of Gautier's mental dictionary seems to have been deployed in the text.

. . . he saw . . . in their every detail rose windows, pinnacles bristling with crosses, kings, patriarchs, prophets, saints, angels of every order, the whole monstrous army of demons and chimeras, clawed, scaly, fanged, hideously feathered: wyverns, taresques, gargoyles, asses' heads, monkeys' snouts, the whole strange bestiary of the Middle Ages.

Gautier lists words of precise and often esoteric meaning and produces a verbal fog, in which the outlines separating artist and work become vague and finally merge. Inspiratory literature is added to this synthesis of Nanteuil and his creations, and, through formal analogy, is made to contribute to a pervasive sense of the painter's vision. Certain of Hugo's ballads, illustrated by Nanteuil, are like Gothic stained-glass windows, and Nanteuil actually used coloured glass in his painting to intensify his hues: 'The constantly broken rhythm in the line of verse is equivalent to the broken glass in the painting.'

Nanteuil is Gautier's supreme example of a Petit Cénacle artist, a figure moulded into ideal shape. Through Gautier's prose, Nanteuil brings about a marriage of the arts, assimilating literature and a wide range of studio techniques to his vision; even his person aspires to the condition of his art, and unites its qualities. He is totally absorbed in his medieval world; and it is not by 'hard study' or 'extensive research' that he achieves this complete identification, but through 'a similarity of being with the artists of the Middle Ages', and because he had 'an intuition of things he had never seen.'

Behind the Petit Cénacle's studiedly eccentric and flamboyant exterior, such visionary intuition lay as an article of faith. It was a means by which artists could penetrate layers of artificially imposed civilization and arrive at their true inner natures, ripe for externalization into art. 'The inner life, the Romantic and metaphysical life is as unruly, as adventurous, and as free as Arab tribes in their wildernesses,' wrote O'Neddy in the preface to *Feu et flamme*;[47] for Gautier, the inner life was less turbulent and adventurous than contained and serene. It was an ordered and intimate dream, carefully placed in poetic time and space by precise details of local colour, and too delicate to be accessible to the delirium and mental *dépaysement* with which Borel and O'Neddy later sought to emancipate themselves from the prosaically rational bourgeois. While subscribing to the theatrical excesses of the Petit Cénacle, harmless as they generally were, Gautier was always able to stand back from them, and retreat into the contemplation of quieter and more private visions.

Until 1834 he continued to live at home with his parents and two sisters, and his home life was reflected in the tranquil, intimate note that he brought to the Romantic cacophony. In

the preface to *Albertus*, verse published in October 1832 and
so entitled after his own current group nickname, he tacitly
rejected frenetic, delirious Romanticism; there would be
'neither torrents nor cataracts' in his poems.[48] 'They are first
and foremost little interiors, gentle and calm in effect, little
landscapes in the Flemish manner, light in touch and rather
subdued in colour'; his verses were to be the reflections and
painterly observations of a lazy, weary young man who hardly
ever ventured from his room into the street, and who found
the world contained in his imagination. In the same month,
Victor Hugo moved into the house next door to the Gautier
family home in the spacious and quiet place Royale (now
place des Vosges). The stable, reassuringly potent presence
of the undisputed and irrefutable Master, who now welcomed
the young poet into his domestic circle as an old friend,
confirmed Gautier's move away from the Petit Cénacle,
which Borel seemed to be leading into increasingly aggressive
and exhibitionist antics, and whose pseudo-political provo-
cations of the now established bourgeois monarchy were
beginning to appear childish, hysterical, and quite impotent.
Not that Gautier's hatred of the insensitive, vaudeville-
loving bourgeois ever abated; perhaps, as Jasinski suggests,
'he only differs from his former companions in that he
interiorizes his dreams instead of shattering them against
reality'.[49] *Les Jeunes-France*, a collection of six *nouvelles* or
romans goguenards published in August 1833, was in any case
a satire on the most useless and excessive manifestations of
Romanticism; it was a further statement of personal emancipation (even Nanteuil, the 'jeune homme moyen-âge', was
made fun of, as 'Élias Wildmanstadius'), while its very
subject-matter, treated with characteristically double-edged
irony, was intended as an example of shocking bad taste to
horrify the bourgeois.[50]

   With the dissolution of the Petit Cénacle after Borel had led
it away from Duseigneur's studio and from the rarefied,
aesthetic idealism that it had dwelt on there, the period
covered by *L'Histoire du romantisme* ends. By 1833, with
Poésies and *Albertus* published and with the encouragement
of Hugo, the former 'jeune rapin à cœur de lion' had made his
choice between literature and painting. In May Hugo had

published a rallying manifesto in *L'Europe littéraire*, a *rappel à l'ordre* in which he exhorted Romantic writers to continue the struggle in the production of finished works. His emphasis on the importance of literary technique and form— 'Kill the form and you almost always kill the idea'[51]—was further ideological support for Gautier's resolve to withdraw and discover his range as a writer. Poetry, he reaffirmed in the story *Celle-ci et celle-là* in *Les Jeunes-France*, was to be found at home:[52] 'Poetry is no more here than it is there: it is within us.' Thus he worked in earnest, acquiring, through the success and controversy of *Mademoiselle de Maupin*, published in 1835 and 1836, a growing literary reputation. Yet painters still outnumbered writers among his friends, and his view of the world remained essentially that of a painter.

In 1834, his father had been appointed receiver of taxes in outlying Passy, and the family left the Place Royale. Wishing to remain in Paris, Théophile joined his old friend Gérard de Nerval and the painter Camille Rogier at their new residence in a crumbling house in the Impasse du Doyenné. The Impasse was situated among a group of old houses which stood in a corner of the present Place du Carrousel and literally in the shadow of the Louvre. They were all that remained of a demolished *quartier* and were due for demolition themselves, thus permanently unrepaired. They were not finally knocked down until 1850; Balzac described them in *La Cousine Bette* as 'tombeaux vivants', living tombs. Respectable and solidly affluent dwellings in the eighteenth century, they were rich and macabre settings for dreams of the past, and provided the background for a Romantic *tableau vivant*, into which Gautier and Gérard could effect escape from contemporary Paris. The Impasse du Doyenné was an oasis of solitude and silence where, as Gautier later recalled, 'an encampment of literary and artistic gipsies led the life of Robinson Crusoe, not on the island of Juan Fernandez, but right in the middle of Paris, in sight of the bourgeois and constitutional monarchy'.[53] Gérard treated it as a literal encampment, sleeping in a kind of tent he had erected in the former salon. The *tableau vivant* also contained a Renaissance bed, some tapestries, and two large Fragonard panels among the other props acquired by Gérard; all it needed now was animation, to be provided by what else but a fancy-dress ball. Gautier, Adolphe Leleux, Nanteuil, Chassériau, and Corot helped produce decorations for the occasion, and the scene stands out in Gautier's repertoire of key memories, a frozen set piece like an early group photograph, carefully posed to look natural: 'we were perched on our ladders, roses in our ears, cigarettes in our lips, palettes in hand, humming ballads by Musset or declaiming verses by Victor Hugo'. The Doyenné was a continuation of carefree studio life, a life of scintillating surfaces like an eighteenth-century *fête galante*. The scene had already become fixed as part of Gautier's personal mythology by 1848; he recalled it in the obituary of his friend and exact contemporary, the Orientalist landscape painter Marilhat, cherishing and idealizing the memory as compensation for the disastrous events of that year. By then, the mural decorations had long disappeared under a coat of whitewash; the dream picture was put aside and the business of journalism began again with a biographical sketch of the departed Marilhat.

The Impasse du Doyenné was Gautier's last opportunity to create a real alternative world. But if no such ideal could survive outside literature and painting, the comparative freedom from family and financial obligations that Gautier had enjoyed up to the age of twenty-five left him with an ineradicable sense of what could be, or, more accurately, of what could have been. He dreamt of an art that could be lived, a total environment in which man himself was a contributing element in the overall formal harmony, dressed to complement the décor and, no doubt, speaking in verse. The *mot propre* and the vernacular and technical talk of the studio had entered Gautier's language, reflecting his effort to reconcile his two artistic leanings. On the simplest level, studio slang can be picked out of his early poetry, words like *chic, galbe, poncif, rococo, bonhomme*, which would be instantly intelligible to a *rapin*; for Gautier was always an artist writing for artists. Examples are taken from painting to add precision to visual impressions, as has been seen in Borel-painted-by-Velazquez. Jasinski likens the long title-poem of *Albertus* to a 'Romantic gallery', so rich is it in figures of speech which exploit favourite painting—for example, 'an old country town such as Teniers painted', 'this bowed head could be a *Mater Dei* after Masaccio', 'Salvator could have signed this *Selve Selvagge*'.[54] Jasinski compares this series of transpositions to miniature pictures in a larger composition, as in the passage in the poem where the contents of the hero's studio are evoked. From his very earliest essays Gautier wrote about art, and 'art for art's sake' is often synonymous with 'art about art'. The poem 'A Louis Boulanger' was first published as a separate instalment in the *Salon of 1836*;[55] it is a poem before it is criticism, only it is a poem about a painting about a poet, and deals with the broadest of critical concepts, with 'la peinture', 'l'art', 'le beau', 'la forme sculptée', and 'la poésie' itself. It finally constitutes a little manifesto which itself aspires to be an example of the kind of beauty it endorses.

Above all, Gautier's use of studio and critical terms expressed his formal way of seeing, and had the function of expanding the range and detail of visual perceptions accessible to poetry and prose. This was most strikingly revealed to the reading public through the descriptive tableaux of *Mademoiselle de Maupin*. 'This involvement of art in poetry has been and remains one of the characteristics of the new School', he wrote in *L'Histoire du romantisme*,[56] 'and explains why its first initiates were drawn from among artists rather than writers. A host of objects, images, and comparisons which had been thought irreducible to words has entered the language and stayed there. The sphere of literature has expanded and now encompasses that of art in its immense orbit.' Romantic painting (with the partial exception of landscape) was of course largely dependent on literature for subject-matter, differing in this respect from the classicism it rejected only in the kind of literature it chose for inspiration; by reversing the process, by introducing art to literature, Gautier was to find himself the champion of a new kind of artist, one whose work could be discussed within the terms of the work itself, without necessary recourse to literature for a measure of success or failure. With his inside knowledge of studio life, personal friendships with artists and would-be artists, and a degree of youthful literary notoriety, he was the natural public representative of 'the new School'.

3 **Professional** *vie artiste*

The need to earn a steady income was becoming pressing. In 1835 he met Balzac, who admired *Mademoiselle de Maupin* and invited Gautier to collaborate on his latest fortune-making project, the review *La Chronique de Paris*. In July and early August 1836, accompanied by Nerval, Théophile visited Belgium on the first of his travels outside France, in search of the physical ideal of Rubens made flesh (he was by now well beyond the sickly timorous phase of his personal mythological history). 'Un Tour en Belgique' appeared in *La Chronique de Paris* in September. His mistress, Eugénie Fort, meanwhile, was pregnant; their son, Théophile junior (Toto) was born in November. No longer able to rely on his father, he was to have a family of his own to support. In August, therefore, he had begun to contribute art criticism to Émile de Girardin's *La Presse*.

Described by Joanna Richardson as a 'nineteenth-century Citizen Kane',[57] Girardin was five years older than Gautier; the relationship between readership-conscious proprietor and often recalcitrant critic was to be fraught, and mollified only by Gautier's close friendship with Mme Delphine de Girardin, who, an admirer of Hugo and Lamartine, was a poetess and columnist herself, and had attended the first night of *Hernani*. Gautier's entrée to her Romantic salon had been effected through Hugo and Balzac; Gautier became one of its most favoured regulars. Romanticism was adjusting itself to the regime; Gautier's first article for Girardin was on Delacroix's paintings in the Throne Room of the Chambre des Députés.[58] Girardin clearly saw potential capital in the presence in his columns of a controversial ex-member of the notoriously maladjusted Jeunes-France, and promptly commissioned a second article[59], on the French school in Rome. This was more provocative ground, which, as Girardin no doubt shrewdly anticipated, would elicit sparkling invective from his new columnist.

But for a small section of the reading public, at least, it would have been no surprise to learn that geniuses could not be bought 'for three thousand francs apiece' or that Turner and Constable were more use to young landscape painters than 'Claude Lorraine, whose reputation has been inflated out of all proportion'. If Théophile's full-time career as an art critic began with these articles in August 1836, he had been unknowingly preparing the ground for his début as a journalist since 1831, with contributions to lesser publications such as *Le Mercure de France au XIX*ᵉ *siècle*, *Le Cabinet de lecture*, *La France littéraire*, *La France industrielle*, and his own *Ariel, journal du monde élégant*. Although his art criticism had reached a narrower readership than that for which *La Presse* was to cater, it had already covered a wide range of subjects; it included four Salons, as well as pleas for the reform of official patronage, strongly worded support for Ingres, Delacroix, Decamps, the landscape school, Pradier and Barye, and statements of critical aims. In late 1836 he also began collaboration with *Le Figaro*, and in July 1837 the duties of a theatre critic were added to his commitments to *La Presse*. He had planned to travel to Italy with Balzac in the spring, but the Salon of 1837 kept him in Paris. His fortunes were to remain tied thus to the ever urgent demand for copy.

In the late 1830s, Théophile was at a peak of virile self-confidence, revelling in his image as a blatantly unrepentant Romantic (*plate 2*). Ernest Feydeau, the Egyptologist, collaborator on *Le Roman de la momie*, and father of the writer of farces, recalled Gautier's appearance in his *Souvenirs intimes*: chestnut hair, literally to the waist, black velvet jacket, and yellow Turkish babouches. He was dressed for the street. Romanticism, Feydeau wrote, recalling the period of his own adolescence, manifested itself around 1840 in 'the strangest kinds of eccentricity . . . Everywhere people were very seriously engaged in amusing themselves'.⁶⁰ In 1837 Gautier had published *Fortunio*, a celebration of wealth and sumptuousness in *nouvelle* form, and if *La Comédie de la mort* of the following year dwelt ominously on 'the invisible void' and 'living death', it was the life-embracing Gautier who dominated during these years; he was confident enough to have produced a second Théophile, a son of his own name, if not in his own image, and sure enough of his own creative energy to announce the imminent publication of a large scale follow-up to *Mademoiselle de Maupin*, *Le Capitaine Fracasse*. He lived in La Nouvelle-Athènes, the artists' quarter between the rue des Martyrs, the rue Saint-Lazare, the rue de Clichy, and the *boulevard extérieur*; he was an artist, working on behalf of artists for the benefit of the bourgeois public he had been committed to outrage, and this awareness was reflected in his art criticism. The division between artist and the rest was clear, and Gautier's invective had definite targets; it had not yet become diffused into weary and generalized complaint at the lot of the critic. Against the true feeling and total dedication to an ideal of real artists, were set the repressive jury system with its penchant for mediocrity, and artists who compromised their calling by pandering to fashion and bourgeois taste. The artist had a duty to lift the public's consciousness from the ugliness and squalor of modern life; he was an educator who should not be afraid of involving himself in the embellishment of domestic, civic, and industrial objects, yet his apartness, as a member of an élite, remained the essential attribute of his nature. He fitted the sculptor Préault's definition: 'The artist has longer, higher, and sharper vision than other men. You see this star? he says to the vulgar. You don't? Well *I* see it!'[61] It did not matter what the artist's particular ideal was, provided that in following his own star he was in wholehearted pursuit of excellence.

Outside artistic circles, art was hardly a public issue during the reign of Louis-Philippe; if certain artists, under the banner of Romanticism, had aligned themselves with radical and subversive elements in society, their productions had not swamped the Salons; and for the triumphant and expanding bourgeoisie, art was no more than an increasingly saleable leisure commodity. As a critic under this relatively liberal regime, whose tolerance was generally closer to indifference, Gautier was free to write more or less as he pleased, as Feydeau suggests. 'He was in his element writing about painting and painters. He was left in complete freedom to say everything he wanted to say about them in the press, for art was a matter of relative indifference to the directors of the serious newspapers, who, besides, did not understand the first thing about it . . .',[62] as long as he produced his copy on time and wrote nothing that might compromise his editor.

In May 1840, having disposed once more of the Salon and

its reactionary jury, he set off by coach to Spain, contracted
by *La Presse* to send back regular instalments of travelogue,
later to be published as *Voyage en Espagne*. Eugène Piot, an
old friend from the Doyenné, travelled with him as official
photographer. Spain had already loomed large in the Jeune-
France imagination; it was to be a revelation like, Gautier
said, discovering his real home, the native land of his spirit.[63]
He felt himself transformed, and the experience helped
confirm his restless longing for the unfamiliar and the
unknown, whether in art or in real life. Travel, he realized,
was not just an escape from claustrophobic routine; it was a
way of changing his whole mental terrain and becoming part
of a new environment, of allowing himself to assume a new
disguise and slip unnoticed into the formal harmony. He
travelled as a true Romantic and 'flamboyant', drunk on local
colour and dazzled by a profusion of new visual experiences.
'. . . my method', he told his son-in-law Émile Bergerat in
1871 or '72, 'is the same as Lord Byron's. I travel for the sake
of travelling, that is to see and enjoy new points of view, to
change places, to escape from myself and from others. I travel
to make a dream come true, quite simply, or to change skin if
you like. I went to Constantinople to be a Muslim at my
leisure . . . in Rome, I become apostolic and Roman'.[64]
Every country he visited was the realization of a quite
different dream, characterized by a combination of climate,
landscape, building, costume, and physical type that was
unique to it. Thus Gautier deplored the progress of
civilization, which he saw in terms of encroaching visual
uniformity: Spain and Turkey were being infiltrated by the
frock-coat, carried by train. Short-sighted as he was, he
needed to picture the world in terms of strong contrasts,
which he found above all in the countries of the
Mediterranean; his love of contrasts was also a recognition of
the vast potentialities of the human mind, with all its
disparate and seemingly incompatible yearnings.

Form was permanent; why should he bother to bring to life
the inhabitants of the landscapes he described, who were not?
Feydeau recalled a conversation in which Gautier spoke of
criticism he had received for his treatment of Turks in the
travel book *Constantinople*. 'Anyone would think that none of

them had a soul', it had been remarked of Gautier's Turks. His response to this criticism serves to throw further light on his aims as a descriptive writer. 'What you would need to know, in fact,' he explained to Feydeau, 'is first of all what a soul is, and then if the Turks have got souls, which has never been scientifically proven.'[65] The soul was an invisible, thus hypothetical entity, hinted at perhaps in certain exterior features, which, as Gautier remarked to Feydeau, are in any case hard to observe in Turks, who are secretive and shy of Europeans. The experience of his eyes was all that Gautier could be sure of, and it engaged him totally; anything else was fatuous conjecture. A Turk was simply a Turk, as a pschent was a pschent; a Turk was defined as such by his appearance, and since Gautier had been one himself, 'a Muslim at his leisure', he could bypass the question of soul as irrelevant. 'La plastique est l'art supérieur',[66] he told Feydeau; visual art is the superior art.

He returned from his Spanish journey in September 1840, to a life of official duty and increasing public success. If the collection of poems *España* that he completed on his return was allegedly composed with the quill that an eagle had dropped for him on the Sierra Nevada,[67] in other areas his passion for colourful detail had to be curbed, as would befit the sober role of secretary to the commission for Napoleon's monument, and Chevalier de la Légion d'honneur, which he became in January 1842. His entrée to the Opera, through two highly successful ballets, *Giselle* and *La Péri*, required the greatest concessions to respectability; he cut his hair to a decent shoulder-length, Feydeau reports, and abandoned the more exotic items of his costume.[68] The dancer Carlotta Grisi who performed both his ballets became his mistress; in 1842 and '43 he accompanied her to London for their premières there, and in 1843 even collaborated on a successful vaudeville based on his Spanish journey. The following year he fell in love with Carlotta's sister, the singer Ernesta, with whom he lived and who shortly bore him two daughters. But his public and private successes remained dependent on the production of feuilletons and on official favour for support; thus in 1845 he accompanied General Bugeaud's expedition to the new colony of Algeria, in a semi-official capacity, and in 1846, as a representative of the Arts on the first train to leave the Gare du Nord, he found it in him to proclaim the new railway as 'the beginning of a new era in poetry'.[69] If his public status frequently obliged him to compromise his convictions and assume stances that remained distinct from attitudes he expressed elsewhere, he could already shut himself off from events and manipulate his prose, as if from a distance, to say anything. This useful capacity generally enabled him to turn his role as a journalist to his best advantage. In 1846, for example, he was off to Spain again, by more traditionally picturesque means than the railway, with press coverage of the royal marriages in Madrid for excuse; *Militona*, a Spanish story long overdue for serialization in *La Presse*, was finally completed in ten days with the aid of a little hashish.[70] Yet there was no escape from the fact that the maintenance of his life-style depended to no small degree on his credit with Girardin; the shortcomings of his situation were highlighted on 2 February 1847, when Girardin publicly and humiliatingly corrected him in *La Presse* for an aside in a recent feuilleton about the miserable fate of artists who were forced to prostitute their talents as underpaid journalists. His position was summed up by Maxime Du Camp: 'His talent had brought him celebrity; he was recognized as a poet of high rank and a great prose writer; newspapers, reviews, and publishers demanded him; he lived in style, if not exactly according to his taste.'[71]

The year 1848 really marks the end of Gautier's hopeful youth and the beginning of bitterness and disillusion. The February Revolution found him in debt, and Ernesta pregnant, and since credit of any kind was hard to come by, he was forced to relinquish his life-style as a cosmopolitan and a man-about-town, and to live directly on his feuilletons as his only remaining realizable assets. His mother died in March, and an article hastily penned paid for her funeral. In July he wrote the obituary of Marilhat for *La Revue des Deux Mondes*, apologizing for the lateness of his article as if it were a desertion from the cause of art, and giving full vent to his personal bitterness, since he was not writing for *La Presse*: '. . . the daily grind, the thousand cares of existence, the sorrows and disappointments of a poet who pursues his dream through the oppressive realities of journalism, a revolution, the inconsolable grief of a bereavement in the most painful of circumstances, such is my excuse, and my tribute will be no less strongly felt for being somewhat belated. I forget no one quickly, except fools and scoundrels.'[72] This was among the first of his obituaries of Romantic artist-casualties, with whom he would tacitly express his solidarity as he marked their fall from the depleted ranks of the Romantic army. The enemy, from now on, was not only 'the sorrows and disappointments' of everyday reality and the 'fools and scoundrels' that it harboured, but also death itself. An avenue of escape lay in nostalgia for his own past; as has been seen, Marilhat's obituary also contained an evocation of the never-never land of the Doyenné: an expression of the disenchantment and anxiety that established itself in Gautier's mental landscape in 1848.

The year 1848 also provided a golden opportunity once more to assert art's independence, as a great compensation for the failure of other human institutions. Governments fall, art survives, reads the opening of the *Salon of 1848* in *La Presse*, 'the breeze soon dissipates the smell of powder and sweeps away the opaque clouds of smoke, and the temple of Art re-emerges in its serene whiteness, against the unchangeable azure.'[73] The task of the critic is as important as that of those in public office: to maintain the clear, well defined and serene ideal of art, an ideal of order, against nebulous chaos. At the same time, Gautier enlisted revolutionary fervour in support of his withdrawn and impassive ideal. The long-despised jury has gone (its members are verbally guillotined), leaving 'Full and absolute liberty, liberty for all, for young and old alike, for the unknown as for the illustrious, for the skilful as for blunderers, for the sublime as for the ridiculous! . . . Fall away, old fetters! Collapse, decrepit barriers! . . . Let the people judge for itself!' etc. A feuilleton for every occasion: Gautier's words took care of themselves, and of Gautier. Like his worship at the temple of art, his pragmatic and always just faintly ironical reflection of what he considered to be the prevailing spirit of the moment expressed above all a need for personal security.

4 Nostalgia

He continued to write for *La Presse* until 1855; in 1853 he had
begun to contribute to *Le Moniteur universel*, the official
organ of the recently proclaimed Empire, and he was to
remain virtually the government's own art and theatre critic
until 1870, through *Le Moniteur*'s transformation in 1869 to
plain *Journal officiel de l'empire français*. His father died in
1854, leaving Gautier's two unmarried sisters to his financial
care; in 1857 he withdrew from Paris to a quiet house in
Neuilly, rue de Longchamp, 32, where his sisters set up home
with him. The prestige given by official favour would, he
hoped, protect him against the more pressing and demeaning
demands of everyday life. In 1851 he had become the object of
a three-year legal action brought against him by *La Revue des
Deux Mondes* for his continuing failure to produce the ever
promised *Le Capitaine Fracasse*; in the same year he was
imprisoned for shirking his citizen's duty as a *garde national*.
The ultimate haven, as he increasingly saw it, was the
Academy, ensuring official invulnerability and immortality
to its select members. Government commissions were forthcoming. In 1855 he was appointed by the Minister of State to
help award prizes for drama (along with two former *bêtes
noires* of Romanticism, Nisard and Scribe), and in 1858 he
was promoted to the rank of Officier de la Légion d'honneur;
by 1864, he was a member of the Conseil supérieur
d'enseignement pour les Beaux-Arts, the president of the
Societé nationale des Beaux-Arts, a member of the once much
reviled Salon jury, and frequently to be seen in the Imperial
circle. He was thus extremely well connected and at the centre
of the Parisian art-world; he found especially high-level
refuge in his *amitié voluptueuse* with the imperial Princesse
Mathilde and in her comprehensively artistic salon where, in
the company of men such as Augier, Ingres, Meissonier,
Girardin, Nieuwerkerke, Viollet-le-Duc, Vernet, Gounod,
Dumas fils, Flaubert, the Goncourts, Sainte-Beuve, and
Banville, his sparklingly paradoxical conversation could take
wing. But the Academy, which had crowned Sainte-Beuve as
the great critic of the age, continued to elude him; in 1868,

Princesse Mathilde appointed him her almost honorary librarian in compensation. His third and final bid for Academic immortality failed the following year.

As his personal need for official honours grew, the theme of permanence through form loomed larger in his thinking.

> Tout passe – L'art robuste
> Seul a l'éternité.
> Le buste
> Survit à la cité.

('Everything is transient. Robust art alone is eternal. The bust survives the city.')

First published in *L'Artiste* in 1857[74] and appended to later editions of *Émaux et Camées*, poems which had appeared in 1852 fashioned and polished like jewels set to last for ever, the poem 'L'Art' gave full and definitive expression to Gautier's notion of art as compensation. Everything is transient, except sculpture and verse, because they are made from the most unyielding and durable of materials, he wrote; and if in his 1867 autobiographical sketch for *L'Illustration* he admitted that artistic immortality had eluded him personally—'I am not one of those people whose house posterity will distinguish with a bust or a marble plaque'[75]—he was able to do so because he had come to see his role as a critic and a poet in a humbler light. It might not be his own marble bust that would survive the destruction of the city, but he would at least have touched immortality in his lifetime, as a rapt worshipper and conscientious tender of the undying flame of Art. This reverential idealism was strongly reflected in his editorship of *L'Artiste*, which he took over in 1856. Unlike other publications, *L'Artiste* was to be unmercenary and non-partisan, religiously respectful of the opinions of its contributors and openly comprehensive of all the experiences that art had to offer. Grouped around the Master, Feydeau recalled, 'we had no aim in mind other than art . . . I have never known a more genuinely liberal editor'.[76] ' "Here, you can say anything, anything at all" ', Gautier told his collaborators, who included Feydeau, the Goncourts, Baudelaire, Charles Blanc, Flaubert, Saint-Victor, Fromentin, Viollet-le-Duc, Banville, and Murger, ' "as long as you don't attack the doctrine of Art for Art's Sake . . . Let us always do our best, and not trouble ourselves in the least about our subscribers: this must be our unbreakable rule." '

Such idealism was harder to maintain in his work for *Le Moniteur universel*. The sheer quantity of the art of the Second Empire presented an impossible task to a critic who had stated his intention to admire as much as possible, who prided himself on being able to describe anything, and who was obliged, as the government critic responsible for summing up the yearly progress of France's artists, to make a comprehensive critical survey of the annual or biennial Salons. It was no wonder, in these circumstances, if Gautier resorted to describing pictures he had never seen, or employed ghost-writers. Joanna Richardson lists Théophile junior, Noël Parfait, Louis de Cormenin, Maxime Du Camp, Arsène Houssaye, Ernest Reyer, and Adolphe Bazin as among Gautier's possible *critiques blonds*;[77] Gautier himself added his Abyssinian servant Abdallah Pergialla to the list, a comment on how much he came to see the production of critical prose as a mechanical routine, operable by remote control. The passions and clear-cut rivalries that had engaged him during the '30s and '40s had disappeared from the Salons, and had been replaced by a general level of technical competence; many of the artist friends whose successes and failures he had taken as if they were his own were ageing, sterile, absent, or dead,[78] and the intentions of the rising generation were often harder to sympathize with. As the most widely read art critic of the time he was solicited from every quarter:

There is no painter, sculptor, actor, writer of vaudevilles, no acrobat, nor trainer of performing horses who does not write to him to solicit his support. He is addressed as: Dear and illustrious Master, or simply: Dear Monsieur Gauthier, with an irritating *h* added to his so very famous name. He is requested to come round to the studio to view the picture or statue destined for the next Salon;

rejected artists want him to call God and Man to witness for the injustice of which they are victims[79]

wrote Du Camp. Most soul-destroying of all was theatre criticism; even greater than his distaste for the glib anecdotal mediocrity or affected real-life sordidness of certain paintings was the nausea caused him by the ugliness and banality of many modern plays, which, commented Feydeau, 'were too like . . . charades and riddles, and besides represented the actions of characters with little to commend them to an artist'.[80] Then there were so many diverse personal interests involved in the success or failure of a play, often including those of newspaper proprietors. The Goncourts were conveniently on hand in 1867 to record an anecdote illustrating Gautier's delicate position: 'One day M. Walewski told him that he need no longer be indulgent and that from tomorrow he could write what he really thought about the plays he reviewed. But, said Gautier, this week there is a play by Doucet . . . Ah! said M. Walewski, perhaps you could start next week?—Well, I'm still waiting for next week!'[81] 'Le bon Théo' 's reputation for forbearance was not only a result of his natural identification with artists. 'I am really ashamed of the job I do!' he exclaimed to the Goncourts in 1857,[82] the year of the *Madame Bovary* trial. 'For very modest sums, which I have to earn because without them I would starve to death, I say only a half or a quarter of what I really think . . . and even then, I risk being dragged before the courts with every sentence I write!'

Gautier had an increased feeling of missed vocation, of unbridgeable distance between his daily routine as a journalist and what he saw as his real preoccupations. He continually sought escape. 'Perhaps I am beginning to get old,' he told the Goncourts in 1862, 'but there's no air these days. It's all very well having wings, but you also need air . . . I no longer feel contemporary.'[83] The pleasures that had carried him away when he was younger seemed hollow, and were not compensation enough; the sensual faculties needed to grasp them were failing, and it was his capacity for physical and visual sensation that had linked him to the present. No doubt he was making an exaggerated generalization when he wrote to his sisters from Russia in 1859 that art, pictures, books, and even travel amused him no longer, being merely the reasons for more work and weariness;[84] yet his constant complaints during the last fifteen years of his life make his desire for escape to more and more rarefied realms seem almost like an overt death-wish. Real life was unable to support his dreams; he seems to have felt himself a useless survivor engaged in meaningless gestures. As if to point up the distance between the life of the imagination and that of everyday practicalities, his great friend Gérard de Nerval had hanged himself in grotesquely picturesque circumstances in 1855, the year of the Exposition Universelle, which Gautier covered in six hundred pages of prose for *Le Moniteur*. Unlike Gérard, Gautier always provided himself with a return ticket before setting out on his escapist excursions; he suffered instead from a kind of spiritual jet-lag. According to Joanna Richardson, he told Eugénie Fort in 1864 that he felt himself becoming a pure spirit, and that his imagination seemed to him more real than reality.[85]

He remained a restless traveller and continued to try to make dreams come true, in tangible terms. Between 1849 and his death he visited or revisited London (three times), Bilbao, Italy (twice), Malta, Constantinople, Athens, Munich, Russia (twice), Algeria, Madrid, Egypt, and Geneva (where Carlotta Grisi provided a haven from Paris, many times). He returned from Russia a Russian, bursting in on a dinner party clad in furs from head to foot, as if the snow were still on his boots (*plate 3*);[86] he promenaded in Egyptian disguise and with Ernest Feydeau's help verbally photographed Egypt in *Le Roman de la momie* ten years before he ever went there; and in 1863 *Le Capitaine Fracasse* was finally completed, the most mammoth and theatrical fantasy of all. But it was at the dinner-table that Gautier seems to have given freest rein to his literary instincts; here the verbal facility that he switched into operation for his articles in *Le Moniteur* enabled him to reach heights of sparkling and vulgar hyperbole. He talked exactly as he wrote: 'Do us a feuilleton!' Feydeau would request,[87] but the subject-matter of Gautier's discourse would be far removed from that of his Salon articles, if the tone was the same. The 'truculent stories . . . amazing paradoxes . . . subversive discussions' with which he made himself the life and soul of Madame Sabatier's dinner-parties would be met by the perfect tolerance[88] of the hostess, who in any case was used to receiving his richly pornographic letters. The artistic salons and dinners of the '50s and '60s were like re-enactments of the Petit Cénacle for grown-ups. At 'La Présidente' 's, and at the regularly reconvened and secret-club-like Magny dinners, Gautier could give his large-scale exotic, despotic, and lustily sensual urges a healthy airing. His conversation was a purgative, or an old Romantic's talking therapy, which enabled him to touch upon all the chords of his experience. 'His voice was monotonous, rarely inflected and . . . serenely insistent,' recalled Émile Bergerat. 'It flowed evenly; one felt that the poet's strong personality assimilated everything and submitted to nothing.'[89] The Goncourts would gleefully listen to this 'Sultan of the epithet' as they savoured Sainte-Beuve's special cocktail at Magny's:

Gautier tirelessly scatters paradoxes, lofty observations, original thoughts, the pearls of his fantasy. What a conversationalist! . . . What a feast for artists this flow of language with its two tones, its frequently mingled notes of Rabelais and Heine, of monstrous outrageousness and tender melancholy! He was talking of ennui this evening, the ennui that gnaws at him: he spoke as the poet and the colourist of ennui![90]

In the last year of his life, according to Bergerat,[91] he had a catch phrase with which he would interrupt discussions, even his own monologues: 'Nothing is any good for anything! To begin with there's nothing, yet everything happens! But that's all quite immaterial!' It was a sick man's rambling and inconsequential pet speech, perhaps, but one which never-theless reflected Gautier's 'lassitude d'hippopotame', his overwhelming sense of the supreme indifference of nature, and the sense of his own detachment that accompanied it; this had haunted him throughout his life. Gautier's *mot*, sig-nificant to note, had been invented by a visual artist, the enameller (maker of *émaux*) Claudius Popelin.

Gautier survived a third political upheaval. He was in Paris during the siege and Commune, living in cramped and cheap lodgings with his emaciated cats while shells fell into his garden in Neuilly. His physical powers were destroyed; he had suffered two heart-attacks in 1868, and the imminence of death filled him with anger. After all the trouble you have taken cultivating your talents, he told Feydeau, you are without warning 'stopped in mid-action by a great blow with a scythe through the belly . . . it's disgusting.'⁹² Death seemed as ugly and pointless as the revolutions which had upset his plans before; at the same time he was able to achieve the acquiescence of *Tableaux de siège*, as if with death all around him, he had nothing more to lose, and could once more take pleasure in the spectacle of life, however tentative its hold. 'It is not so much men taken as individuals who are tyrannical and stupid,' Feydeau heard, 'as humanity as a whole that abhors the Beautiful and the Good. Humanity is idiotic. Nowhere is it able to make use of the riches lying under its nose.'⁹³ Gautier's mission had been to realize and fix in permanent literary form the riches to be gained from sensual perception; but his aesthetic nirvana was always less accessible than it had seemed in his dreams as a 'jeune rapin à cœur de lion'. Hence the disillusion that grew on him during the last half of his career, manifesting itself at one moment in grossly flamboyant overcompensation, and at another in resigned and diffident melancholy—Rabelais and Heine.

'The great event in Gautier's existence is not his participation in Romanticism, it is this journalist's career that appeared one day open before him and which he has had to follow without respite ever since. Alas! Poor Gautier!', Émile Montégut had written on him in 1865.⁹⁴ In 1872 he resumed his task as an art critic, covering the Salon in *Le Bien public* and contributing instalments of *L'Histoire du romantisme*. Like the model in Rioult's studio, human grasp of the beautiful and the good had proved imperfect; ultimately Gautier was unable to assimilate the fact that the permanence and serenity of sculpture were ideals reserved strictly for sculpture, and withdrew into a private world, which, at its worst, was one of lethargy and indifference, and in which he was sheltered and comforted by his mythic, superhuman, and unliveable autobiography. He died in his house in Neuilly on 23 October 1872.

II The Critic

1 Stated aims

Like the preface to *Mademoiselle de Maupin* itself, Gautier's art criticism is full of inconsistencies and contradictions. He was essentially a pragmatist, embracing one polemical line to support the argument of the moment, only to reject it the next moment in favour of some new resonance. The public of 1833 was 'devoid of that capacity for admiration which makes for great artists'; a few paragraphs further on, the readers of *La France littéraire* learnt that they were not so insensitive after all, their eyes having been opened by Gautier's intervening lines, no doubt: [1] 'Let us hope, anyway, that the French public, which is becoming more and more artistic, will finally do sculpture all the justice that it deserves'. The journalistic grandeur of his statements was an aspect of his provocative sense of irony, which in turn was a weapon at the service of Romantic *instinct*, set in opposition to the aridity and inflexibility which, in Gautier's eyes, the classicist cult of reason had ultimately brought to art. Gautier's reaction against blindly a priori criticism in the preface to *Mademoiselle de Maupin* was a rejection of systems, above all in that it was unsystematic itself; its polemical effect rested not on well-reasoned, consistent argument but on humour, and the irrational forces it could unleash. Continuity is destroyed, and the ground falls beneath the attentive and reasonable reader at every turn; the dogmatic and grandiose utterances of Gautier's Rabelaisian pseudo-arguments are reason parodied to mild delirium. 'Nothing is really beautiful except that which cannot be used for anything; everything that is useful is ugly, for it is the expression of some need[2] . . . . enjoyment seems to me to be the aim of life, and the only useful thing in the world.'[3] His arguments are primed to destroy themselves in the face of the reader who tries to catch Gautier at his game. He has built in

self-directed irony; he discreetly parodies his love of exquisitely accurate local colour, for instance. God wanted
pleasure to be the aim of life, he writes, 'He who has made
women, perfumes, light, beautiful flowers, good wines,
spirited horses, Italian greyhounds, and angora cats'[4] (not
just any dogs or cats; for Gautier was not like just any
Spaniard, but like a Spaniard from Cuba).

The argument grows and the style is fully inflated, only to
fizzle out like a mysteriously deflated balloon: God 'who,
finally, has bestowed upon us alone that threefold and
glorious privilege of drinking without being thirsty, of
striking lights, and of making love in all seasons, which
distinguishes us from the beasts far more than the practice of
reading newspapers and drawing up charters'.[5] Glorious
privileges? 'Battre le briquet'? The preface bears no direct
relation to the novel: even Gautier's hero Albert, presented at
the beginning of the novel as a terminally bored and sceptical
young man who has given up looking for anything to amuse
him, is made a fool of in the preface, in company with 'blasé
journalists . . . : everything bores them, everything wears
them out and prostrates them'.[6] *Les Jeunes-France* of the
previous year had been a parody of the Romantic cult of
unreason itself, a rejection of extremism that had become
systemized. Gautier was continually executing such elusive
ironical pirouettes, and if there was a line of ideological
consistency behind his criticism it lay in this unsystematic
rejection of critical systems.

'In our articles on the Salon', he wrote in *Ariel* in 1836, 'we
shall speak only of statues and pictures and not of any
pantheistic or palingenetical system—a simple yet strange
enough idea, since it has never been done before.'[7] This is a
declaration of critical emancipation that stands in line of
descent from Stendhal's blunt resolve to rely for judgement
on nothing but reference to his own experience. But Gautier
aimed for greater open-mindedness; where Stendhal had
proclaimed his right to be partial, not to know much but to
know what he liked, Gautier sought an initially impartial state
of mind, which, coupled with wide connoisseurship and
inside knowledge of painters' practice, would leave him
susceptible to an ever broadening range of artistic sensations.

Stendhal referred art to his best real-life experiences; for Gautier, art was experience itself: he referred life to art. Yet his rejection of imposed systems of thought was as essential a purging of the perceptions as it was for Stendhal; the common concern of both men was that art should yield the maximum quota of pleasure. As early as 1834 Gautier had a clear conception of art criticism's role. Art criticism was to operate like a sympathetic but discriminating guide, who desired only to be allowed to admire; it was to be unhampered by the critic's fault-picking preconceptions.

Our criticism will be different from that of the other newspapers . . . in that far from discoursing at length on faults and taking great pains to reveal them, it will apply itself rather to bringing out qualities. We can hardly conceive of criticism as anything else. The critic is a kind of cicerone who takes you by the hand and guides you through a country that you do not yet know. What would you think of a guide who conducted you through the muddiest and least well-built streets in town, in order to lead you to some insignificant hovel, instead of bringing you to a halt in front of fine palaces and ancient churches? . . . of a host who took you straight to the latrines?⁸*

Thus Gautier opened his *Salon of 1834* for *La France industrielle*. Writing only weeks before the composition of the preface to *Mademoiselle de Maupin*, he stated that as a guide he intended to be useful; except for some 'balloons bloated with praises, which need pins to be stuck in them so that the wind distending them can escape, leaving them emptier than a poet's purse or a courtesan's conscience, we shall speak only of things worthy of discussion.' It may be amusing for a critic to insist on pointing out faults, in positive disregard of the artist's manifest intentions and in favour of some set of preconceptions of his own, but it is a limiting exercise.

In May 1834 Gautier felt himself to be the victim of such criticism. His current enthusiasm for Villon, Rabelais and the French Renaissance (reflected in colourful turns of phrase such as 'emptier than a poet's purse') was finding expression in a series of articles for *La France littéraire*, the first of which, on Villon, was the object of the moral condemnation of *Le Constitutionnel*. Gautier counter-attacked in his preface; but beneath his humorously overstated polemic, he was only the more convinced of the seriousness of the ideal of art's autonomy, of the value of considering works of art in none but their own terms.

Gautier's task was to introduce the uninitiated to the fascinating vicissitudes of the life of the separate realm of art; the limits of this realm were to be discerned from the inside, by Gautier's own capacity for assimilation, not by means of any outside moral, religious, or political terms of reference. 'In matters of art, we have no religion apart from that of art itself, and Venus pleases us as much as the Virgin. We are pagan or Catholic according to the talent of the sculptor. The arts are not systems', he wrote in 1836 for *Le Cabinet de lecture*.[9] Taking paintings and sculptures as he found them, he saw his criticism as asylum for their delicate existences. The twice-weekly periodical *Ariel*, founded in 1836 by Gautier and Charles Lassailly (who, as an unhappy protégé of Balzac, perhaps felt in need of refuge himself), survived for only two months; Gautier's dedication for *Ariel*'s first issue appeared beneath the editorial proviso 'Politics are excluded from this journal', and recalls the fleeting and delicate spirit of the Impasse du Doyenné. 'Oh sweet Ariel,' it begins, 'be obedient to us as to your worthy master the magician Prospero. Do not let us invoke you in vain. Come and gild with your reflection the capricious bubbles of our fantasies . . . your mortal enemy, the vulgar Caliban, has no access to our elegant retreat . . .'[10]

Gautier's fullest statement of critical aims appeared on 14 December 1856 in another publication of which, as the new editor, he was largely in control. His prospectus for *L'Artiste* was consistent with the liberal critical ideals he had set himself twenty years earlier. 'As for our principles, we like to think . . . that they are sufficiently well known; we believe in the autonomy of Art; Art for us is not a means but an end . . . We have often been accused of indulgence', he went on; 'we do not deny this reproach. Criticism, in our view, should be a commentary on beauties rather than a search for faults . . . we are a poet, not a schoolmaster.'[11] The *raison d'être* of Gautier's *L'Artiste* was art education, to give the public a grounding of connoisseurship in the visual arts as it had in literature; he remained a guide around the immense world of art, but one with special qualifications and gifts of receptivity. Was not art 'the whole of visible nature, to which man's emotion is added? Isn't it a dream borrowing the forms of reality in order to manifest itself?' Gautier was familiar with the dream because he had lived it. Everything he saw, he possessed: 'The Scriptures speak somewhere of the concupiscence of the eyes, *concupiscentia oculorum*; this sin is our sin, and we hope God will forgive us for it. Never were eyes greedier than ours, and not even Béranger's gipsy put into practice more conscientiously than we the motto: to see is to possess.' Art was experience itself, experience always to be enlarged upon; seeing through art was not just possessing, but becoming another.

We accept each artist from the point of view of his particular ideal; a colourist with Delacroix, a draughtsman with Ingres, we only ask of them what they themselves propose . . . we judge their painting as if we possessed their souls. Of course we have our secret sympathies, but why limit oneself, why not take full enjoyment in everything? Why deprive oneself of the delicious pleasure of being another for a time, of inhabiting his mind, of seeing nature through his eyes, as if through a new prism? Heaven . . . has blessed us with the gift of understanding and admiration, and as the Persian poet says: if we are not the rose, we have lived close to the rose.[12]*

Looked at in the least sympathetic light, Gautier is like some ambitious and sycophantic character from Balzac: abnegating his own natural characteristics in order to slip into those of a higher bracket through his acquired wealth. If to regard him as a social climber in the hierarchy of the senses is too strict and heartless a categorization, we shall see that a similar, if more tentative connection can indeed be made between Gautier's critical mentality, and a mid-nineteenth-century preoccupation with ambitious self-betterment and personal transformation.

In *L'Artiste* of 14 February 1858 he further listed a critic's necessary qualifications, in an article in defence of Ingres against 'La Néo-Critique'; the article was a more cogent restatement of parts of the preface to *Mademoiselle de Maupin*: 'true criticism was born yesterday . . . and has conferred upon itself the priesthood of abuse, the apostolate of invective . . . it tolerates imagination in no one.'[13] 'La Néo-Critique' treated Ingres, whose name, for Gautier, was not to be taken in vain, as a *rapin*, a painter of beer-signs, a soulless Chinese. 'To speak with such presumption, this criticism has no doubt . . . made a long study of art, explored Greece, Italy, and Flanders, visited museums and collections, compared schools of every age and nation, learnt the history of each master in his various manners, and observed or practised technical procedures.' Constant refining of the perceptions and never-ending dilettantish curiosity were essential prerequisites for the function of admiration. Art criticism should be a labour of love demanding the whole life of a critic.[14] 'Be damning if you wish,' he admonished 'La Néo-Critique', 'but leave room for admiration, for every admiration is one more happiness.'

Admiration for Gautier was above all a creative process; it enabled him to assimilate the inner laws of the autonomous art-worlds he entered and possessed, and to recreate their structures in prose. 'To study a work, to understand it, to express it in terms of our own art, such has always been our aim,' he wrote in the *L'Artiste* prospectus. 'We like to put alongside a picture a page on which the painter's theme is taken up by the writer.'[15] Verbal evocation of a work clinched visual possession, and consolidated the frontiers of experience already broadened by the artist, and it was awareness of the formal properties of a work of art that allowed this transposition to take place, together with Gautier's fundamental Platonic belief in the inseparability of form and idea: 'we have never been able to understand the separation of idea from form, any more than we could understand body without soul, or soul without body . . . ; a beautiful form is a beautiful idea, for how could there be such a thing as a form that expressed nothing?'[16] Such literary, philosophical, or moral ideas as a painting or sculpture might express were not, in theory, the art critic's primary concern, but this was not to say that ideas were to be excluded from the visual arts: form and idea were inseparable. Working towards formal harmony, the artist established a complete world that was self-sufficient not only in terms of its formal structure, but also from the point of view of the ideas it must contain, the psychological, social, and dramatic aspects of the dream.

Gautier experienced the world primarily through his eyes; if there was no such thing as a form which expressed nothing, the corollary was also true: no idea could exist without formal embodiment. Hence everything—the whole of human thought and experience, not to say language—was embodied or found correspondence in visual appearances, and visual artists alone thus possessed the key to a full grasp of the universe. What is more, with their vocabulary of visual phenomena, they could rearrange and recreate the universe to ideal patterns, stretch the range of the possible, and raise human consciousness to new and higher levels of aspiration.

2 Form and Idea

'Belle forme . . . belle idée': the art critic's task was extended to touch upon every kind of artefact.

Everything form touches comes within our province . . . the sculpted façade of a house . . . the clock . . . the fire-dog, the lamp, the bronze displayed on the console-table, wallpaper, tapestry, the floral pattern on the curtain held back by a twisted cord . . . women's coiffures, clothes, and fashions . . . designs and motifs for jewels . . . elegant or sumptuous interiors, the supreme expression of modern luxury . . . a glance at carriages to see if the lines are pleasing and the harnessing correct . . .[17]

Every form potentially suggested a more serene and harmonious vision of life.

If the slogan 'De la forme naît l'idée'—from the form the idea is born[18]—became an Art for Art's Sake motto, it was one that Gautier was finally unable to reconcile with the fact of personal death; everything must cease with the failure of perception. 'A sea with no sail upon it is the most melancholy and heart-rending spectacle that can be contemplated. To think that there is not a single thought in this great expanse, not a single mind to take in this sublime spectacle! A white dot scarcely visible . . . and the immensity is populated: there is interest, a drama.'[19] Thus he expressed his fears of a formless, idealess *néant* (of having nothing to say). The possible implications of the theory of no ideas without formal embodiment have already been hinted at with regard to Gautier's poetry and consciously construed self-image. He sought to express his every mood and aspiration in visual images or in physical terms, but his solid embodiments could become images of just the fears he was trying to sublimate. From 'de la forme naît l'idée' it is but a short step, past the empty suits of armour, to the conclusion that nothing exists except tangible matter, and that, in the absence of perceiving man, forms exist without issue and meaning.

Gautier was rooted in his visual perceptions and intuitions, irrevocably attached to the material world by the avidity of his eyes and his capacity for admiring assimilation. He was himself absorbed as he assimilated: a Russian in Russia, a Spaniard in Spain, and an ancient Egyptian in Paris, his whole mental and physical being was locked in vision, and his identity could be lost in the act. Saint-Victor spoke to the Goncourts of Gautier's 'moral elephantiasis. "He is in that Indian incarnation nirvana: his soul is in his body, like a cow in a sacred meadow, with its enormous, pendulous dewlap."'[20] If for Gautier there was no separation of body and soul, of form and idea, then the only consolation for the inevitable death of the sensual and perceiving faculties lay in the maintenance of the almost mystical state of mind and of the correspondingly bovine or hippopotamus-like exterior discerned by Saint-Victor and the Goncourts.[21] If individual identity and responsibility were lost in form, and if material form survived for eternity, then the same physical appearances might constantly be reproduced, and the same ideas might thus subsist throughout history, with unbroken continuity. Such a train of thought would begin to explain Gautier's almost obsessive preoccupation with the phenomena of the material world; here also was the source of the central consoling power of his theories on art and artists.

Art was thus timeless, an eternal present tense. The concept of progress and the critical ideal of a genius of the future were superficial and misleading: 'human genius has proved itself',[22] he pointed out in the *L'Artiste* manifesto, and the present should give the past all the respect that is its due. If greater geniuses than Phidias, Leonardo, or Titian were to present themselves, the critic would, of course, acknowledge them joyfully; but his primary role was to dwell on the facts before him, not to make speculations, either gloomy or optimistic, nor to compare artists at their mutual expense.[23]

Here lay the final and decisive justification for Gautier's emancipation of critic and artist from other more transient professional concerns. The critic must of course believe in 'the autonomy of art, that art is the expression of itself . . . Whoever thinks otherwise may well be a philosopher, a statesman, a mathematician, but he certainly won't be a poet, nor a musician, nor a sculptor, nor a painter. Art exists neither to dogmatize, teach, nor prove anything; its purpose is to give birth to the idea of the beautiful'. Contemplation of the beautiful gave the illusion of immortality; it referred one back to some primal unspoilt state, as reflected most clearly in the art of ancient Greece, but also in a hundred other formal arrangements. A work of art could be a single point of access to man's true and ideal condition (for, as Gautier was fond of quoting from Plato, 'beauty is the splendour of truth'),[24] a focus for his vague instinctive yearnings for an Eden, or a nirvana, or an Athens. It was like a sketch of the future; and even if the ideal future was never to be reached, art remained the closest realization of a permanently recurring human dream. Contemplation of art was for Gautier the supreme intellectual activity. 'Art . . . elevates the human spirit in its very essence: reading verses, listening to a melody, looking at a picture or statue is a superior intellectual pleasure in itself, which releases you from the coarse reality of things.'[25]

The range to which Gautier's 'idée du beau' extended is to be perceived piece by piece, in the manner in which Gautier himself perceived, through the highly disparate forms which he was able to assimilate into his prose, and through the corresponding forms which his prose itself took (or, ceasing to correspond, ossified into). The 'idée du beau' was, moreover, made tangible by a particular and superior kind of being. Together with his belief in the endless continuity and reproduction of form and idea, Gautier conceived that theory of the artist that has been glimpsed at work among the members of the Petit Cénacle. It establishes the artist as a member of an élite, separated from the philosophers, statesmen, mathematicians, and 'the coarse reality of things' by an intuition of things he has never seen, and possessed, as if by reincarnation, of a vision of an ideal synthetic, or anterior, existence.

III The Artist

1 The Élite

'The absolute poet who had attained the hardest and highest degree of perfection would be as great as God, and God is perhaps only the world's first poet.' Such was the ultimate superiority of the élite to which Gautier's artists belonged, as he expressed it in an article on 'L'Excellence de la poésie' in 1837.[1] Like gods, and like the critic who himself could admire anything, his artists were sublimely indifferent; Decamps, for example, displayed this qualification at the Salon of 1839:

What we love most of all about Decamps, and what distinguishes him as an artist of high calling, is the absolute indifference, the supreme impartiality of his talent. Like the sun, he gilds without choice nor preference. . . a human face, a monkey's snout, or a horse's rump . . . he well knows that everything he touches comes to life; he is as implacable as nature and moved to tenderness by nothing. Without realizing it, he is the greatest pantheist in the world; for him everything has its importance and beauty. He is a true painter.[2]

Decamps had already achieved Gautier's earthly nirvana; unselfconsciously absorbed in exterior form, he was able spontaneously to recreate its nuances. But if the artist's god-like impartiality absolved him, and the critic, of any outside moral, intellectual, or utilitarian obligations, this was not to say that his role was simply the indiscriminate reproduction of appearances. His impartiality was not that of a carefully objective scientist; 'for if the sciences always end up opening the doors of their sanctuary to anyone who comes and knocks on them often enough, poetry, music, and painting are more particular, and only surrender themselves to certain select beings' ('des organisations d'élite').[3] The artist's impartiality to things sprang rather from a rare and mysteriously inborn instinct, and the qualities which characterized him as an 'organisation d'élite' were exactly those that coloured and identified his vision as unmistakably and uniquely his own. For painter as for poet, the work of art demanded the energies of the whole man: 'As well as an abundance of ideas, knowledge of the language, and a gift for images, you need a certain inner sense, a secret predisposition, something which cannot be acquired and which has its roots in temperament itself and in idiosyncrasy.' A master could reveal himself in a single brush-stroke or line of verse, 'for genius is like God, who is contained whole in each fragment of the host', Gautier wrote apropos of Delacroix at the Salon of 1839.[4] Delacroix had 'life, a rare and precious gift', which manifested itself in all its idiosyncrasy in his work; Decamps's pictures were also unmistakably stamped with his virile talent, 'victoriously scored by the lion's claw'.[5] There was no separation possible between Gautier's true artist and his production; if the artist shared the characteristics of his art (as Nanteuil those of his Gothic fantasies), the work of art also reflected something of the character of its maker. Gautier's fundamentally Romantic view of the artist thus evolved into general critical theory about the nature of art, as formulated, for instance, in the *L'Artiste* prospectus of 1856: 'Is it not the whole of visible nature, to which man's emotion is added?'[6]

This formulation directly anticipates Zola's 'A work of art is a corner of creation seen through a temperament'; but if, like Zola, Gautier sought evidence of living human individuality in pictures, and if *tempérament* was an essential prerequisite for the production of great art, it was not in itself the final quality that all art should set out to reveal. For Gautier the function of individual temperament was necessarily to idealize: however objectively an artist might wish to report on the world's visual content, his temperament or unconscious 'disposition secrète' would intervene and idealize it. Zola's forthright declaration of 1866 'What I look for above all in a picture is a man and not a picture'[7] would have stuck in Gautier's throat; Zola's man of flesh and blood was Gautier's idealism, and it was precisely to this idealism that Zola proclaimed his hostility. 'I don't like the word "art",' he wrote, as if in deliberate defiance of the poet of 'L'Art'; 'it embodies some vague idea of necessary arrangement, of an absolute ideal.' In Courbet, Zola found 'l'homme' where Gautier failed to locate an aspiration towards 'l'idéal absolu'; if Gautier was able to recognize Courbet's 'obvious and powerful qualities' years before Zola first published art criticism in the Parisian press (which was in 1866), and to assert (for example, in his *Salon of 1857*) that 'If M. Courbet lacks an artist's intelligence, at least he has the temperament', his final characterization of the painter was that he was an inverted idealist, the Watteau of the ugly,[8] who was nevertheless capable of producing real art in spite of himself and his dogmatic realist 'system'. 'He is a born painter, and whatever use he makes of it, his talent subsists';[9] as such, he too, even, contained 'un sens intime', the seed of the ideal.

That art is not a mirror—'painting is not natural history, and . . . the artist should write man's poem, not his monograph'—was an essential tenet in Gautier's aesthetic, although, as with other critical statements that might threaten to falsify first-hand experience with their neatness, he was prepared immediately to qualify it. 'Nevertheless we do not blame the *"naturistes"*, for art is such a vast thing that there are a thousand ways of being great within it.' He was writing in 1839; among the '*naturistes*' he might have had in mind the landscape painter Delaberge, whose painstakingly detailed pictures attempted a scrupulous, pre-Pre-Raphaelite, leaf-by-leaf realism. Delaberge would certainly seem to have wished his canvases to be mirrors, yet in his obituary in 1842 Gautier was able to credit this painter too with an idealistic and distinctively individual vision: 'His life has been dedicated to the pursuit of his dream'; he has 'left his mark, he has established his originality, he is himself.'[10] Delaberge's alternative nature, systematically and pseudo-scientifically conceived as it was, was still manifestly the product of a human mind. But if there was no limit to the forms from beneath which a 'disposition secrète' might emerge, it was through those artists whose work veered towards the poetic rather than the monographic that Gautier arrived at his clearest and most breathtaking conception of the creative mind. Its first full formulation appeared in the same 1839 Salon article, under the heading 'Delacroix et Riesener'; the artistic temperament of Delacroix carried Gautier's imagination into fantastic and magical realms. We do not blame the *'naturistes'*;

but there are other, more anxious and fantastically minded geniuses, for whom nature is a point of departure rather than an end in itself, and whose wings, open to all the winds of caprice, beat impetuously against the panes of the studio window and break them; they see differently and different things; in their eyes lines flicker like flames or writhe like serpents, the smallest details take on bizarre forms; red turns into purple, blue into green, yellow becomes tawny, and black assumes the velvety quality of the stripes on a tiger's skin; water glints mysteriously from the depths of the shadows, and the sky peers out of the foliage through strangely azure eyes.[11]*

This is the language of Baudelaire and Rimbaud; it also refers us back to O'Neddy's comment from the preface to *Feu et flamme* of 1833:[12] 'The inner life . . . is as unruly, as adventurous and free as Arab tribes in their wildernesses', and to the Petit Cénacle's hallucinatory and Gothic excursions, the climate out of which emerged Gautier's own early Hoffmannesque *contes fantastiques*. But Gautier firmly steers his more anxious and fantastically minded artistic geniuses clear of an anarchy of the senses, of the drug-induced dementia which the Jeunes-France had publicly flaunted but which Gautier, in any case, seems to have privately eschewed. The term *organisation* is of course a usual one, but in the phrase 'organisation d'élite' it is used to particular point: Gautier conceives the inner life of the artist in metaphors that seem, at first glance, to be as well ordered and as concrete as proven facts.

The vision of those idealizing artists like Delacroix who see 'differently and different things' is directed through a 'prism': an image that (literally) crystallizes, while remaining within a purely visual framework of references, the notions of 'disposition secrète', 'sens intime', idiosyncrasy, and temperament, that constitute an artist's originality. These artists 'have the greatest difficulty in introducing crude and positive reality into their creations; they have to have assimilated an object and contemplated it through their prism in order to be able to paint it.'[13] This precise optical image hardly promises visual delirium; a prism may distort objects and explode them, but into neat facets; if some aspect of the object is given unnatural prominence, its essential character remains, or is even emphasized. The prism suggests the approach of those artists who, like Delacroix and Gautier himself (as, in both cases, Baudelaire informs us)[14], regarded the world as a dictionary of forms to be rearranged according to some ideal pattern. The crux of Gautier's theory of the artist lies in the intuition of this pattern, in the direction in which the artist must gaze.

Goethe says somewhere that every artist must carry within him the *microcosm*, that is, a whole world in miniature from which he draws the content and the form of his works; it is in this microcosm that live fair heroines and dusky Madonnas . . . Artists who possess the microcosm look into themselves and not outside when they want to produce something; they may very well do a house from a duck, and a monkey from a tree. They are the real poets, in the Greek sense of the word, those who create, those who make: the rest are mere imitators and copyists.[15*]

In that they create new worlds out of the fabric of the old, Gautier's true artists thus approach the stature of gods.

The prism is bi-directional. From the inside, the light of the microcosm passes through the prism to transform objects in exterior nature. Decamps is 'like the sun'; his painting is equivalent to 'the whole of visible nature, to which man's emotion is added'. From the outside, objects are assimilated by the prism and transformed by the microcosm; they are the forms of reality in which the Ideal is clothed, 'a dream borrowing the forms of nature in order to manifest itself', Gautier's other formulation of the nature of art from the *L'Artiste* prospectus,[16] which suggests both a fantastic and an idealizing, classical artistic vision.

Such distinctions are not to be insisted upon; the prism is not intended to stand the scrutiny of a closely critical reading. It is a poetic image for artistic temperament, which, as Gautier's humour does in a more extreme form (as in 'house-duck', 'monkey-tree'), makes links and suggests correspondences in a way that reason cannot.

Part of the power of the concept of the microcosm lies in the vague association that Gautier lends it to an ancient philosophical tradition, one that runs through Goethe, father figure of the Romantic neo-Renaissance, back to the ancient Greeks who invented the word poet. The microcosm thus assumes the weight of an eternal truth. In an appendix on 'The Sources of the "Microcosm"',[17] Michael Spencer stresses the widespread nature of ideas revolving around the microcosm among Gautier's French and German predecessors and contemporaries. The term itself, he writes, can be traced back to Democritus; it is therefore one of the oldest in aesthetics. The idea was taken up by Leibniz for his 'Monadology', and Leibniz was the common source for aspects of the thought of Balzac, Goethe, and Karl Philipp Moritz. Gautier's immediate sources of information on this philosophical background were no doubt Nerval and Heine, and above all Balzac; Spencer provides a full and authoritative discussion of the subject, and this discussion is to be recommended for the further insights it contains. But, as Spencer points out, the specific sources commandeered by Gautier for his microcosm 'theory' cannot be determined precisely; as we shall see, this theory was hardly, in any case, a carefully worked out and logically argued piece of philosophy.

Ultimately, the concept of the microcosm as Gautier made use of it can perhaps best be explained as a derivative and corruption of the Platonic notion of *Idea*, *Idea*, that is, in the Greek sense of the word, as 'form' or 'pattern'. In individual artists, the microcosm is a version of Plato's universal world of *Idea*, of the Ideal, the unchanging formal pattern of the absolute, of which the mortal, sensually perceptible world was but a pale reflection. This Platonic view of the world as a flawed and second-rate approximation to its ideal counterpart is more than latent in Gautier's writing: hence his insistence on the necessity for idealization in art (and, as has been seen with Courbet, on the inevitability of idealization, owing to the inborn spiritual intuitions of artists) and hence his profound distaste for art that wilfully dwelt on earthly imperfections. The microcosm was the exclusive and inexplicable gift that only 'organisations d'élite' possessed, the intuition or 'sens intime' on which they drew for their work;

Plato's pattern world too was an intuition granted to privileged souls, who had caught glimpses of it during the intervals between incarnations, before they drank the waters of Lethe. The psyche journeyed through incarnations towards a less and less shadowy recollection of the Ideal, until it finally arrived as part of the serene abstract unity itself.[18] And so did Gautier evolve what virtually amounts to a personal theory of reincarnation, as a rationale for the mysterious powers he sensed in art and for the serene self-forgetfulness that the contemplation of art enabled him to achieve.

Théophile was not superstitious, Émile Bergerat recalled; he was superstition itself. 'He believed in charms, spells, curses, magic, in the meaning of dreams, in the divination of the slightest accident: crossed knives, spilt salt, three candles burning, goodness knows what else.'[19] Gautier's daughter Judith underlined this deep superstition. 'He pictured man as surrounded by a network of invisible forces, currents, and influences, good or evil, which were to be made use of or guarded against'; he believed, for instance, in the evil eye, the *jettatura*, which became the subject of a story of that title: 'my father lived in real dread of the "evil eye", which he considered to be a sort of maleficent magnetism, projected quite involuntarily by the possessors of this baneful gift'.[20] Although those with the evil eye did not necessarily apply their unfortunate facility wilfully, and were often unaware of its effects, the concept of the *jettatura* was nevertheless linked to the highest moral considerations in Gautier's mind. Offenbach, in his estimation, had the evil eye; Gautier could not even bring himself to write the composer's name, according to Adolphe Boschot, for fear of attracting some harm to himself.[21] He personally detested Offenbach's music, which he considered debasing (we have another authority in Berlioz to corroborate this opinion) and destructive to man's most worthy aspirations towards the Ideal, in the same way as Delaroche's popular painting. 'Belle forme, belle idée': it was no coincidence that Offenbach, with his evil eye, was also physically ugly. 'And he is ugly because his thoughts are base. A beautiful soul, on the other hand, sculpts itself a beautiful face.'

Offenbach was an untouchable in Gautier's aesthetic caste system; his psyche might not have progressed far towards Plato's Ideal either. But this would have had nothing to do with his physical ugliness, which, after all, he shared with Socrates. It is here that Gautier's tacit inheritance of a Western tradition of Platonic-Catholic thought ceases to be of service to him. For Plato, as for the Christian, the body was ultimately to be discarded with relief and the soul liberated; for the sensualist and materialist Gautier, body and soul were inseparable, since form and idea were one. Gautier might have found mythic confirmation for this in their embodiment in the same Greek word, *Idea*; thus the Platonic *Idea* becomes in Gautier a tangible physical ideal.

Beautiful was good and ugly was bad; what is more, material form, for Gautier, was continually disintegrating and reintegrating into similar configurations, and producing correspondingly familiar ideas, forces, currents, and influences. When applied to living matter (perhaps, since Gautier equated statue and woman, this distinction between animate and inanimate does not need to be made: everything is matter), this view provides the basis for a belief in reincarnation.

A latter day Pre-Socratic at one moment, and seeming momentarily to touch the heights of Platonic idealism at the next, pagan or Catholic according to the talent of the artist, Gautier mixes his mythologies, if not his metaphors. His reincarnation theory flirts with other, non-Greek and non-Christian mythologies; like the microcosm and the prism, it is primarily a poetic idea, although Gautier's genuine superstitiousness and the literal, even heavy-handed way in which poetic images are presented throughout his writing make it tempting to treat it as a seriously held philosophical belief. *Avatar*, like *Jettatura*, is the title of a *nouvelle fantastique*; *jettatura* belongs to the folklore of Naples, and comes from the Neapolitan *iettatura*, ultimately derived from the Latin *jacere*, while 'avatar' is a word from Sanskrit used to mean the descent of a Hindu deity in visible form, or simply incarnation; its figurative usage, as the supreme glorification of any principle, also has its bearing on Gautier's thinking. It is part of his personal, mythological rationale for the timelessness and subsisting value that he sensed in all art, from whatever period, that had moved him.

The same ideas circulate and reappear throughout history, as they do in the convolutions of Gautier's own mind; thus certain artists are born with very specific and identifiable 'microcosms', like Célestin Nanteuil with his intuition of things he had never seen. Nanteuil, it has been remarked, had 'a similarity of nature with the artists of the Middle Ages';[22] he is an exemplary avatar, an incarnation of one talent in another, an artist of no great originality or influence, who simply reflected his artistic and spiritual masters. For Vetter and Meissonier, in the Salon of 1847, Plato's mythic terms are again enlisted; they are two artists who, like Pythagoras, 'have not drunk the waters of forgetfulness'.[23] Vetter is manifestly a contemporary of Molière; Meissonier 'spent a previous existence watching them play chess at the Café Procope or boules in the Cours-la-Reine'—such is the painter's ability to transport Gautier into a complete eighteenth-century milieu. The theory is more properly expounded in a Salon article of 1848: talents are limited in type and number, and reappear infinitely throughout history; it would be interesting to chart their genealogy in detail . . . but enough philosophy, and back to the task in hand, which happens to be one Wattier, the 'avatar' of none other than Watteau.[24] To Gautier, this coincidence of names as well as of talents is all in the natural mysterious course of things, a *correspondance* that he passes over with barely a remark. Just back from Pompeii in 1851, where he was inspired to write another reincarnation fantasy of his own, *Arria Marcella*, Gautier was awestruck by Gérôme's *Intérieur grec* at the Salon: 'The young artist must have been a citizen of that charming Italo-Greek city before the eruption of Vesuvius'.[25] At the Salon of 1853, Gérôme is 'an Athenian born in France two thousand years too late, that's all',[26] just as Borel, to name but one familiar example, was a displaced fifteenth-century Spaniard, or Arab, or Italian. Gustave Moreau, in 1866, is another fifteenth-century artist,[27] and Fromentin's 'profound and nostalgic intuition of Arab life' in 1869 must no doubt result from the fact that he is descended from a Saracen who remained in France after the defeat of Abderrahman. 'He only paints bedouins so well because he is a bedouin himself.'[28]

Every artist worthy of Gautier's élite contains the microcosm; those who are also avatars provide the most extreme, thus the clearest illustrations of his feelings about the creative process, not to say about the continuing process of creation itself. The avatar embodies, in one word, the notion of a universe tied together by a web of sensually perceptible correspondences whose strands even pass through human heredity. It is the supreme glorification of the whole theme of artistic identification and nostalgia, for time as for place, in Gautier's writing.

The Orientalists were particularly susceptible to an incapacitating nostalgia, because of the associations attached to the Middle East as the cradle of civilization and source of life; here Gautier's own gnawing metaphorical homesickness was generalized into universal poetic truth. It was difficult, if not beyond their powers, for these artists to adapt to any climate other than that of their spiritual home. Decamps is not dead, Gautier reassured his readers as he covered a sale of the artist's work in 1853. 'The illness that gave so much cause for alarm . . . is only a nostalgia for the sun.'[29]And for Marilhat, who really was dead after two years of nervous dilapidation, he wrote: 'It takes a strong heart and a level head to stand up to that vague anguish, that fatal anxiety which is heaven's price for genius, not to succumb to that strange nostalgia which the sun of the East leaves to those whom it has bronzed with its rays. It is because the East is the true homeland, the cradle of humankind.'[30] Deprived of his life-source, Marilhat wasted away; he had gone to join his ancestors, the ancient migrations of whose primitive tribes had ultimately caused the artist's 'bizarre instincts'. It was as if he were a weakling abandoned in the alien North. The living Marilhat could not resist 'the mysterious call of blood . . . an unknown ancestor claims his rights . . . He is going to rejoin his brothers of long ago'.

Whether through irresistible hereditary disposition, through instinctive need to return to some primal life-source or through a mysterious rebirth brought about by the inevitable reconfiguration of matter, every great contemporary talent had his (historical or geographical) 'intellectual fatherland', if not his own identifiable avatars. Lamartine, Musset, and Vigny were ultimately English, Delacroix was Anglo-Hindu, Hugo Spanish, Ingres Roman or Florentine, Pradier Greek, Dumas Créole; Chassériau was a pagan Pelagius[31] who belonged to the time of Orpheus, Decamps was a Turk, and Marilhat himself was a specifically Syrian Arab.[32] What is more, since all things were linked and form was inseparable from idea, Gautier's artists, of course, shared the physical characteristics of their worlds. Decamps, as he appeared still flushed with life in 1853, with his 'Lebanese Druse's head, his pale blue eyes, his eagle's nose, his blond moustache, and his Oriental manner',[33] is a good example to add to the list of Petit Cénacle physiognomies; the Rommel of the Romantic Afrika Korps, blue-eyed and blond-moustached, he combines sound, Nordic executive qualities with the Oriental character of the lands to which his instincts lead him. The painter Ernest Hébert is another example: 'Hébert, with his sallow complexion, his large, nostalgic eyes, his long black hair, his bushy brown beard, and his profoundly Italian appearance, seems the ideal and the model for his own pictures',[34] and so is Ary Scheffer, who has 'a fine Romantic head, impassioned and ravaged like one imagines Faust's to have been, swarthy . . . with a dreaming, melancholy, and spiritual expression quite in keeping with the nature of his talent'.[35] Gautier admits that he has never even met Scheffer, and that he must rely on hearsay for his description of the artist's appearance. This, for Gautier, is simply how Scheffer ought to, and must, have looked.

Talents are limited in type across history; the idea of an élite, of a limited family of archetypal geniuses who continually reappear throughout history, who embrace similar sympathies and express familiar human preoccupations and emotions in the same essentially sensual language, is Gautier's conceptual key to some final Oneness, to some artistic Elysium in which all the pleasures and qualities to be gained from art might be united. Consolation and hope lay in this continuity. The sense of an ever nearly attainable ideal, of some future but inexpressible mystical synthesis, is hard to reconcile with Gautier's belief in no ideas without formal embodiment; yet since all forms, however humble, corresponded with each other through their potential as part of a vision of the ideal, it is logical that Gautier's last word on the subject should come from an unlikely source, an article on 'Maisons sculptées modernes' which appeared in 1843: '. . . great geniuses also have a family, beyond time and space. If there is any consolation for death, it is the thought that when you are no more than a handful of dust, beings who suffer like you have suffered will pause in front of your works and feel their hearts swell and overflow, drawn towards you by some invisible force.'[36] Gautier was never a man for whom the invisible world did not exist: but it was only to be apprehended through exterior form and through the evidence of the senses.

2 Mysteries

Unlike Baudelaire, but like Goethe and Nerval, Goethe's great mediator in France, Gautier was a mythologist rather than a psychologist. 'There are no ideas', he is reported to have remarked provocatively to the Imperial circle during a discussion on modern and progressive ideas; 'truth advances in a procession of feelings'.[37] Gautier was also speaking as a poet and a pragmatic observer. He submitted himself entirely to the impression made on his sensibilities by an object, person, or work of art; in translating his impression into words he was concerned with retaining its impact, rather than with analysing and explaining it in terms of a general theory. Truth was subjective; the powerful imagery of mythology corresponded to his impressions of the world as the most satisfactory means of explaining and linking them. His theory of the artist is conceived in terms of poetic images (prism) and mythological constructs (microcosm and avatar) which serve primarily to illustrate his intuitions and perceptions about the nature of creation, without trying to integrate them into a definitive world-view. 'Forgive this anomalous and cab-balistic term', he wrote in his *Salon of 1841* about the word microcosm, 'but it perfectly expresses our thinking'.[38] Much as Baudelaire's aesthetic seems to overlap Gautier's, es-pecially over *correspondances*, where Baudelaire analysed the artist and *le beau* into postulated mental faculties and theoretical elements, Gautier fundamentally and perhaps paradoxically sought to preserve a sense of mystery. Thus 'microcosm' and 'prism' stand in place of 'imagination' and 'temperament'. Gautier could postulate nothing as fact unless he could see, touch, or experience it (e.g. the soul of a Turk); where it was necessary, in order to explain or illuminate something, to have recourse to an intangible, abstract idea, he would work by analogy. Gautier's mythological metaphors allowed him to acknowledge and retain a sense of mystery and awe, while providing him with a perhaps minimal but workable, practical framework of references that gave his experience coherence (and enabled him to ward off the danger of perceptual anarchy, a danger which he clearly and early recognized, and which he expressed, metaphorically, in his resolve to flirt with 'neither torrents nor cataracts'). [39]

His superstition, based on his belief in the articulateness of matter for those who knew how to interpret it, was no affectation, in that it worked for him. Gautier did not seek to rationalize the irrational, but to use its powers; in ancient myth it simply found its most concrete and accessible expression. While dealing more or less specifically with Gautier's conception of the artist, it will not be possible to touch upon all the mythological constructs with which he underlined his experience, nor to demonstrate the full range of their sources, whether Greek, Latin, Nordic, or Oriental (the familiar principle of assimilation and empirically apt reordering was again at work here); two final examples of intuitions elevated to the status of myth may, however, serve here to complete our picture of Gautier's poetic world-view.

As a self-characterized 'man for whom the visible world existed', [40] Gautier found corroboration for his sense of the power of the human eye in an ancient Greek idea. He expressed it thus in *Voyage en Italie*: 'The Greeks had a special word for the central or important place in a country or a town: *ophthalmos* (the eye). Is it not the eye, after all, that gives life, intelligence, and meaning to the human physiognomy, that reveals human thoughts and seduces with its luminous magnetism?' [41] To this personal 'eye' mythology belong the opposing notions of attracting ocular avidity (*concupiscentia oculorum*), and projected, repelling *jettatura*.

The subject is more fully explored in Rita Benesch's thesis *Le Regard de Théophile Gautier*; so too is Gautier's use of the idea of a universe structured in concentric radiations (not unlike the glimpse he gives us of the convoluted structure of his own mind in *L'Histoire du romantisme*), which accompanies the notions of microcosm, avatar, and formal correspondences, as it does that of the central 'eye'. Such was the breadth and tenuous coherence of his questing and consoling mysticism. 'He thought . . . that people emitted a network of rays that collided with or brushed caressingly against the rays of others, and that this was the cause of sympathy or antipathy', wrote Judith Gautier;[42] the source he commandeered to make tangible his intuitions, about the universe as about people, its microcosms, could no doubt be traced through Nerval and Goethe to the dark origins of the Faust legend itself; the context here is actually the Pompeiian reincarnation story *Arria Marcella*:

. . . nothing dies, everything exists for ever; no power can destroy what once was. Every action, every word, every form, every thought dropped into the universal ocean of things produces rings that go on getting bigger and bigger, up to the very edges of eternity. Material figuration disappears only for vulgar eyes; the spectres that detach themselves from the material populate infinity. Paris continues to abduct Helen in some unknown region of space. The silken sails of Cleopatra's galley swell on the azure waters of some ideal Cydnus. A few passionate and powerful minds have been able to recall to themselves centuries that to all appearances have passed for ever, and bring back to life individuals dead to everyone else. Faust had Tyndarus's daughter for his mistress, and brought her to his Gothic castle from the mysterious chasms of Hades . . .[43*]

Like the Decamps of his 1839 description, Gautier is 'the greatest pantheist in the world'. Ancient myths and beliefs contained the seeds of truth; with the gently melancholic tone of Heine's *Les Dieux en exil* (only published in 1856), Gautier demanded in a theatre feuilleton of 1841 that the gods of antiquity be treated with respect:

When the ancient divinities are mocked, a sort of uneasiness comes over us . . . Seeing the travesty of what was once the adoration and terror of a vanished world, what so many illustrious and superior men—poets, artists, philosophers—venerated for nearly two thousand years, one cannot help but reflect sadly on the instability of ideas and beliefs . . . All forms of religion deserve respect, whether they are flourishing or have fallen into disuse, for their principle is the recognition of human weakness, the desire for heavenly support, and the need to explain . . . the marvellous phenomenon of creation. These are sublime sentiments, and distinguish man from the beasts if nothing else does . . .[44]

—and the poet, indeed, from the hippopotamus.

Myth assimilated the inexplicable; it exteriorized mysterious human instincts that were inaccessible to pure reason. Gautier's respect for myth was a respect for instinct; the microcosm and the avatar were mythic embodiments of the instincts upon which, as Gautier saw it, artistic creation was based. In the struggle to realize the Ideal in some visible form, no effort was too great, he advised artists in 1860: 'In art one never goes too far, and . . . he who thinks himself audacious is just timid; when you wrestle with nature like Jacob with the angel, you must use all your muscles, all your sinews, all your breath, your head, and your whole heart—it is not too much. When you face infinity, you cannot be excessive.'[45] The whole man, reasoning faculties included, was to be engaged; but the key to the liberation of the whole man, to the realization of the ideal type of the Romantic artist, whose life was one with his art, was instinct. Hence the most familiar advice to artists in the pages of Gautier's forty-year-long artistic commentary was: Abandon yourselves to your instincts. The world of art is large enough to contain the infinite variety of forms under which they will subsist . . .

At the end of an article of 1847, entitled 'Du Beau dans l'Art' (a review of a pseudo-treatise on aesthetics, *Réflexions et menus propos d'un peintre genevois* . . . , by Rodolphe Töpffer), Gautier could be heard exhorting artists towards a state of Pentecostal grace:

. . . let us leave psychic embryology to the philosophers, those anatomists of the soul; let us abandon ourselves to love, to admiration, to enthusiasm, to work and leisure, to thought and to dreams, to all the raptures of the intelligence, to all the fullness of life! Let us sparkle like waves and vibrate like lyres; let us be shot through, like prisms, with the rays of suns and the emanations of universes! Let us allow words to issue forth from our lips; let us entrust ourselves to the unknown . . .[46]*

With his mythological, anti-intellectual view of the world, Gautier was proposing what amounted to a religion of art; the central dogma of this religion was a faith in the creative and redemptive powers of the irrational. It was a programme for self-fulfilment and more: it also promised artists the power to transcend themselves, and thus to participate in the constant process of recreation of the universe itself.

IV Delacroix

'To understand genius, you need something like genius,' Gautier wrote at the age of twenty-three in the course of his second-ever Salon review.[1] Twenty-two years later, his personal attitude to geniuses had not changed; thus he could declare in his prospectus for *L'Artiste* in December 1856: 'we judge their painting as if we possessed their souls.' 'No doubt we also have our secret sympathies,' he continued, hinting at what his own poetry might reveal, but also suggesting a distinction between art that corresponded to his privately most cherished intuitions, and that which it was merely his public pleasure to admire. It is with the language of his public expressions of admiration and solidarity that we must be concerned, and with the hierarchy of artists that its modulations suggest. Gautier's subtle distinction will thus tend to emerge of its own accord.

1 Revelation

At the Salon of 1834 Delacroix exhibited *Les Femmes d'Alger*. Delacroix was not infallible; at the previous year's exhibition, the young dilettante critic had wished, for Delacroix's sake, that he had kept his exhibited portraits at home.[2] Yet Gautier felt a genuine affinity with the painter, one that went beyond partisan recognition of Delacroix's stature as hero of the Romantic movement, and which was inspired by more than the easy contrast with the bourgeois Delaroche, who, for Gautier, was not even worthy of charging Delacroix's palette, and for whose *Jane Grey* of the Salon of 1834 mediocre was too good a word.[3] The difference between them was that Delaroche was a talented workman, while Delacroix was 'a painter, an artist in the fullest meaning of the word'. Gautier's first appreciation of Delacroix was thus of Delacroix the painter, who worked within the physical resources of his

autonomous art; he fulfilled the artistic precepts of the Petit
Cénacle, and those of the Preface that was to be written in
May 1834, within about a month of this Salon article. In *Les
Femmes d'Alger* Gautier relished the colour above all, remarking that here Delacroix equalled the Venetians; his
appreciation of the picture is not so much that of a self-
conscious literary dilettante, as that of a fellow painter: 'the
harmony of colour is admirable, and yet nothing can have
been harder to achieve, given walls covered with gaudy tiles,
inlaid furniture, fabrics, and pieces of embroidery all of the
most discordant colours imaginable. Yet not one of these
gems . . . draws the eye more than it should.'

It was, however, the simple presence of richly patterned
tiles, pieces of furniture, and fabrics that also attracted
Gautier, who was a lover of studio exoticism as well as of pure
painting. Painter's criticism is followed by self-indulgent
poet's criticism: 'The women are charming, and perfectly
Oriental in their beauty . . . this is exactly . . . the fine, full
flesh of women who do not go out of doors.' Gautier is
delighted that Delacroix has made this observation, which is
worthy of a writer of descriptive prose. It is even more with
Delacroix's other exhibits at the Salon of 1834 that we begin
to see the strength of the poet's affinity with his work, the
wider implications of what he meant when he called him 'an
artist in the fullest meaning of the word'. Delacroix's portrait
of Rabelais is the portrait of another hero of the Romantics,
and one of the closest to Gautier's dreams; here is 'a whole
personality brought back to life, the Master Alcofribas Nasier
of whom we have dreamt—sad beneath his mirth like
Molière, like Cervantes' (like, as the Goncourts and others
recorded, the later Gautier himself). Gautier is able to
respond spontaneously: Delacroix inspires in him a rapid
association of literary ideas, so successfully does he ma-
terialize and synthesize Gautier's imaginative experience of
Rabelais. This resurrection is complemented, in *La Rue de
Mekinez*, by the realization of an anthropological dream; the
painting 'reveals the elegant and poetic side of those Orientals
whose odder aspects Decamps has so astonishingly thrown
into relief'. Again Delacroix has caught what Gautier,
through Decamps, seems to have imagined to be already

there; the power of the picture lay in its seemingly exact correspondence to a forgotten poetic dream, as if it prompted Gautier's memory. Delacroix does not invent, he does not even 'throw into relief'; for Gautier, he *reveals*.

2 Shared genius

In that Delacroix revealed what Gautier could spontaneously sense to be already there, they could be said to share a common vision. Thus Gautier could write, in answer to the rhetorical question 'Why isn't Delacroix as famous as M. Delaroche?': you need something like genius to understand genius. 'Something that cannot be acquired and has its roots in temperament itself', Delacroix's genius (and Gautier's implied corresponding genius) was something inexplicably heaven-sent and exclusive. Their 'dispositions secrètes' happily seemed to overlap. Hence it was Delacroix, when Gautier needed mythic elaboration and illustration for his intuition of heaven-sent genius, who was the living model genius into whom the prism and the microcosm were transplanted, who, with his mysterious powers of revelation, called for the need for their introduction. Delacroix survived surgery, and the mythic organs gave good service. Through Delacroix's magic prism, Gautier was able to see and explore the painter's world in greater and greater detail, to identify with it more and more closely and to tighten the correspondences between it and his own experience, his own prose, so that there are points at which Gautier does indeed seem to possess Delacroix's soul. From the thirties until the painter's death in 1863, this marriage-made-in-heaven and consummated in the pages of *La Presse* and *Le Moniteur universel* survived what was for Gautier some of his most fundamental criticism; each artist reflects the other in perhaps his best light. [4]

After Thiers, moreover, [5] Gautier was possibly Delacroix's most consistent and courageous defender, and certainly did more than any other contemporary critic to make Delacroix's canvases and murals accessible to a wide public. If Delacroix's subsequent reputation has rested heavily on Baudelaire's, the dedication to *Les Fleurs du mal* attests to the

esteem in which Gautier was held by his younger contemporary, and similarities in the language that Delacroix inspired in
both poets give ground for argument in favour of Gautier's
precedence. (Baudelaire was ten years younger than Gautier,
and his first published art criticism was the *Salon of 1845*; he
was then twenty-four.)

Delacroix himself appreciated Gautier's efforts on his
behalf, or rather, acknowledged them as a gesture from one
artist to another. The urbane, disinterested Théophile was
certainly more sympathetic to him personally than the
bumptious, impetuous young Baudelaire (well-kept long hair
was exotic, artistic, a mark of disdain perhaps, that was closer
to dandyism than to Bohemia; but green hair . . . ?). Gautier
was acceptable socially. Delacroix gave Gautier several of his
canvases; Bergerat recalls seeing a *Lady Macbeth* and *Combat
au Giaour* in the drawing-room of Gautier's house in Neuilly
in 1872. Need we be reminded, writes Adolphe Boschot (who
sometimes expressed his boundless admiration for 'le bon et
grand Théo' as protectively and coyly as the proud father of
an exemplary schoolboy), that Delacroix was highly
'reserved, distant, and sparing in the expressions of his
enthusiasm'?[6]

Delacroix of all living artists had embodied and promised
to fulfil Gautier's Romantic dream of a new Renaissance, of a
modern, original art that would comprehend and synthesize a
whole new realm of sensual experience. Of Delacroix's *Saint
Sébastien*, 'the finest page' of the Salon of 1836, he wrote in
Ariel: 'it is not the sonorous and ferocious style of a
Michelangelo, nor is it Raphael's airy limpidity; there is
something more feverish and anxious about the contours, a
more sustained effort to arrive at something superior, as in all
periods of decadence and renewal, when the old art no longer
exists and the synthesis of the new has not yet been
formulated.'[7] In 1836, Gautier's dream—not so much of a
single 'genius of the future' as of a barely defined artistic
nirvana, a synthesis of all the best pleasures art could give—
seemed still realizable, and was focused around Delacroix,
the *chef d'école*. But if the life of a government critic under the
officialdom of Napoleon III was what Théophile finally woke
up to, Delacroix was to survive intact as a continuing

reminder of what could be. Gautier's model genius who, by following his instincts, allowed the release of all his inherent energies, Delacroix survived as a force of nature survives. In January 1857, when the painter was finally elected to the Institut, Gautier had no fears for his continuing vitality. Let loose among the Institut's venerable and sedate members, 'he will tell them of the fever, the tumult, the maelstrom of modern life'; he will not be changed, because his irrepressible painter's temperament will carry him away, even in spite of himself:

He cannot master it, reason with it or steer it: attached to this beast like Mazeppa to his horse, pursued by a black cloud of crows and a pack of wolves with phosphorescent eyes, he careers at full tilt and in a whirlwind of sparks across vast steppes, through forests whose branches lash him as he passes, over ravines, quagmires, and crashing rivers; and when at the end of his unchecked flight he falls panting from his mount, it is only to rise up again as a king, like the Hetmann in Victor Hugo's ode. Not that he always likes this kind of riding: he would sometimes prefer a gentler pace. But his horse has no mouth and feels only the spur.[8]

Such was the *bousingo* language with which Gautier still celebrated Delacroix's world in 1857. It was in these terms that Delacroix reflected 'the feverishness of modern life', his modernity remaining that of a Romantic of 1830. He possessed the vitality and all-grasping range of Gautier's most long-standing living hero, Victor Hugo, and celebrated in such literary terms, his capacity for assimilating literature was not the least of his strengths: hence of course the aptness of Gautier's use of Mazeppa and the Hetmann. He had all the qualities of a great artist, Gautier had restated, and not for the last time, in the *Ariel Salon of 1836*: 'he is a poet as well as a technician. He does not take painting back to the childishness of Gothic nor to the senility of pseudo-Greek. His style is modern and corresponds to that of Victor Hugo in *Les Orientales*: it has the same fire and temperament.'[9] Delacroix's *La Mort de Sardanapale*, Gautier was thrilled to point out, is the equivalent of Hugo's 'Le Feu du ciel', and *Le Massacre de Scio*, of 'La Bataille de Navarin'. The *Saint Sébastien* of the same Salon was not described as its 'finest page' gratuitously: Gautier read it almost as if it were a passage of confessional prose.

Here lay Delacroix's essential modernity and the strength of Gautier's affinity with him. Although half a generation apart (Gautier was thirteen years younger) they shared the same cultural background and enthusiasms. Gautier had even, briefly, attended Delacroix's old school, the Lycée Louis-le-Grand, where he had received the beginnings of a similarly orthodox, rational, and classical education; but it was above all their common response to that horizon-opening reading, from Rabelais and Shakespeare to Goethe, Chateaubriand, and Byron, which dominated the 1820s in Paris, that accounted for Gautier's empathy. Thus he was able to write in his obituary of Delacroix in 1864, that if Delacroix executed as a painter, 'he thought like a poet, and the basis of his talent is literature. He had a profound and intimate understanding of the inner meaning of the works from which he drew his subject-matter. He completely assimilated the characters he used . . . he gave them his heart's blood and the tremor of his nerves, recreating them through and through, while preserving their original identities.'[10]

3 A modern synthesis

Delacroix was an 'organisation nerveuse', Gautier summed up in his obituary.

Owing to his nervous, impressionable nature, Delacroix responded more spontaneously than anyone to the flux of ideas, events, and passions of his age. In spite of an apparent scepticism, he was infected by its fevers and tempered in its flames; like Corinthian bronze, he was compounded of every metal in fusion.

He was 'the true child of the century . . . one feels that the whole of contemporary poetry has cast its shadow on his palette . . .',[11] Gautier had written in 1841. But not only were the painter's powers of identification extended to literature, and to such an extent that Gautier was able to observe in *Les Beaux-Arts en Europe* in 1855 that not even Goethe had penetrated into the character of Hamlet as deeply;[12] not only was he moved, like Byron who greatly inspired him, to comment on the Greek struggle for independence, or on the 1830 Revolution. Delacroix seemed to be composed of 'every metal in fusion' and was carried away by his landscape-devouring temperament as if by an involuntary nervous reflex; Gautier saw him as making an even greater synthesis of the experience of his time, as capable of assimilating almost everything through his magic prism. He exploited the full range of his art. 'There is not a single genre upon which M. Delacroix has not left his mark . . . battles, religious pictures, scenes of everyday life, Oriental subjects, costume, and animal pieces, *grandes machines*, easel paintings, illustrations of the poets,'[13] and he always equalled or surpassed the specialists. Only Decamps could match him for the ease with which he was able to transport the young Gautier into other realms; he possessed a virtuoso's command of 'every genre and every epoch, from the fabulous Orient to the prosaic reign of the Charter'.

Gautier was writing his first article for *La Presse*, and his awed response to Delacroix's powers of assimilation was to subsist.[14] In 1855 he added to this synthesis a musical analogy to delight Pater: 'How many octaves on his pictorial keyboard, and what an immense gamut he has run through since the *Barque of Dante!*' Yet, as in harmonious improvisations on the piano, a profound sense of unity reigned among Delacroix's disparate productions, and Gautier was forcibly struck by this when confronted by the large retrospective collection of the painter's work that was gathered in 1855 for the imperial showpiece Exposition Universelle.[15] The mythic explanation for this phenomenal unity, and the unchanging if often unspoken premiss upon which Gautier based his whole critical relationship to Delacroix, was, of course, the microcosm. The theory had been reiterated and elaborated in his *Salon of 1841*. The impression that the world about him makes upon an artist is determined by his capacities, Gautier wrote; certain colour notes in the sky or certain countenances strike him particularly forcibly, and he is thus able to see *correspondances* that are invisible to others. But not all artists have the genius, or the memory, necessary to co-ordinate their impressions and give them logic or coherence. Their impressions lack unity, because these artists are not born with intuition, and because they are thus led astray by some unexpected detail, by some form (or *mot propre*) that academic models do not give. But

when M. Delacroix composes a picture, he looks inside himself rather than pressing his nose against the studio window . . . his colour, before it makes the journey from his eye to the end of his brush, has passed by way of his brain, where it takes on nuances which may at first seem bizarre, exaggerated, or false. Yet each touch contributes to the general harmony, and if it does not render an object in its prosaic aspect, at least it makes manifest a painter's feeling or idea.[16]

The unity that underlay his productions was the result of the stamp of individuality that marked everything the painter touched; his perceptions registered on his sensibilities like vibrations on a musical instrument and were thus informed with a particular and unique timbre. Everything he produced harmonized automatically with the atmosphere and emotional climate of his instinctual world, Gautier continued in *Les Beaux-Arts en Europe.*

Try to isolate one of M. Delacroix's figures or to imagine it in another setting, and it will seem bizarre or impossible, for it is surrounded by an atmosphere which is proper to it and which it alone can breathe. The artist's colour, quite rightly so highly praised, is subject to the same conditions; it is not individually vivid reds, greens, or blues that constitute its harmony, but a scale of nuances determining each other's values. His rich colours are not beautiful in themselves; their impact is the result of their juxtaposition and contrast . . .[17*]

The vital unity that linked Delacroix's productions was reflected in the consistency and length of Gautier's thirty-five-year-long celebration of his work. A lion described in 1836 and some men in armour in 1870 share the same qualities of vitality and immediacy. The lion, which unpromisingly symbolized constitutional government in the Throne Room of the Chambre des Députés, is 'the very ideal of a lion: an enormous head with a streaming tawny mane, eyes of clear, metallic yellow, like suns, and an indefinable air of contained and grandiose strength and cunning'.[18] The evocation of armour in *Le Roi Jean à la bataille de Poitiers* appeared in 1870,[19] in a nostalgic account of 'A Romantic Gallery': 'Delacroix's powerful hand transforms this collection of old iron into something supple: the braces do not restrain the arms, the knee-pieces do not stop the knees from bending . . . his knights can breathe beneath their coats of mail or breast-plates . . . there are heads in their helmets, and eyes full of life gleam from behind the bars and the holes of their visors.' It was this consoling life that Gautier's own suits of armour in *Le Capitaine Fracasse* and the poem 'Le Souper des armures',[20] for example, precisely and symbolically lacked, expressing the poet's terror at its potential absence.

Even Delacroix's inferior productions were marked by that supreme quality, 'la vie', and since his life-giving genius sprang from the depths of the man, his 'faults' were finally integral to his vision. The microcosm theory had been re-enlisted in 1841 to explain the power Delacroix possessed 'in spite of all his faults'; the nature of these faults nevertheless constituted a fundamental affront to Gautier's sensibilities. ' "Above all painting should not fill you with horror" ', he told Feydeau; Gautier's horror was a horror of mutants. As a neo-Renaissance man, he saw violation of the human form, the potential ideal of physical and sensual beauty *par excellence*, as a sacrilege, a blatant manifestation of evil. Thus, in a discussion with Feydeau, he claimed that the presence in Delacroix's work of figures with six fingers, or backward-bending joints, or with the knee where the ham ought to be, was quite unacceptable in painting, whatever pictorial, compositional justifications there were.[21] This was his strong feeling in principle; in practice, the impact of Delacroix at his most feverish carried all before it. Painting was 'a dream borrowing the forms of reality in order to manifest itself ', and the forms of reality were to be respected; yet if through Delacroix's magic prism they took on a bizarre or exaggerated appearance, it was in this way that they adjusted themselves to form a new harmony. They were essential by-products of the mysterious and irresistible vitality of Delacroix's work, and their absence was even to be regretted. 'There is a good deal of talent in all this, but no genius!'[22] Gautier complained at the Salon of 1840, where certain other exhibits seemed to fade into insipidity beside Delacroix's *La Justice de Trajan*. 'It's all perfectly beautiful, but perfectly boring: there is no zest, no fire, no daring, none of the restless stirring of life . . . We said that these canvases lack genius: they also lack faults.'[23] The authoritative voice of Zola can be heard in not too distant echo: 'You are a great incompetent, Monsieur (Pissarro)—you are an artist I like.'[24]

4 *Le mot propre*

'Violent and frank by nature, he offers himself to the public just as he is, qualities, faults, and all',[25] Gautier summed up in 1859 with the added confidence of hindsight: Delacroix was now a member of the Institut, and his posterity had thus received public assurance and official approval. In revealing himself such as he was, he had, for Gautier, shown his courage as a combatant for the Romantic cause. The echo of Zola is particularly resonant here, because his Pissarro had inherited the same love of the *mot propre*; and here too had lain the nature of Delacroix's apparent 'faults'. Just as Gautier himself submitted to the impact of his perceptions, so too was Delacroix not afraid of transcribing his complex reactions to the visible world in the forms into which they were moulded by instinctual inner necessity. Delacroix was not of course a simple copyist of the exterior world; his love of the particular was a striving towards a different kind of truth and *justesse*, the subjective truth which Gautier characterized as marching 'in a procession of feelings'. 'In his work, Delacroix has always sought the characteristic sign, the tell-tale hint of passion, the significant gesture, the strange and rare note.'[26] Delacroix's love of the *mot propre* was much the same as that which Victor Hugo thought he discerned in Gautier himself:[27] '(Gautier) has a horror of the common, the banal, the conventional. He seeks the choice, elegant, ingenious, paradoxical, curious, and sometimes strange side of things, the side of things not generally perceived. He tends toward the fantastic, but a well-lit, well-defined fantastic, in high relief, the fantastic of Rabelais and the old Italian comedy, and not the fantastic of the Germans; he tends toward Callot rather than Hoffmann'.[28] This was less the invented other-worldly fantastic of speculative mysticism than it was that unlikely fantastic which the receptive observer could discover in real life. It was the fantastic of things-in-themselves, of things as they strike the feelings and not as they are preconceived by the intellect. Delacroix too was a pragmatist, a rejector of systems; thus his 1836 lion was the essence of what a lion should be, the living and hirsute 'ideal of a lion', and no relation to the formalized, polite lions 'en perruque' that adorned classical monuments. Thus Delacroix (in 1841) was never led astray 'by an unexpected detail, by a form that the academies and the models do not give'.[29]

Above all Delacroix's striving for the particular and the *mot propre* was oriented towards dramatic truth, just as the same striving had been primarily focused on drama in Hugolian Romantic ideology. 'Delacroix is the great mime artist of painting', Gautier wrote in 1859.[30] 'It is this quality, for which he has not, perhaps, received enough credit, that really distinguishes him; his so-called mistakes are a result of it; he will often sacrifice contour in his search for the right gesture.' Delacroix's search for gesture was based on observation and psychological insight, as Gautier was able to corroborate in 1855; Delacroix could appear unconventional because of his total submission to the motif. 'Anyone who has merely visited Algeria', Gautier wrote of *La Noce juive* in *Les Beaux-Arts en Europe*, 'will be struck by the extraordinary talent for assimilation that M. Delacroix shows in this scene. Not one of the figures has a European posture; travellers have observed . . . that Muslims, Arabs, Turks, Asiatics have movements which bear no similarity to our own.'[31] Delacroix had caught unfamiliar but characteristic attitudes, for which Gautier goes on to explain the anthropological and cultural reasons. *Les Convulsionnaires de Tanger* he might accuse of exaggeration, had he not himself seen 'Aïssaouas indulging in their strange exercises, rolling on burning embers, swallowing snakes, chewing on glass, eating fire, slashing their own bodies, and, throwing themselves on the ground, shuddering in intermittent spasms like galvanized frogs'; Delacroix has perhaps even not gone far enough. In his *Saint Sébastien* of the Salon of 1859, it was more purely dramatic, psychological truth that Delacroix achieved.[32] The attitude of the kneeling woman pulling an arrow out of the saint's body expressed to Gautier a double preoccupation: a fear of aggravating the martyr's agony; and 'the surgical resolve, so to speak', to pull out the murderous barb. It was a gesture whose complex *vérité* and *justesse* were communicated by its very awkwardness.

Consider that Delacroix is not only a colourist, Gautier asks us in *Les Beaux-Arts en Europe*; add to this that

he has the gift of portraying movement . . . His figures bustle, gesticulate, run, hurl themselves about; the canvas hardly seems able to contain them . . . Their contours are constantly shifting in the shimmering luminosity of the atmosphere; no rigid line attaches them to their backgrounds: they are painted on the other side too and could turn around if they wished; they get on with what they are doing without bothering about whether they look handsome or ugly, or to pose in a corner and show off their torsos or heads, for the benefit of the spectator. Like English actors, they often turn their backs on their audience and only look at their interlocutors, flouting theatrical convention.[33*]

Based on his identification with the literature of his generation, with its own emphasis on dramatic *vraisemblance*, Delacroix's innate sense of drama, expressed in shifting contours and uncompromisingly articulated movement and gesture, was as great a unifying factor in his work as was colour. Gautier especially relished him because he was a creator of true dramatic tableaux. The effect on the critic of the *Bataille de Taillebourg* at the Salon of 1837 had been overwhelmingly dramatic, and it was in almost exclusively dramatic terms that Gautier then evoked the picture, indulging in a verbal blood-bath, as if describing a violent movie-still with a cast of stunt-men caught in mid-action.[34] The main compositional lines that he pointed out (lances, bridge) served in Gautier's prose, as in the picture, above all to heighten the drama. He was absorbed in the action and its historical trappings; Delacroix was able to transport Gautier to other realms, to reveal them to him with such *vraisemblance* that Gautier could imagine he had already been there himself; Delacroix revealed things as if with the selective economy of memory itself.

Delacroix painted complete and self-sufficient milieux; thus he joined the ranks of the Old Masters during his own lifetime. As in other fields, Delacroix was also a master of the grand tradition of mural painting, with its demands for 'breadth of conception', 'bold and decisive application of paint . . . all the highest qualities of art', and Gautier had remarked upon this in 1836;[35] Delacroix was the only contemporary to have produced true decorative painting 'understood in its architectural sense, and strictly in harmony with the site it occupies'. Delacroix is not an easel painter in the current sense, Gautier observed again in 1859, meaning that his painting did not rely for effect on fashionably skilful surface artifice.[36] 'His energetic brush demands great spaces' and there results 'a picture, a rare thing among so many painted canvases, in other words, a composition, a milieu, and a whole point of view!' The milieux that Delacroix created, essentially modern and corresponding to ineffably nineteenth-century sentiments, nevertheless provided Gautier with a platform for dreams and escape as effectively as did Titian, Veronese, or Rubens; through the additional common Romantic inheritance that he shared with Delacroix, Gautier could thus not only enter the painter's world, but also participate in its creation.

5 Collaboration

With the resources of his own, verbal, medium, Gautier emphasized, elaborated, and added to aspects of Delacroix's milieux. He brought out what remained implicit in the painter's dramatic tableaux; thus for instance, the great synthesis that Delacroix realized on his 'pictorial keyboard' was broadened by Gautier to take even sound into its sphere. *La Mort de l'évêque de Liége* at the Salon of 1838 was 'rowdy, a painting in an uproar; you can hear it as plainly as you can see it'.[37] When he saw it again at the Exposition Universelle, he was similarly impressed. 'Movement, fine; but this little canvas shouts, groans, and blasphemes. You can almost hear the hundred and one ribaldries and the obscene songs of this wine-sodden soldiery.'³⁸ As Gautier's evocation and his involvement deepened, the picture even began to smell: 'how it swarms, yelps, blazes, and reeks!' ('. . . comme cela flamboie et pue!') Even his rough colloquial phrasing seems to echo the hubbub of a distinctly common crowd.

The Salon of 1841 had provided the opportunity for one of the longest and most involved celebrations of Delacroix's world, with the microcosm aired in full public view and the crucial comment made that Delacroix was 'the true child of the century'. Thus Gautier was able to feel an immediate rapport with the pictures exhibited that year, and to enter into their spirit, his own poetic imagination liberated to the extent that he could freely elaborate on his own account, within the milieux they materialized. This, for example, is part of his evocation of *La Barque de don Juan* (a subject inspired by Byron's *Don Juan*, canto 2, stanza 75):

The sea is short, choppy and opaque, as after a long storm. The sky is hung with low clouds, heavy with rain and lightning, which cast only leaden reflections on the sad scene they cover. In the midst of this double expanse drifts a small, dangerously overloaded barque. Thirty-odd poor wretches, gaunt, ghastly, and emaciated, are huddled together in this frail craft . . . the dazzling red lights of famine dance before their eyes . . .³⁹*

When the picture was shown again in 1855, Gautier's identification with the milieu was further extended:

Forget about Don Juan, who would be hard to recognize among these gaunt, sunken, fleshless faces, grimacing with execrable lusts . . . You can sense the sharks with their triple rows of teeth writhing beneath these glaucous waves with their crests of white foam! What a hollow sound the wind and the thunder make, growling behind those low clouds, heavy with rain and tempest . . .⁴⁰*

Here the actual image is indeed transcended; the picture evokes a particular dramatic milieu so powerfully in Gautier

that his evocation becomes a sensual elaboration and recreation, more than a description and virtually a parallel and
independent work of art. Of course there are sharks just
beneath the waves, now that Gautier mentions it; so deep is
his spontaneous imaginative involvement with the drama
that he can see the spots in front of the deprived and scurvied
victims' eyes, as if he were physically experiencing their fate
himself. As for the noisy and smelly *Mort de l'évêque de
Liége*, his evocation rounds off the experience of the picture,
enlisting the power of words to evoke non-visual sensations,
like the groaning of thunder and the sound of 'une mer
courte, opaque et clapoteuse' slapping against the side of the
boat; by introducing extraneous and invisible sharks and the
debilitated vision of the victims, he not only illustrates the
predicament of Don Juan and his crew, but surpasses it in
poignancy. He is writing not as a critic, but as one artist in
deep collusion with another.

Gautier presents *La Barque de don Juan* as a fragment from
a larger drama, as is suggested by the fatal ring of 'a small,
dangerously overloaded barque'. Drama was once more the
key to Gautier's verbal involvement in 1861, when he saw
Jacob wrestling with the angel in the Chapelle des Saints-
Anges at Saint-Sulpice; his language simulates and heightens
the tensions and recreates the physical dynamics of the
fight.[41] 'Jacob is fighting hand-to-hand with the fine young
man whose appearance hardly belies his great strength;
he clasps him, locks him in an embrace, straining all the
knots of his muscles, buttressing his feet against the
ground, arching his neck for greater impetus, bearing down
on his adversary's wrist, putting his heart, his sinews, and his
back into it.' Rich and powerful similes help impress upon us
the reality of Jacob's struggle, and all the more forcibly
because they have a contemporary and extraneous ring: 'his
powerful chest heaves like a blacksmith's bellows, the sweat
gleams on his limbs like the oil on the body of a circus athlete,
yet he cannot throw down the frail adolescent.' Gautier, who,
admiring boxers and athletes above all other mortals, revelled
in any manifestation of physical strength, particularly his
own, can fully identify with Jacob, who has been caught by
Delacroix at his moment of supreme effort. The fight has

arrived at a climactically static instant, through the opposing pressure of equal forces; but this locked energy is about to be triggered into explosion and dissipation by the casual and unfair hand of the supernatural. 'The angel resists like an immortal attacked by a man, with ease and indifference. He can bring this unequal struggle to an end simply by wishing it, and already he has nonchalantly dropped his arm to seek Jacob's ham, which withers at the touch of this hand of flame.' Gautier's evocation is like an extract from a flowing commentary; the effect of the words is to heighten the spectator's personal involvement in the scene, to make him more aware of its embodied energies and its dangerously imminent future possibilities. Again, this is more than an apt description, a verbal reproduction; the painting becomes the platform and inspiration for a closely parallel but independent prose excursion.[42]

It is, moreover, that feature of Gautier's criticism which, more than any other, qualifies him as a quintessential Romantic critic. The work of a fellow artist, his evocations of Delacroix are efforts towards that harmonious understanding or correspondence between the arts which was promised in the cenacles of the early thirties, and promised above all, most significantly for Gautier's rapport with Delacroix, through Hugo's (and to a lesser extent Stendhal's) Romantic *drama*, wherein painters, poets, actors, and musicians would literally work side by side in a unified effort to exteriorize on stage, and thus liberate, universal and unchanging human passions.[43] The Romanticism of 1830 embodied an ideal of fruitful collaboration between artists, and this ideal was reflected in and coloured Gautier's criticism from the outset; Gautier's embellishments of and elaborations on art he discussed must thus be seen as his contribution to this Romantic programme for collaboration. If they sometimes led him to be inaccurate about details,[44] their function was first and foremost to evoke and to explore the spirit and emotional atmosphere of works of art. 'We like to put alongside a picture a page on which the painter's theme is taken up by the writer';[45] poetic elaboration was the very essence of Gautier's Romanticism.[46] It was in this way that Gautier, who wished to think of himself as a poet above all else, was sometimes best able to communicate his response to a painting; and was not Baudelaire, indeed, to suggest that 'the best account of a picture might be a sonnet or an elegy'?[47]

Gautier's evocations of Delacroix's dramatic milieux are among his personal fulfilments of the promise of a new Renaissance, of the promise, ultimately, of a new and comprehensive view of man that would admit extreme but real passions, appetites, and reactions which a classicist and polite eighteenth-century mentality had deemed unacceptable. Indeed it was a constricting politeness that Gautier still found pervasive in contemporary society with its ideas about progress and civilized morals. Society continued to need the *mot propre*, not to mention Gautier's own extravagant and publicly vaunted sensuality, as an antidote.

6 Conclusion

La Barque de don Juan, Gautier notes in *Les Beaux-Arts en Europe*, seems to mark the end of Delacroix's purely Romantic period.[48] Yet the fundamental and vital unity of his work subsisted in his treatment of Greek and Roman subjects, that is, unmodern, pre-Christian, but none the less literary subjects: 'he has dared to be alive, impassioned, full of movement and spirit, telling himself that man has always been the same, and that the blood in the veins of the heroes and heroines of antiquity was of a no less vivid purple'. This notion, as it emerges from the impression of unity that Delacroix's work imparted, contributes to the consolation for transience, the sense of endless continuity that Gautier sought in visual art; Gautier's obituary of Delacroix (which deserves to feature as an essential part of any introduction to the painter's work)[49] extends this idea of an ultimate consoling unity to include the artist himself, and thus reflects the sweeping powers of synthesis with which the painter held the critic in awe. As with most of Gautier's artists, we are given few character references or clues as to the painter's personal social impact; Delacroix is an 'organisation nerveuse', a sensitive microcosm-containing instrument who, as a member of the élite, fulfils higher functions in the service of Art. But he does, of course, share some of the characteristics of his work: 'He was lithe, suave, and captivating like one of those tigers whose supple and formidable grace he renders so superlatively'. And it is significant, of course, that the dead Delacroix still excels in the present tense; art is superior to artists because it survives while they do not. Above all, the experience of Delacroix enabled Gautier to verbalize his feeling that life was interior, if not inferior, to art: he was able to feel that a whole living temperament, in all its idiosyncrasies and ramifications, was contained in Delacroix's painting. Delacroix also lent strength to Gautier's conviction that art was the revelation and focus of an unbreakable web of *correspondances* that linked every element in time and creation. What is man in terms of his banal everyday social intercourse, Gautier might have said to himself, in the face of a discovery such as this? He could not see Delacroix's soul any more than he could see that of a Turk; thus it is not the man but his art which is discussed, because his art, the product of his deepest instincts, is his soul revealed in palpable form, as if in spontaneous confession. The artist, Gautier reiterated in Delacroix's obituary, contained a microcosm in which webs of *correspondances* were focused:

In the roughest sketch as in the most important finished painting, the sky, the landscape, the trees, the sea, the buildings play an active part in the scene they surround; whether they are stormy or clear, harmonious or broken, bare or in full leaf, calm or turbulent, ruined or magnificent, they always seem to be one with the furies, the hatreds, sufferings, and miseries of the figures . . . Everything hangs together, everything is linked and forms a magical whole . . . Rembrandt's are the only other paintings we know that have this profound and indissoluble unity . . . Rembrandt, like Delacroix, has his own architecture, his wardrobe, his arsenal . . . his light and his darkness, his gamut of colours which do not exist elsewhere, and from which he is able to draw marvellous effects, turning the fantastic into something more real than reality.[50*]

Rembrandt too had that uncompromising, preconception-free naïvety of gesture; his world too was suffused with an atmosphere that was unique to it, and outside which his figures could not thrive. The system of inner correspondences by which the whole becomes a magical unity is a justification and explanation of essentially nineteenth-century Pathetic Fallacy; just as the passions of Delacroix's dramatic 'personnages' are linked to the climate and landscape around them, so by extension is the painter inseparable from his world. And the passions that Gautier sees him as finally espousing (viewing his work as a whole after his death) do not include happiness, or serenity, or even pleasure; they are 'furies', 'hatreds', 'sufferings', and 'miseries'. Here perhaps Gautier sensed the painter's most profoundly intuitive modernity: Delacroix expressed in more passionate, colourful, and dramatic terms the drab disillusion and barely contained bitterness with which Gautier sensed himself overtaken, and which seemed, to a self-styled slave of the press and of vested interest, to be the unavoidable and chronic side-effects of modern urban civilization.

Sublimation lay in the higher and larger truth of dispassionate Art. 'The aim of art, and this is all too readily forgotten these days, is not the exact reproduction of nature, but rather the creation, by means of the forms and colours which nature makes available, of a microcosm in which the dreams, sensations, and ideas which the world inspires in us may live and flourish . . .' Thus Gautier arrived at a climactic statement of faith in Delacroix's obituary. Consolation lay in the very range and revealing power of Delacroix's work, with its tacit promise of some future synthesis of man and art, of body and soul; it was also to be found in the realization that the fantastic, for a man who looked for inner truth rather than pressing his nose against the grimy studio window, could be 'something more real than reality'. 'It should not be forgotten', wrote René Jasinski, 'that if Romanticism was a school, it is above all a state of mind in which reason is subordinated to the dictates of the imagination and the heart, not only in poetry and art, but also in life.'[51]

V Ingres

I Verbal responses

An 'organisation nerveuse', the Delacroix of Gautier's obituary has elements of the Goncourts' Watteau. 'He was anxious, feverish . . .'; with his sensibilities and weaknesses, Gautier's Delacroix is at least the semblance of a real person.

He was also 'impassioned, in love with art and glory', and as such had much in common with Théophile Gautier the 'jeune rapin à cœur de lion' himself. Throughout the long period of nostalgia for his own rosy youth, from around 1848 until his death in 1872, Gautier's appreciation of Delacroix rested more and more heavily on his identification of the painter as a combatant for the common cause. He delighted in using the stagey imagery of High Romanticism in his obituary to conjure up Delacroix's rank-shattering effect upon the old adversary: 'A meteor crashing into a marsh, with flame, smoke, and thunder, would not have caused greater consternation among a choir of frogs', a turn of phrase almost worthy of Tristram Shandy's Uncle Toby. His support of the painter was not patronizing, neither was it obsequious, but extended rather as an act of comradeship-in-arms. The Exposition Universelle of 1855 was an opportunity to disseminate some retrospective propaganda that anticipated L'Histoire du romantisme. 'The tail of the Davidian school was at that time dragging its last coils through the academic dust' when Delacroix arrived on the scene . . . and so on.[1] Gautier's clinching and most typical late characterization of Delacroix is thus a fighting one: 'The master has not left the field of combat, even to loosen for a moment his battered armour and wash away the dust, sweat, and blood of battle in a spring; not once has his hand left his sword, hacked by the blows of his adversaries until it resembles a saw; not once has he withdrawn with his bruised self-esteem to the shelter of his tent.'[2] Gautier's dogged image suggests both Walter Scott-like heroics and the human vulnerability of a contemporary who has laid his sensibilities open to abuse from the reactionaries and rejection from the Salon jury.

Delacroix is a man in the thick of things; Ingres, on the other hand, is a god, and like a god, he is set apart. Delacroix quivers and trembles as new passions, ideas, and events register themselves on his extraordinary sensibilities; Ingres is as immovable as a statue of Homer or Zeus. He is the presiding deity in Gautier's serene temple of Art, of the ultimate consoling ideal, with its white marble pediment that stands out against a clear sky of unchangeable azure. Gautier's most typical characterization of Ingres sets him for eternity 'on art's highest peak, on that golden throne with its ivory step where, crowned with laurels, are seated those whose glory is assured and who are ready for immortality';[3] this is less a characterization than an apotheosis. He is the type of the 'absolute poet . . . at the highest degree of perfection'.

Gautier early expressed the nature of his rapport with Delacroix with the phrase 'to understand genius you need something like genius'; to use such a phrase in connection with Ingres would have been *hubris*. For Ingres, the key words are not identification and collusion, but admiration and worship. Ingres, in 1855, is 'the first name that presents itself when you come to deal with the French school', the French school being represented in full strength at the Exhibition, and not only is he the nation's leading contemporary painter; he is already an immortal. 'The epithet of sovereign, which Dante gives to Homer, sits just as well on M. Ingres.'[4] 'Cher et vénéré maître', Gautier addressed the painter, employing a conventional but superlatively respectful form, in a letter from St. Petersburg in February 1859;[5] the letter concerned a *Virgin and Child* (this was possibly a *Vierge à l'hostie*), in which Gautier discerned the hand of the Master. If the picture were repurchased for the greater glory of France, would M. Ingres be good enough to add his signature, 'that sovereign name, which stands for sublimity, ideal style, supreme beauty . . . I would consider the devotion of my whole life to your glory well rewarded by this condescension' Gautier wrote, adding in doxologizing manner: 'Ingres and Raphael are the only two names that

could be inscribed at the bottom of this masterpiece.' Victor
Hugo himself hardly received such formal and unreserved
devotion.[6]

The great modern Old Master, an imposing genius on
Hugo's scale, Ingres is spoken of in hushed religious terms.
Gautier does not visit Ingres's studio in the summer of 1847,
he makes a pilgrimage to the sanctuary: 'At the back of the
courtyard of the Institut is a narrow studio, above which is an
uncomfortable lodging containing truly regal treasures. It is a
sanctuary, a chapel of art, to which worshippers make
pilgrimage, when the high priest sees fit partly to open the
doors.'[7] (Far be it to presume a greater condescension than
merely half-opened portals.) Ascetically housed himself above
the sanctuary of his single-minded passion, and shut away
from the bustling *quais*, Ingres runs a tough, monastically
disciplined school; he is the Master 'who, with an irritated
glance, could reduce his pupils to tears, and whose smile of
approval would cause ecstasies of joy'. Ziegler was one
painter who 'went through M. Ingres's school, where he did
penance for his excesses'.[8] 'We have just experienced one of
those keen emotions which are milestones in the life of a
critic,' Gautier wrote in 1862;[9] he had just been to see *Jésus
enfant parmi les docteurs* on its easel. 'The easel,' he inter-
rupted himself; 'we should like to say the altar'.

No superlatives were good enough, and superlatives were
the frequent expression of Gautier's joyful (or tiring)
admiration, to communicate the effect of Ingres's painting.
Personifying perfection itself, Ingres often left Gautier with
nothing to say but once more to proclaim the painter's
superiority; only occasionally did he stimulate the verbal
fecundity that a Delacroix or a Decamps could whip up. At
the Salon of 1834, writing in defence of *Le Martyre du Saint
Symphorien*, Gautier went to some lengths to explain Ingres's
approach.[10] But his *evocation* of the picture—and his voice of
approval here must have sounded small indeed given the
otherwise almost unanimously hostile press which greeted *Le
Saint Symphorien*'s appearance—virtually stopped short at
'the most beautiful fresco, the most magnificent cartoon you
could hope to see'. His reaction to the *Portrait de femme* was
equally muted: 'the colour glows, the hands are beautiful, the

dress is in the best possible taste and executed in a superior manner'. It is true that he also made somewhat fatuous or tongue-tied comments in his admiration for *Les Femmes d'Alger* (they were 'charming and quite Oriental in their beauty'); but Delacroix, unlike Ingres, inspired some spontaneous associations as well, while Decamps's *La Bataille des Cimbres* provoked a positive explosion of verbal energy. 'What savage and spirited application of paint! What brutal impasto! What a rich surface, the paint boldly and resolutely kneaded on! What verve, what animation, what frenzy . . .' The article sandwiches Ingres between Delacroix and Decamps; Gautier's verbal responses emerge in high contrast.

This early verbal reaction to Ingres persists. Gautier tends not so much to accumulate related ideas and poetic images around Ingres's work as to deploy a vocabulary of abstract superlatives and terms such as might be used by a philosopher or an aesthetician: *beau, idéal, absolu, style, art.* At the Exposition Universelle, for example, *L'Apothéose d'Homère* is simply described as incomparable: 'We don't believe, having visited all the galleries in the world, that there is a picture anywhere that could stand comparison with it.'[11] *Le Martyre du Saint Symphorien* is 'the *ne plus ultra* of style and art'.[12] 'Never,' Gautier wrote of *La Vénus Anadyomène* (using a favourite construction that enabled him to catalogue and celebrate his own syntactical World's Fair, rich in comparative material), 'Never, whether in Indian ivory, in Paros marble, on wood, or on canvas, has art represented a more virginally naked, a more ideally youthful, or divinely beautiful body.'[13] What is more, 'no one has painted portraits better than he';[14] and a final superlative for the *Stratonice*, which was not even at the exhibition: it is a 'marvel without parallel in the world'.[15]

Ingres's world is complete and definitive; Gautier's prose evocations are correspondingly restrained, and the energy of his enthusiasm is generally concentrated in his superlatives, in a syntactical vacuum away from the content of the pictures themselves (in the case of the *Stratonice*, in the picture's complete and literal absence). His descriptions keep poetic elaboration to a discreet and apt minimum; there is little to add that would not threaten the unity and serenity of the whole, no spontaneous personal contributions to make to an ever broadening synthesis, as was the case with Delacroix. They are verbal engravings rather than prose celebrations or fantasies around a theme; where in the process of translation from one medium to another Gautier highlights or intensifies some aspect of the original, he does so strictly within the original's terms, as the sharply defined nature of Ingres's world demands, at least at its most doggedly classical.

L'Apothéose d'Homère, for example, is described in 1855 in its physical disposition, and Gautier shows his absorption in the milieu by underlining and illustrating aspects of its expressive power, by explaining the iconography; but that is all he does.

Before the peristyle of a temple whose Ionic order symbolically recalls the country of Melesigenus sits Homer deified, with the serenity of a blind Jupiter. His pose indicates his blindness, if his eyes, white like those of a statue, do not already suggest that the divine poet sees only with an inner eye the marvels of creation which he has so splendidly recounted. A golden band encircles his broad temples, full of thoughts.[16]

Here is nothing to stretch the imagination to new efforts, nothing to add new insights much beyond the conventional, space-filling observation that Homer's temples are full of thoughts. In the more dramatic *Oedipe devinant l'énigme du Sphinx*, Gautier becomes involved in the dramatic confrontation, but is in no sense carried away by the drama into an unfamiliar milieu, as he was with *La Barque de don Juan*, for example. The Sphinx has already asked its riddle, and is raising its claws. But Oedipus 'has found the answer; he is going to reply; his lips open, and there is nothing the beaten Sphinx can do but throw itself off its rock. Faint footprints, skulls, and skeletal remains can vaguely be discerned in the black mouth of the cavern, reminders of the risk run by travellers whose bad fortune led them to take this fatal road.'[17] Gautier makes a factual commentary, describing and explaining the situation as it stands; there is no drawing of extraneous parallels, there is nothing to conjecture nor add, no suggestion that the figures might imminently burst out of the frame, or that the decisively beaten Sphinx might make a last-minute come-back; he has only to throw himself off his rock, but that is another picture. The *Oedipe* is a static formalization of a dramatic moment, quite unlike one of Delacroix's violent movie-stills (Gautier's description of the picture may be compared, in particular, with his ring-side commentary on the fight between Jacob and the angel); it contains no hint of distant thunder or obscene exclamation (the ether of Ingres's world is too rarefied to carry sound); there is no whiff of sweat or decay (statue-like beings do not perspire, and Ingres's bones and skulls are a necessary iconographical adjunct, not just gratuitous local colour or atmospheric special effect). As with *L'Apothéose d'Homère*, the scene is perceived from the outside. This is how Homer and Oedipus must have looked, or how they certainly ought to have looked; Ingres, for Gautier, has distilled their ideal appearances. Oedipus is not 'archaism, but resurrection. This is indeed just how he stood, the fine, proud young man'; but Ingres does not make the critic feel that he might *be* in Oedipus's situation, as he might have been part of Delacroix's shipwrecked crew or ferocious fight. There are no spots in front of Oedipus's eyes.

'*Oedipe devinant l'énigme du Sphinx* might have been painted by a Greek artist from the school of Sicyone, so powerfully does it exude a sense of pure antiquity.'[18] Ingres's 'sens intime' enabled him to impart this feeling to Gautier, ever watchful for opportunities to make connections across the centuries; he too is thus subsumed beneath the avatar and contains the microcosm. But Ingres moved in spheres that were too distant to enable Gautier to see through his prism and experience his world from the inside. 'We accept each artist from the point of view of his particular ideal,' he was able to write in perfect good faith in *L'Artiste* in 1856. If he went on to assert 'we judge their painting as if we possessed their souls',[19] he was not speaking hyperbolically about his rapport with Delacroix. It is significant that *admiration*, and a conception of a very much more distant and hierarchical relationship between critic and artist, should be stressed in the other manifesto-like article in *L'Artiste*, which was entitled 'La Néo-Critique – A propos de M. Ingres'.[20]

2 Worship

If we did not know of Ingres's existence from other sources, we might assume that Gautier had invented him. Ingres is a statue or a cut-out like the dress in his portrait of Madame Moitessier. This he has in common with Gautier's artists of the Petit Cénacle, and with Gautier's own two-dimensional self-image, with its wardrobe of guises not dissimilar in character to Madame Moitessier's. Gautier's Ingres is a reflection of part of his self-image; he personifies an absolute, if not the Absolute, in the poet's personal mythology.

Much that can be said of the poet/critic's relationship to Ingres is already implicit in the painter's work. Gautier's artists and their productions merge imperceptibly, are assimilated whole and fused into his world-view: they merge into Gautier. Ingres paints sculptural figures; he is virtually characterized as a statue. In the light of Gautier's extraordinary ability to empathize, which is never to be underestimated, his free use of superlatives whenever Ingres is in question seems to reflect the fact that Ingres painted superlatives: Homer, the Virgin Mary, Christ, Napoleon, and mythic figures who themselves stand for some ultimate or absolute. Ingres the painter of apotheoses is himself apotheosized by Gautier; the idea of worship, as Gautier afforded it to Ingres in his serene temple of Art, is already stated by Ingres: Virgil, Dante, Raphael, Poussin, and others worship Homer in his Ionic temple. It is as if, in the serious, time-honoured, and highbrow content of his painting, Ingres reflected Gautier's experience of a need to worship, and then came to be the object and fulfilment of this worship himself.

Ingres himself worshipped *le beau*, in all the connotations that Gautier lent to the word. The aim of art was 'to give birth to the idea of the beautiful', contemplation of which was 'a superior intellectual pleasure in itself, which releases you from the coarse reality of things', Gautier wrote in 'La Néo-Critique . . .'; Ingres's whole life was dedicated single-mindedly to a religion of self-sufficient form. Voluntarily immured in the depths of his sanctuary, he 'lived in ecstatic contemplation of the beautiful, on his knees before Phidias and Raphael, his gods', and moved in Gautier's Platonic realms, those of 'the personifications of supreme beauty, the transparent blue ether breathed by the Sibyls of the Sistine Chapel, the Muses of the Vatican, and the Victories of the Parthenon'.[21] In the face of this supreme beauty which Ingres courted, it is not surprising if Gautier sometimes found too little to say. Sensual experience of the material world, to which Gautier could always put words, was a distraction to the purest aesthetic idealist. Borrowing the forms of nature in order to manifest itself, the Ideal was, so to speak, to be morally perceived through the eyes; it was an experience that was not to be heightened by the collaboration of geniuses in their separate fields, but that was to be approached through private contemplation. Thus Gautier could only admire and eulogize, conceiving the Ideal as separate and difficult of access by its very nature; and thus the gift of admiration was itself exclusive, and born of the same inexplicable instinct. Making a characteristic fusion, he speaks of his admiration for Ingres in the same breath as that of Ingres for Raphael, and adds Dante and Virgil for good measure: 'The faculty of admiration is a rare and precious one which lifts the soul almost to the level of the genius adored. To admire is to love and understand, and it is to be feared that he who has not given himself from youth a "master and an author", as Dante called Virgil, will not in his turn receive the admiration of posterity.'[22] As with a real god, Gautier's worship of Ingres was an assurance of personal immortality, linking the worshipper, if humbly, to the eternal family of genius.

3 Ingres's Romanticism

'No haze could hide the star of beauty from him';[23] the star was that which was also followed by Préault's Romantic artist and by Gérard de Nerval. (See the star in Nerval's *Aurélia*, and other contemporary star imagery, as for instance in Balzac's *Le Lys dans la vallée*;[24] the star, the image of an ideal, is associated in both Nerval and Balzac with love for a woman, and this, it will be seen, has a very significant bearing on Gautier's conception of *le beau*.) It was a widely manifested yearning for a timeless and consoling ideal that forged the link, not as surprising as it may seem at first glance, between Gautier the flamboyant literary guerrilla in the cause of Delacroix and Hugo, and Ingres the austere inheritor of Neo-Classicism. Not alone among Gautier's artists, Ingres was not of his time; transcending the fashions and immediate values of his own age, and unlike any other living painter (except perhaps some of his own pupils), he was eternal, and this was a quality that touched so deeply on Gautier's private predilections that he made, in 1855, a rare and unequivocal statement of partiality. 'There is a moving, thrilling side to everyday life . . . and art has the right to bring this out and draw magnificent works from it; but we prefer that absolute and pure beauty which belongs to every age, to every nation and creed, and which unites past, present, and future in a fellowship of admiration.'[25]

The Olympian Ingres alone bore 'the torch of Greece' in his hands. His particular spiritual masters were Phidias, Raphael (in whose honour, Gautier noted in his obituary, Ingres kept his hair parted down the middle), and Michelangelo. Yet alongside his classical ideality he possessed a sensualist's grasp of local colour and an avatar-like power of historical identification. In his *Paolo et Francesca*, 'M. Ingres, who was so Greek in *L'Apothéose d'Homère*, so Roman in *Le Martyre du Saint Symphorien*, so Oriental in his various *Odalisques*, is here a pure medieval image-maker . . . (his) facility for absorbing the local colour of a subject is one of the great artist's numerous qualities, and one that has been little remarked upon . . . (yet) no one has this power of transformation in a higher degree'.[26] At one moment he seems to Gautier to have copied a Renaissance tapestry, at another he is an associate of Porbus or Clouet, or again of Lebrun, or he is a Venetian contemporary of Tintoretto; as a portraitist, he has the right to mix with Velazquez, Holbein, and van Dyck in their artists' Elysium, as well as with the fixed stars of the Italian Renaissance. It is as a Romantic carried away by the *mot propre* and by Petit Cénacle theatricality that Gautier insists on Ingres's feeling for local colour and on his 'power of transformation'; this secondary link between Ingres and Gautier's generation is made explicit in his obituary. With his 'profound sense of reality' Ingres was attacked as Gothic and barbaric; he received prompt expressions of solidarity and support from the Romantics of the early 1820s, and Gautier himself was responsible for renewing this alliance with his virtually single-handed defence of *Le Saint Symphorien* against established critical opinion, in *La France industrielle* in 1834. 'The Romantic movement was a return to the Renaissance', and as such it found its most resounding echo in Ingres.

But, Gautier recognized, all Ingres's Romantic qualities were accompanied, if not realized by 'knowledge of drawing and style, which he never forgets';[27] Ingres did not so much resurrect a picturesque Renaissance as maintain its artistic traditions: 'M. Ingres's honour will consist in having taken up that torch which antiquity held out to the Renaissance.'[28] Gautier is suggesting the continuity of Classicism in terms to which a 'perruque' or a 'grisâtre' might not have objected, and he seems to have sensed the possible delicacy of his stance (even in 1855); had he not been committed, in his youth, to decrying the Davidian school to which Ingres belonged? He thus inserts a qualifying clause; honour is due to Ingres for bearing the torch of the Classical and Renaissance tradition, 'and not having let it go out when so many mouths were blowing on it, with the best intentions in the world, it must be said'. This ideological difficulty is overcome in the obituary by means of an epithet that reconciles Ingres the creator of platforms for Romantic dreams, with the ascetic, Classical genius: he is 'le romantique de la ligne', the Romantic of line.[29]

Gautier's first awakening to the superiority of the linear and sculptural tradition as Ingres represented it was based on his own careful visual judgements. The contrast in verbal excitement aroused by Delacroix and Decamps as against Ingres at the Salon of 1834 has been suggested; in his more sober response he had, the previous year, nevertheless reserved for Ingres his highest praise.[30] 'A myth, the personification of drawing', Ingres was seen as standing alone; there was no immediate ideological conflict here with the young Romantic's avowed hatred of the Classical 'grisâtres'. The 'sanctity of line', the 'religion of form evident in the smallest details', and the uncompromisingly honest handling of the 1807 portrait of a Roman lady which was exhibited in 1833 made it 'very hard to believe that this was painted right in the middle of David's reign'. Not only was Ingres a great idealistic independent; his approach was already seen, it is implied, as the superior one. Surprisingly for 1833, when colour might have been assumed to be the prevailing propaganda issue, the ultimate superiority that Ingres represented was that of tonal, contoured drawing over colour. The superiority of Ingres's approach (in the portrait of a Roman lady) emerged in contrast to that of Gros. 'The whole head is alive and mobile, and this is achieved not with magical effects of colour but with a simple local colour, skilfully shaded to follow forms and movement. Personally we much prefer this method to the prismatic knitting with which the school of Gros covers its figures; it seems incontestably more life-like and pleasing to the eye.' ' "That devil of a fellow" ', Gautier is reported to have remarked to Feydeau years later (Feydeau only met him around 1840) ' "is so steeped in a knowledge of drawing that with six strokes of his pencil he can achieve the same relief, the same rendering as Delacroix with all the fury of his colour." '[31] Applied for its own sake and empirically, for the grace and serenity inherent in a sinuous contour or in carefully graded relief, Ingres's procedure was seen as distinct from the programmatic Classicism of David, if belonging to the same tradition; above all, Gautier perceived that it enabled the painter to achieve an illusionistic solidity, a sense of physical presence, with an economy that was beyond the colourists (if it was not outside their aims).

The following year, at the Salon of 1834, Gautier examined Ingres's procedure as a draughtsman in detail, apropos of *Le Saint Symphorien*. Ingres, he wrote, is no mere slavish imitator of Raphael, in spite of what the papers say; for Dürer is more his spiritual patron than Raphael; Ingres's heads are less generalized and idealized than Raphael's:

it is a much more literal translation from nature: his drawing follows the form more closely. The character of his style is exaggeration, within the bounds of truth, of external details, for M. Ingres is concerned principally with the outline of his figures, and draws around the edge rather than from the middle. If relief is sacrificed, what results from this procedure is a breadth, a simplicity, and an air of absolute mastery which would enable you to distinguish this picture at a glance from among thousands. [32*]

Now this is a different approach from the 'simple local colour, skilfully shaded to follow forms and movement' which had been seen at work in the 1807 portrait the previous year. Gautier does not acknowledge the difference; he is content with his separate observations. Ingres's emphasis on contour, producing figures of a characteristic 'breadth and simplicity' found approval in Gautier, with his own tendency to see the world in terms of clearly defined and irreducible elements. The character of Ingres's style was 'exaggeration, within the bounds of truth, of external details', 'a much more literal translation from nature' than Raphael's; such a technique would result in a great intensity of life when applied to living models, and would even make of necessarily more generalized figures from religious or mythological painting types with a certain individuality of their own. Relief might be sacrificed, but the sensation of being in the presence of living flesh would be heightened, because Ingres's drawing, following forms closely, would delineate individual physiological particularities and even flaws, while continuing to simplify and idealize.

4　Sensuality and the Ideal

In the particularizing, individualizing tendency of his drawing lies Ingres's Romanticism; and here, with the pragmatic, unintellectual Gautier, we are confronted with the uncomfortable complexity of Ingres's long artistic evolution, with the uneasy mixture of dry ideality and epidermal sensuality that obtained in his work. He was after all the painter of the portly Bertin as well as of blandly divine Madonnas. Gautier was not wholly able to reconcile such opposites; Ingres, indeed, reflected the similar duality inherent in Gautier's own vision. The critic's emphasis on the verbal resonance of the moment must of course be borne in mind, but was he not to generalize, nevertheless, in *Les*

Beaux-Arts en Europe, that Ingres's art 'owes nothing to accident' ('a literal translation from nature', often closer to Dürer than to the divine and adored Raphael?), and that it was 'heedless of passing preoccupations and the fashions of the day' (lovingly executed contemporary costumes containing ordinary middle-class contemporaries?).[33] Thus as well as noting the painter's sensual, Romantic qualities, Gautier also discerned a purer, more Raphaelesque strain of idealism in his work.

Along with Ingres's modern love of the particular and his close observation of nature, there was also a latent, unchanging ideal of physical beauty implied in Gautier's account of his painting, an ideal which was based on the syntheses and generalizations of indefinably beautiful human physiques made by the Renaissance, and which ultimately harked back to the youthful beauty eternalized in Greek sculpture. Gautier does not attempt to define the characteristics of this beauty; he is content with the experience of contemplating it. When this youthful physical beauty is absent in Ingres, Gautier leads us away from any sensual response to sculptural solidity or individuality, and into the realms of pure aesthetic mysticism; the very essence of beauty then resides in Ingres's painting of inorganic form.

Gautier discovered this essence in 1862 while he was contemplating *Jésus enfant parmi les docteurs*, with its cast of aged and hoary sages. He draws our attention to the draperies; they remain inseparable from the unpromising forms they clothe, but Gautier's appreciation of them nevertheless recalls the abstracted vision, the ever lurking threat of the anguish of the aesthetic, which was suggested by his comments to the Goncourts about the fold in an actress's costume.

Some of these draperies induce that sort of enchantment which accompanies experience of the absolute. They could not possibly be more perfect. The melody of the human body has never had a more harmonious accompaniment in the whole history of art. M. Ingres's profound skill here cannot be admired too much, for, having old men as models, to whom he could only give character, he has put *beauty* in the draperies.[34]

Gautier is indeed lost for words; the urgent need for more and more emphatic superlatives even forces him into italics. (What could be more perfect than 'la *beauté*'?) An analogy with music is the nearest approximation he can find to express his profound enchantment. Bearing in mind the importance he attached to words as reflections of a full universe rich in sensual experience (see the opposing image of a shipless sea, without interest or drama, in *Voyage en Espagne*), and his deeply consoling claim to be able to describe anything, the aesthetic ecstasy to which contemplation of Ingres can bring him seems to carry with it the fear of an empty absolute. It is as if the most perfect beauty ultimately refined itself to nothing, leaving a perfect void.

Ingres could of course engage more straightforwardly sensual responses, but even his sensuality sometimes proved offensive to Gautier's purest aspirations towards the Ideal. It was a delicate question of aptness, which once more seems to reflect the odd complexity of Ingres's vision. A version of *La Vierge à l'hostie* was actually criticized in 1855 for not being ideal enough. 'Our only reproach is that this truly celestial face has a rather too human pink on the cheeks.'[35] (Perhaps, Gautier surmises in deference to Ingres, who never makes errors of taste, 'the artist wished to express the mystical Rose of the Litanies'.) The reverse criticism, again of inapt use of resources, had been applied to Ingres's portrait of M. Bertin. The essence of formal beauty that Ingres distilled was wasted on M. Bertin, who appeared at the Salon of 1833, when Gautier's idealism was perhaps at its most youthfully radical. 'It is a pity that such faultless drawing was not applied to a quite different subject. Such purity and precision are, in our opinion, completely wasted on the folds in a waistcoat or a frock-coat, which could have been treated in another way without being any the less life-like.'[36] The banal familiarity of M. Bertin's appearance—turning away from the portrait, the young critic at the Salon would have found himself surrounded by real M. Bertins—and the scrupulous treatment of his dress perhaps gave Gautier a hint of the formal *dépaysement* and nausea that were to afflict him later; he seems to have suffered a kind of aesthetic short-circuit. (In 1855, when fashions in men's wear had changed sufficiently,

M. Bertin inspired no disgust, but was the miraculous dream revelation of a whole epoch; he was 'the respectable man under Louis-Philippe' eternalized as a 'bourgeois Caesar'.[37])

In 1833 the young critic's idealism, his desire to be transported to ideal realms, was so strong that he insisted that 'M. Ingres should only do subjects involving the nude, or at least, the antique'. Most of all M. Bertin was simply too ugly to be immortalized. Every fold in his chin was preserved for eternity by Ingres's truthful pencil; his massively physical presence inspired Gautier with no dreams, and gave no scope to any sensual response beyond mild revulsion and the perception of abstract purity and exactitude of form.

5 Permanence

The very antiquity and power of survival of the tradition to which Ingres subscribed was the final proof for Gautier of its superiority; it satisfied his need for a sense of continuity. And if Ingres represented an absolute in Gautier's personal mythology, there was finally nothing ethereal about it; the ideal that Ingres made visible was embodied in form, above all in human form. Ingres thus reflected Gautier's yearning to share the permanence of sculpture, which might survive the passage of time as Phidias's had done. The theme of permanence touches Gautier's account of Ingres at every level; the painter of archetypal figures and myths always has his eye on eternity. He even takes time into account in the preparation of his pigments. The colours of *Notre-Seigneur remettant à Saint Pierre les clefs du paradis en présence des apôtres*, shown at the 1855 Exhibition, improve, we are told, with every day that passes; contemporaries who simulate 'the darkened look of age by means of varnishes and bitumen' are compromising the future and should imitate Ingres, who sacrifices an initially pleasing surface in his new productions for the sake of their posterity.[38]

Ingres reflects the permanence-courting solidity of Gautier's own images. Of Napoleon in *L'Apothéose de Napoléon*, the ceiling in the Hôtel de Ville, Gautier wrote in 1854 that his torso seemed to be 'made of marble and light' while his head had 'the beauty of a medal or a cameo'.[39]

Ingres's Napoleon, like Ingres himself, has the essential
qualities of Gautier's heroes: Victor Hugo is 'like a statue on a
bronze column' in *L'Histoire du romantisme*;[40] the torso of
the Pharaoh in *Le Roman de la momie* 'was polished and
shining like pink granite that has been worked by a skilful
craftsman . . . Those unblinking eyes seemed to be focused
on eternity and infinity'[41] ('Ingres was immovable . . . his
eyes focused on an object invisible to others'—obituary); and
Gautier himself is described in similar terms by the sculptor
David d'Angers, who had been commissioned in 1845 to
immortalize the poet in a portrait medallion: 'he took off his
shirt and I saw a man built like an Egyptian statue'.[42]
Prophetically, for Ingres's ceiling was destroyed during the
Commune, Gautier wished to see it engraved for eternity 'on
a large piece of agate like the Apotheosis of Augustus in the
Sainte-Chapelle'.

Gautier's personal aspirations for immortality through art
elicited from him a cry of regret, almost of panic and anguish,
when he visited Ingres's studio in the spring of 1862, to see
Jésus enfant . . . on its 'altar'. 'Confronted with this hale,
hearty, and fruitful old age' (Gautier had by now lost
something of his monolithic torso and virile self-confidence
to a monolithic 'hippopotamus' lassitude') 'you are filled with
shame for being so tired, so feeble, so washed out, on the
pretext of some few million frivolous lines cast to the four
winds of journalism; you blush at your faint-hearted yearnings for rest, for insensibility and slumber, for stupefying
well-being. You tell yourself that perhaps it is still not too late
to create a masterpiece.'[43] *Le Capitaine Fracasse* was indeed
yet to come; but gone, temporarily, was Théophile's mag-
nificently self-assured 'nous', in favour of a neutral and
colourless 'on'; he was but a humble worshipper, and
Ingres in his old age even more like God the Father, whose
immortal state of creative grace seemed correspondingly
more difficult to reach. The very transient nature of
Gautier's profession heightened the sense of eternity and
permanence that he received from Ingres, as if in compensation.

Gautier had already shivered at the passing of time in
Ingres's studio in 1848, where *La Vénus Anadyomène* was
privately revealed to him. The picture had been started in

1808, but only completed forty years later; the thirteen-year-old who had posed for Ingres in 1808 was now an august matron; genius had preserved her youth for eternity;[44] she was like the virgin of *Arria Marcella* in the Vesuvian lava, or the mummified princess in *Le Roman de la momie*. One of the baby *amours* later became an *odalisque*; the *frisson* of fear of transience that Gautier experienced was also a *frisson* of pleasure.

6 Conclusion

According to David d'Angers, Gautier had the physical monumentality of an Egyptian statue; the sculptor had also discerned Théophile's deep-seated sensuality: 'I also saw an image of the Divinity' (a medallion of the Virgin Mary that Gautier wore around his neck), 'hanging next to flesh which seemed to embody both an intelligence and an indescribable sensuality.'[45] David's artist's observation suggests the extraordinary degree to which the paganistic Gautier made a personal association between the highest, almost religious idealism, and the most luxuriant, self-indulgent sensual awareness. Both these qualities were reflected in his account of the work of Ingres.

When Ingres's solidly physical idealizations and eternalizations do allow Gautier's own great sensuality free rein—that is, when physiological individuality is added in the right proportion to the unchanging, unspoken ideal of youthful physical beauty to provoke an unashamedly sensual response (and here Gautier has come close to Baudelaire's definition of *le beau* in *Le Peintre de la vie moderne*)—then the painter truly becomes a figment of the poet's personal mythology. It is significant, moreover, that when Ingres is criticized for wasting ideality, it should be over a portrait of a male sitter, ugly and banal as he was. The ideal of physical beauty that Gautier saw at work in Ingres was epitomized above all in female form; in Ingres's painting of women, and especially of the female nude, Gautier found the fullest of consolations. (Was not the microcosm, after all, populated with 'blond heroines and dusky Madonnas'?[46]) It satisfied both his sensuality and his yearning for some reassurance of permanence. If the death of the sensual and perceiving faculties was the beginning of nothingness, art at least survived; Ingres's nudes, surviving the passage of time with their youth untarnished, were the permanent embodiments of sensuality.

Not all of Ingres's figures have the epidermal impact of M. Bertin; the statue-like Homer and the polished marble Napoleon, who is worthy of an *émail* or a *camée*, exist in a rarefied alternative realm. *La Vénus Anadyomène*, in 1855, is also 'a statue come to life';[47] she is just such an ideal as Gautier might have had in mind when he wrote 'I have always preferred statues to women, and marble to flesh'. But if she is worshipped like a goddess materialized in sculptural form by the hand of some priest-like artist, it is also because she is a crystallization of awakening sexuality; she is the goddess of puberty, with her 'twisted blond hair from which a few bitter droplets are rolling on to a breast already flushed with the emotion of life'. In contrast, the figure of Angélique in *Roger délivrant Angélique*, also at the 1855 Exhibition, is all woman, and what is more, modern, identifiable woman: 'this can be sensed in something finer and more slender about her, and, why not say it, although the word may seem strange in this context, something more Christian. Look how she bends her swan-like neck . . .' This is pure titillation, seasoned with a taste of Catholic guilt, for Angélique might be the pretty, respectable bourgeoise next door; it is the stuff of which soft pornography is made. But Gautier has written himself a grandly saving clause above: 'she is . . . the most delectable figure, with her pearly, chaste pallor, that an imagination in love with the beautiful could dream of'. The sensuality and overt eroticism that colour his response are all part of his connoisseur's reaction to *le beau*; they are indeed the vital ingredients of this ultimate *beau* itself. It consists of soul and idea, plus body and form in full measure.

Enshrined in their harems like more goddesses incarnate, Ingres's odalisques are the ideal objects of Gautier's pagan worship. An *Odalisque à l'esclave* becomes in 1855 a pure reflection of his own sensual lassitude; the critical superlatives are as abundant as ever, but now, at home in the world of his odalisque's senses and in her lush and exotic milieu, Gautier is once more at no loss for words; this particular

captive ideal is touched almost exclusively by the terrestrial
and material aspects of *le beau*. She is 'a young, blond-haired
woman, overwhelmed by the enervating languors of the
seraglio, resting her head on her arms which are crossed
among the billows of her flowing hair; her half-naked body is
contorted in a spasm of boredom. Perhaps some secret and
unsatisfied desire, some mad aspiration for freedom stirs this
beautiful creature buried alive in the tomb of the harem and
causes her to toss and turn on the matting and the mosaics.'[48]
She reflects Gautier's own aspirations for freedom. If she is
not sculpture, if the realm she inhabits is not suffused with
'the dawn light of immortality', like Homer's, it is nevertheless true that, as in Homer's Elysium, no 'sun of the living'
illuminates things there. She is 'buried alive in the tomb of
the harem' for all time; a slave, she is also a goddess-like ideal,
kept apart from the outside world and breathing only the
rarefied atmosphere that is proper to her sphere. 'The
mystery, silence, and stifling claustrophobia of the seraglio
could not be better portrayed: there is not a single ray of sun,
not a corner of blue sky, not a breath of air in this richly
upholstered room, suffused with the sickly, musky smells of
tombac, amber, and benjamin, in which, removed from the
common gaze, the most beautiful human flower is fading.'[49]
There is even some literary collaboration with the Master
here; smells are introduced to heighten and intensify the close
atmosphere. But the scene is still essentially looked in upon
from the outside; the captive ideal is to be savoured as if by
privileged voyeurs or by invisible intruders. The ladies of the
harem are not to be identified with nor is their fate to be
shared; they are a phenomenon to be enjoyed objectively, at
man's pleasure; they are exclusive like Art itself.

'If ever a divinely beautiful creature stretched out in her
chaste nudity before the eyes of men unworthy to gaze upon
her, it is without doubt the reclining odalisque; the brush has
never produced anything more perfect.'[50] The *Grande Odalisque* of 1814 was a picture that had been condemned, Gautier
notes, as 'cold, dry, empty, hard, Gothic, indeed, to use the
clinching word' when it was first exhibited; in 1855 it
revealed itself in its true glory. It combined sensuality with an
ideal of sculptural permanence to a far greater degree than the

1839 *Odalisque à l'esclave*, and gave scope both to Gautier's lustful *regard*, the power of sexual attraction that was among the attributes of the omnipotent eye, and to that *regard* which was held in fascination by the hard, shiny surfaces of marble or enamel, pearls and diamonds. An absolute in material form, for Gautier the *Grande Odalisque* unites the qualities both of marble and of flesh. Like her more epidermally sensitized sister, she is not immune to lassitude and repletion; she epitomizes 'enslaved beauty in its serene dejection, displaying with indifference treasures which she can no longer call her own, and reclining naked after her bath, the last pearl-like droplets of which are hardly yet dry . . . not even taking the trouble to remove her belt with its massive diamond-studded clasp'. She may reflect Gautier's personal feeling that he was himself displaying with indifference treasures he could no longer call his own, for the benefit of the insatiable press; but she shows no corresponding desire for liberty. She belongs completely to her shrine, with her 'feet whose soles have never trod on anything but Turkish carpets and the . . . alabaster steps of the harem's pools'. They are feet whose toes, to a myopic eye in love with detail ripe with promise, 'are gently curved, cool, and white like camellia buds, and seem to have been modelled on some miraculously rediscovered carving in ivory by Phidias'. The odalisque is a tangible eternal feminine; with her arm slightly lifted to reveal to best advantage 'an exquisitely sculpted, virginal breast, the breast of a Grecian Venus', she is partly examined and savoured for her finer features, as if Gautier were about to make of her an expert purchase, and partly revered as a devotional object. Her face is a marriage of 'Oriental individuality and the Greek ideal'.

The final synthesis of nature and ideal was *La Source*, seen in Ingres's studio early in 1857. 'Nature and the ideal are fused in perfect proportions.'[51] Gautier finds no lassitude here, only a promise of future sexuality. His keen sensual reflexes are finally sublimated and channelled into a supreme idea; it is an idea, however, whose persuasiveness remains firmly embedded in the physical and sexual responses in which Gautier gloried, and which, through the intercession of the pagan god Ingres, he was almost convincingly able to integrate into the highest reaches of his experience. 'M. Ingres's nymph is fifteen at the most . . . no hint of womanhood has yet appeared in her pure, virginal, even asexual forms . . . the small, hardly developed breast, coloured at its tip with a faint pink glow, awakens no more desire than the bud of a flower . . . you feel that before your eyes are not organs, but expressions of the ideal!'

Gautier was a man for whom the visible world existed; he was also a man who could speak of 'organs' and 'expressions of the ideal' in the same breath. Locked in vision, he could bring his whole being to bear, his whole weighty sensual experience as well as his intuition of some serene Elysium, on what he perceived in isolation. His Elysium was peopled with such solid embodiments as Ingres painted. They combined the permanence of marble, with its own special sensual quality, with the voluptuousness of living flesh. The portrait of Mme. Devauçay, painted in Rome four years before Gautier was born, thrills him in 1855 with the 'frightening intensity of its life. Those calm black eyes . . . penetrate your soul like two darts of fire. They follow you, they obsess and charm you, taking the word in its magical sense. The imperceptible smile hovering over her fine lips seems to be mocking you for your impossible love.'[52] Ingres provided Gautier with the ultimate *frisson*, tantalizingly placing impossible fields of sensual conquest almost within his reach, across time. In the bland, marble-like flesh in which this preserved sensuality lay forever dormant there was, as well as consolation, a foretaste of death: the harem is not described as a tomb by pure chance. This is the macabre, fetishistic vein of Romantic idealism that was to be tapped by Ernst and Delvaux, with the wit and sense of anxious foreboding that seem its appropriate accompaniment; it is perhaps most tellingly exemplified, in all Romantic literature, by Gautier's own limited circulation *Poésies libertines*,[53] which use the imagery of stone, gems, and flowers to make the most bizarrely pornographic suggestions, as, for instance, in 'Le Musée secret', which amounts to a celebration of the marble vagina.

It is also the key to Gautier's apparently incongruous Classical streak. 'Without the nude, no art' was his most overworked slogan, used in particular connection with sculpture. With the sense of solid permanence that Ingres communicated, and the intensity of animal life that he realized by detailed observation of nature and subsequent painstaking idealization, the god-like painter personified values and instincts that it was Gautier's continual personal effort to try to synthesize into a new and sunny paganism.

One particular image evokes to perfection the nature and context of this effort. At the Salon of 1861 Gautier was presented in perhaps the most characteristic of his public guises (*plate 6*): a step away from the real world outside, he presides over a perfectly reconstructed alternative milieu, Homeric and resplendent in his pagan imperturbability.[54]

VI Nineteenth-Century Pagan

1 Sculpture, the nude, and a critique of the age

(a) GAUTIER'S TRADITIONALISM: *LE BEAU IDÉAL*

Gautier wanted the best of both as well as the best of all possible worlds. His yearning was directed along two broad channels by the two towering contemporary artists of his age. On the one hand was his enthusiasm for a collaborative effort towards a new plenitude of experience, towards a liberation of modern responses, the creation of rich and emotionally fulfilling milieux in art and life; and on the other was a sketchily formulated but deep-rooted Platonic idealism, an adherence to a concept of pure unchangeable beauty and a need for consoling worship. He wanted mortal sensibility with permanence; new, nineteenth-century experience in an old, proven, and timeless framework. The great modern artist Delacroix was also an Old Master; Ingres painted an unequivocally modern woman distressed by the attentions of a mythological sea-monster (*Roger et Angélique*).

'Take art neither from its cradle nor from its grave,' he had exhorted young contemporaries in 1836. 'Be neither Gothic nor academic; do not copy the masters, but take your inspiration from them . . . use their methods, but not their motifs!'[1] Yet frequently, and especially later in his career, Gautier was to emphasize art's backward-looking nature at the expense of its power as a focus for distinctly modern experience. 'Art, like poetry, is archaic by nature; it hardly notices what is stirring around it, or else it ignores it, through love of some vague retrospective ideal', he wrote in 1857.[2] To make real paintings and show what you can really do, he continued in 1859,[3] you should return to the values of antiquity as handed down by tradition—as to the source of the plastic imagination's energy. He asked for varied human types, naked or draped men, women, and children, with fauns and satyrs thrown in as contrasts. 'This apparently banal theme has served for more than two thousand years, for antiquity adapted it in every conceivable way, and its possibilities have not yet been exhausted.' Even in 1836 he had been vociferous in putting forward such time-hallowed programmes for painting; he was writing on the Throne Room of the Chambre des Députés, where Delacroix was showing his grasp of allegory: 'A very simple thing, which people don't seem to want to understand, is that what a painter needs above all in his work are arms, shoulders, torsos in fine movement, noble heads, generously sweeping draperies, free and supple costumes . . . and allegory meets all these requirements to the letter. It permits nudity, without which the graphic arts cannot exist.'[4]

Gautier's vision of what should constitute real painting is firmly rooted in the classical, Renaissance tradition; if it is not reactionary, it is nevertheless profoundly conservative. It is directed towards the grandeur, sweep, and nobility of a full-blown Renaissance or Baroque, that of Andrea del Sarto, Titian, Veronese, or Rubens; it reflects an idea of the red-waistcoated magnificence that the poet continued to seek for himself. Above all it was a view that allowed art the greatest possible homogeneity and continuity, and the largest emotional and sensual scope; the image that stands in central focus in this broad, history-conscious vision, its key unifying element, is the naked human figure.

'Without the nude, no great art.'[5] 'Young people, study the nude' was the crux of Gautier's lesson in 1836.[6] 'The nude is the essential prerequiste for statuary' he dogmatized in 1855;[7] it is 'the secret of beauty'.[8] He proclaimed his disappointment in 1861: 'There is so little of the nude at the Salon!' and repeated his warning: 'without the nude, no true art';[9] for 'the nude is the grammar and syntax of art'.[10]

Such is Gautier's central text, and his persistent preoccupation with the nude in art is the central metaphor of his art criticism. It is made to stand against all the failures of the age. The nude is the measure and co-ordinator of Gautier's universe; his insistence upon it also reflects his fear of an inhuman, inarticulate chaos. It can be the very epitome of mortal sensuality; it is the timeless *beau* incarnate, and is conceived of as synonymous with *forme* itself.

In an article on sculpture in 1855, Gautier sought to explain this absolute need for the nude once and for all; he succeeded in summing up the fundamental propositions upon which his Classicism rested, and provided the fullest specification of its sources. 'The most perfect form that man is capable of conceiving is his own. His imagination will not stretch beyond this; the representation of the human body, purged of the particular and accidental, constitutes ideal beauty.'[11] He went on to quote the 'serious and noble sentences' of none other than Winckelmann, for conclusive corroboration; for, he felt, no one could explain the ideal of antiquity more succinctly. It was the fruit of 'an anthropo-morphic religion' whose gods and heroes assumed 'the purified form of man within which to incarnate themselves' and relied on marble to secure their earthly immortality. In this society, physical beauty as the expression of the Ideal was everyone's preoccupation; thus Plato could formulate his famous doctrine 'beauty is the splendour of truth'.

The human form, idealized and represented as a type, is thus the basis, the grammar and syntax of art, because it embodies man's highest concept of himself, and above all because it is comprehensive, embracing all particularities by transcending them; it links man to his ancestors and descend-ants who all spring from the same formal *Idea*, and thus by implication to the whole of human experience. All natural creation was but 'that visible form of the mind of eternity';[12] the human figure was creation's supreme unifying thought.

Such metaphysical beliefs underlay the importance that Gautier attached to a technical, anatomical understanding of the human form, as crucial to any successful artistic production. 'You've got to know your anatomy . . . through and through', he wrote typically.[13] 'Then figures become logical and foreseeable deductions from a play of muscles in such and such an attitude or perspective, and not mere realist reproductions of a model undergoing the torture of the studio estrapade.' In line with widely held contemporary and traditionalist ideas on art education (and in spite of his personal rejection of Germanicus's torso and Jupiter's nose at Rioult's drawing classes), Gautier's views are finally the expression of a conviction that to understand the human form is to understand an underlying unity in diversity, to grasp an ultimate mystical oneness that secretly informs the profusion of mortal perceptual experience.

For Gautier as for Winckelmann and the ancient Greeks, *le beau idéal* became apprehensible when 'clothed in human likeness'; it communicated its presence among perceiving, sensual mortals most fully and most palpably through sculpture.

(b) PHYSICAL EMBODIMENTS

Sculpture was the least Romantic of the arts;[14] it was the most literal and positive; it was austere and exclusive, as befitted its role as host to the Ideal. To love sculpture, wrote Gautier in 1868, you need 'a feeling for beauty in itself, without the seductions of colour, beauty in its abstract purity and eternal perfection'.[15] It was the supreme art form and the most difficult; its superiority and its difficulty were of the same order, as Gautier, continually reminding us of the consistency and rigour of his idealism, had already been at pains to establish in 1833.[16]

Sculpture is . . . a loftier and more difficult art than painting; you could name one sculptor for every hundred painters . . . Sculpture is the most algebraical of the arts . . . and offers fewer resources than any other: it demands absolutely thorough study of a mass in its every profile, without the help of a background; the sculptor cannot dissimulate, for you walk around his figure, and any imperfections are immediately evident . . . sculpture is . . . as cold as truth . . .

Yet Gautier was never so doctrinaire in his admiration for Winckelmann as to demand that the Ideal should *always* subsist on a minimal and sparse physical sufficiency, without the mortal veins and tendons which Winckelmann's ideal embodiments necessarily lacked. If, in terms of the highest principle, sculpture should be pure and seduction-free, we have seen from Gautier's response to some of Ingres's sculptural creatures that in practice the senses were always willing to be seduced, that sensual responses indeed played an integral part in experience of *le beau idéal*. Whatever metaphysical claims were made for it, sculpture remained the most physical and literal of the arts, existing in space, tangible as well as visible; a sense of communion with the Ideal, of mysteriously ineluctable presence, was at its highest for Gautier when it emerged through his most powerfully physical, if not his most erotically tinged responses. If he criticized Pradier's *Odalisque* in 1841[17] for being *too* physical: 'sometimes (Pradier) substitutes voluptuousness for form, and desire for the ideal', it was because he was subject to a similar tendency himself: 'he forgets that marbles should only be loved platonically', as he wrote of the sculptor. He was indeed prepared to acknowledge, tacitly and ironically, that the erotic could be his only avenue for admiration. 'With a very few exceptions', he commented on the sad state of sculpture in 1857,[18] contemporary sculptors 'leave you colder than their marbles, as unfeeling as their bronzes, unless they address the senses by means of female nudity, and this is an effect they do not intend, we are sure'.

Generally, his erotic responses to the female nude were well integrated into that structure of worship, admiration, and ocular avidity within which he nurtured his highest aesthetic experiences; they are part and parcel of his admiring, reverential 'regard amoureux'. His feelings are veiled in poetic terms; thus in characterizing the function of drapery in sculpture he speaks of the 'pure coquetry of the sculptor who wants to show off his finesse with the chisel and to excite the amorous curiosity of the eye';[19] it is like 'a caress from the surrounding atmosphere'.[20] But at the same time *volupté* and *désir* could impress themselves so powerfully on the spectator's awareness as to constitute a subject in their own right. 'The subject, the drama is the torso', Gautier enthused in front of Clésinger's sensationalist *Femme piquée par un serpent* at the Salon of 1847[21] (*plate 5*), and although he saw the piece in terms of his broadest and most Classical conception of genius ('each section contains the whole statue; genius is like God, who remains one while dividing himself into many'), he also accepted it as a distinctly modern sculptural and sensual experience. Clésinger, he notes, has been bold enough simply to sculpt a woman with a token mythological snake,[22] and in whom antiquity really counts for nothing; she is even wearing a modern bracelet, he observes. She is 'a totally modern beauty', almost in the living flesh; she is free of realist pockmarks and other mortal blemishes, but nevertheless manifests 'the pores and the bloom of skin'. Gautier responds to this blatantly erotic work, 'this voluptuous swoon caused by the intoxicating poison, that perfidious philtre which works its way from the heel to the heart, freezing the veins as it burns them', with less than ingenuous pre-Freudian innocence. 'A fastidious soul might well ask: What was she expressing before the addition of the snake? We really could not say. Well, perhaps she had been struck full in the breast by one of those golden arrows from Eros's quiver, that young god whom even the immortals fear, and was writhing in pain from her invisible wound.' (It would be surprising if Gautier had not been in on the secret: Clésinger's model, rumoured to have been moulded rather than sculpted, was Madame Sabatier, 'La Présidente', the recipient of much of Théophile's erotic correspondence. See *Oeuvres érotiques . . .*) Clésinger was to rework his popular success for the Salon of 1861; his *Cléopâtre* elicited the same warm responses then as in 1847: 'The venomous beast has bitten the beautiful breast that was offered it, and the first shudder of the poison passes through the queen's charming body like a spasm of pleasure'.[23]

Gautier characterized the Salon of 1863 as 'Le "Salon des Vénus"';[24] its central confection, Cabanel's *Naissance de Vénus*, subsequently acquired by the admiring Emperor, was described with typical relish. The figure of Venus occupies the inner sanctuary of Gautier's private temple, epitomizing the highest qualities that he demanded of art: she is both consoling and sensuous: she is the physical embodiment of all that is most worth eternalizing. Gautier had also been delighted to come across a Venus, painted by Riesener, in the prosaic year of 1838;[25] the figure of Venus is a subject that will be 'eternally beautiful, eternally young, eternally alive, because it stands for beauty, youth, life, and love, everything that is poetic in human existence, symbolized in a transparent allegory, in a simple female figure'.

It is in this light that his championing of sculpture, as a critical cause alongside that of Romantic painting, can best be understood; the most physical and most difficult of the arts, its very failure to catch the public's imagination pinpointed for Gautier the basic shortcoming of the age.

(c) A NEW RENAISSANCE

'About the only person who ever visits the sculptor shut away in his damp basement is some provincial who has got the wrong door', he observed in 1836;[26] in 1861 the Salon's sculpture gallery merely seemed to provide the visitor (and the critic) with a cool place to smoke his cigar before returning to the paintings.[27] If contemporary sculpture was by and large simply boring, Gautier was not prepared to blame sculptors. It only seemed boring, because like Heine's gods, it was exiled in an inhospitable environment. The nineteenth century, with its lack of public interest, failed to offer the resources for sculpture's difficult realization of the Ideal; it had no time nor understanding for the disinterested, high-minded artist: 'Civilization has no need of artists, only of workers. It substitutes technique for genius.'[28] It was precisely against what Gautier discerned as the petty economy of his age, its narrow-minded jealousy and dispersal of energy into mundane concerns, that sculpture could take a stand with its vision of a more contemplative, more serene, and less troublesome existence. 'The most public-spirited action an artist can perform is to create a fine work, even if it bears no relation to the issues that are exciting the crowd';[29] the critic was pleased to announce that Pradier had helped keep alive the spirit of the serene temple of art in 1848 by greeting the February Revolution with a *Chloris* in Paros marble.

Fundamental to all the failures of modern civilization was its blindness to material form, its lack of preoccupation with pure physical beauty. Sculpture, only tenuously surviving in the nineteenth century like 'a hot-house plant, cultivated at great expense and etiolated more often than not, in spite of all the attention that is lavished upon it',[30] provided Gautier with the vital antidote. 'If you can remember that man was made in God's image, it is not for seeing civilized man of 1848, with his sack-shaped overcoat, his trousers with foot straps, his collar, and his stove-pipe hat,'[31] he wrote in the year of Pradier's *Chloris*. At the previous Salon he had imagined the disappointment and apprehension of the bourgeois lost among the sculptures who found himself face to face with that 'unknown animal' the human figure. The poor frock-coated Salon visitor did not imagine it was like this; he was used to spending his precious moments of leisure 'dancing the polka with some skinny, wasp-waisted slip of a girl'.[32] Modern artists only had at their disposal 'forms prostituted or degraded by poverty or debauchery . . . withered flesh still bearing the imprint of the corset';[33] the role of the sculptor was to maintain the tradition of the human body as most surely represented in antique art. It was to glorify, 'in spite of tailors and puritans, the chaste and holy raiment of form'.[34]

For sculpture in the nineteenth century was a challenge not just to its modistes and its polka, its preoccupation with speed and profits, but above all to the constraints of a pervasive Christian ethic, which elevated the spirit at the expense of the body. Modern sculpture was 'that divine legacy from Greece, that fine remnant of paganism which has saved the world from complete invasion by Christian and Gothic barbarity, and defended God's work against the tall, emaciated spectres, the shroud-like drapery and the cadaverous physiognomies of a mistaken asceticism'.[35] The nineteenth century had failed to understand that ancient Greek paganism offered a perfect balance of soul and body, an incomparable vision of wholeness, and that the ultimate aim of its idealism was the achievement of 'the serene tranquillity of the artist for whom temptations no longer exist'.[36] Yet if palpable form was only the means to the full realization of the Ideal, confrontation and enjoyment of the palpable and the material nevertheless remained basic prerequisites. Thus elsewhere, as we have seen, Gautier was less careful to reconcile Christian with pagan ideality, and less restrained in his desire to extol the physical. Pradier was sculpture's Ingres, and was identified as Gautier's 'beloved pagan'.[37] For 'all artists are pagans at heart, and their Catholicity is generally dubious'. In 1836 Gautier deplored manifestations of the currently fashionable Catholic revival in art because Christian 'distrust of the material' meant distrust of form, and without form, art could not exist.[38] Thus he could conclude, the following year, that 'any reaction in favour of form will necessarily be pagan'.[39]

Gautier's paganism was his worship of beautiful exterior form, his religion of Art itself; questions of conventional morality were excluded from it. 'Let him make the woman bitten by the mysterious asp go on writhing on her cushions', he exhorted Clésinger, who had produced a disappointingly orthodox *Pietà* for the Salon of 1851. 'Art is sacred. Everything that is beautiful is moral. This artist from Athens or Pompeii has no need of the half-light of a damp chapel.'[40]

A pagan dream of a new Renaissance indeed lies at the very heart of Gautier's reflections on life as on art. The ancient Greeks, 'masters in all things',[41] had offered the supreme vision of wholeness, of a perfect balance between spirit and matter, of ultimate unity, and the Italian Renaissance had inherited and transmitted their values.[42] There was no such thing as 'progress'; all that was best in human nature had already been realized, and indeed nineteenth-century ideas on progress were positively antipathetic to the renewal of Gautier's vision: contemplation was sacrificed to speed, beauty to utility; trades did not become arts and poets became *feuilletonistes*. Human needs, aspirations towards the Ideal, remained the same; this was the crux of Gautier's conservatism. 'For Gautier', the Goncourts corroborated, 'the brain of an artist is the same now as it was at the time of the Pharaohs.'[43] Thus if anything had failed, it was civilization and not art, whose aims remained constant, and which, if it was allowed to survive, was civilization's only hope for redemption. Thus did Gautier's contemporary artists suffer a profound dissatisfaction and nostalgia; like sculpture itself, artists like Marilhat only survived like sickly hot-house plants uprooted from their true environments; they painted memories of previous and more wholesome existences, expressing yearnings to return to that Hellenistic nirvana in which 'belle idée' meant 'belle forme'. Gautier's paganistic religion of art ultimately stands in direct opposition to Baudelaire's contemporary plea for a painting of modern life; his fundamental view was not that art should modulate itself to accommodate and celebrate the vicissitudes of life, but that it should exist as a constant reminder of what could be, set apart from life as its antidote.[44]

'We are cowardly dreamers, effeminate drinkers of water,

cowering, bourgeois that we are, beneath the petticoats of some woman,' the ardent young fanatic of *le beau* railed against his public in 1833;[45] the public was too frivolous and narrow-minded to understand sculpture. 'The Popes of yesteryear were less prudish than the grocers of today,'[46] he challenged in 1839; we are too cowardly and hypocritical to see in Riesener's nudes anything but nudity, where our ancestors would have seen beauty. His paganism was finally a demand to be allowed to take unconstrained pleasure in the perceptible world. A dream of eternal youth, love, and beauty, of a place in the Mediterranean sun and of a simple untroubled existence: such, ultimately, was Gautier's undemanding, unaustere Classicism, hinting that every ideal could find its physical embodiment, conceiving of the universe as a feast for the senses and embodying a conception of the Complete Man.

There was finally no contradiction between Gautier's pagan Classicism and his Romantic's hatred of the 'grisâtres', the old Davidian school, for he did not consider that David's Classicism was Classicism in the true sense of the word at all. It was a superficial fashion: 'rigid rococo substituted for flamboyant rococo'. What David lacked, and Ingres possessed, was that pagan breath of sensuality. Madame Récamier seemed to Gautier to be awaiting the furniture van in David's portrait of her, so chilly and Spartan were her surroundings and the emotional climate of her world. 'What is lacking in this as in all David's paintings of women, is love, it is a caress of form and surface, it is that ideal and chaste flower which Leonardo, Corregio, Titian, and van Dyck, those great voluptuaries of contour and colour, discovered at the ends of their brushes.'[47]

Gautier's Classicism lies at the heart of his Romanticism. The predominance of the human figure at the centre of his vision of a new Renaissance is the image of its central requirement: all the separate pictorial or sculptural worlds in which he could become absorbed manifest an idealizing human presence. They display 'le tempérament', 'la vie', 'la pensée', 'la griffe du lion'; the products of sentient, ordering, emotionally responding beings, they offer avenues for the transference of feeling, and are open to Gautier's verbal identification or worship, collaboration or echo by means of words, the organs of 'la pensée'. They are, at best, worlds into which the spectator may escape, in which his awareness of faculties of his own is heightened, and through which he may enjoy and reconcile seemingly incompatible urges: a facility uniquely offered by amoral art.

2 The large world of art

Gautier can thus hardly even be contained in definition as a nineteenth-century pagan. 'We are pagan or Catholic according to the talent of the sculptor,' he had warned.[48] 'What immense variety there is in the world of art! What diversity of viewpoints! What a contrast of styles!'[49] he reflected at the Salon of 1864, his twenty-first as a professional art-lover. For the critic whose job it became to find admiration for almost everything, any number of seemingly contradictory artistic propositions was possible, from Ingres and Delacroix downwards. 'Art', he wrote, using a characteristic image, 'is an immense palace in which everyone tries to occupy the finest apartment',[50] yet if M. Ribot felt most at home in the kitchen, Gautier was not, on this occasion, prepared to offer any objection. 'We would rather praise than blame' he once more reminds us in 1855, 'and when the critic has found nothing fine in a play, a picture, or a book, he should say, like Titus: "My friends, I've wasted my day."' Beneath the surface of Gautier's generously *laissez-faire* approach to criticism there lay no more conscious critical criterion than this: what did or did not give him pleasure.

His fundamental need was to believe that if man *en masse* was perverse and stupid, he nevertheless instinctively sought pleasurable sensations, and that pleasure was there for the taking. Visual art was the highest proof of this consoling thesis; the fact that within its myriad powers of revelation and realization it could give glimpses of paradise-on-earth, of happy hunting grounds, milieux for untainted *bonheur*, confirmed Gautier in his pleasure principle, and, of course, frequently absolved him of the need to look far outside his world of art or recognize it as a world within and partaking of a larger world of less easily reconcilable conflicts and contradictions.

Thus he could write, moved by some painters of carefree idylls at the Salon of 1850-1, that 'it is not true that man was born to be wretched' and that paradise could be regained straight away if only we wanted it enough.[51] On this basis, shaky as it can seem, rests the tone and the dominant message of his criticism.

Painters who recall such possibilities, he continued, simply speak in the language of nature; unlike writers, they are not obliged to invent a self-conscious doctrine for themselves. As a critic, Gautier aspired to the same creative condition. 'Properly speaking, we are not a man of letters' he introduced himself in his prospectus for *L'Artiste* in 1856. 'We have pushed our love of art to delirium.'[52] Some of the further characteristic forms this delirium took should reward examination here; if we are to begin to understand its persuasive hold, we must first of all come to terms with the sheer extent and quality of its symptoms.

(a) LANDSCAPE

He always regarded modern landscape painting as a particularly Romantic phenomenon, a means of reassuring man that he was still in a position to order and animate nature from its centre; for nature without man was disturbingly chaotic and inarticulate. 'Art is more beautiful, truer, and more powerful than nature; nature is stupid, without consciousness of itself, lacking a mind or passions. It is something dull and insensible that needs us to breathe life and soul into it,'[53] he wrote in 1837, and in 1861 went on to generalize: 'True landscape painting is nature plus man, and by that we do not mean the little figures which you can put in it, but human feeling, joy, sadness, reverie, love—in a word, the state of the painter's soul before such and such a horizon.'[54]

Such was Gautier's version of the Pathetic Fallacy. He was a connoisseur of 'le sentiment humain' and 'l'état de l'âme', and unfailingly brought his own sentiments to bear in his verbal evocations. Of Belly's *Effet du soir dans le désert de Thy* at the Salon of 1861 he wrote: 'it is as if nature were blushing bashfully as she receives the sun's last kiss!'[55]: this is nature plus man, and painting plus Gautier. 'Let us lose ourselves in the great soul of nature' he invited his readers at the Salon of

1849.[56] He is frequently to be heard thus anthropomorphiz-
ing the nature he perceived through art, in true pagan spirit;
his first concern was always to characterize and heighten the
particular sentiment or human imprint with which individual
artists imbued their landscapes. With its 'perfectly blue sky,
across which stretches a trail of golden clouds, their crests
austerely elegant like the heads of Grecian women', Corot's
Diane at the Salon of 1836 was as irresistible as 'one of
Theocritus's idylls'. 'The sloping banks of the river are
clothed in short, velvety moss, picked out here and there with
wild flowers.' In contrast, Corot's *Vue de la campagne de
Rome* was a scene of 'profound desolation', an almost
hallucinatory vision. 'The trees have an expression of wretch-
edness and suffering which is painful to behold . . . On a pale
band running across the horizon, like a linen bandage across
the forehead of a wounded man, stand some small, stunted,
crippled holm-oaks, warts sprouting on the mountain's
back . . .'[57]

Elsewhere, individual temperaments are more carefully
and lovingly evoked. Corot, in 1836,[58] is 'an austere painter,
with nothing facile or dazzling about him; he has only found
himself with difficulty, and only made progress by dint of
hard work . . . (he is) a sublime ox laboriously ploughing his
furrow in heavy and intractable soil, from which he will reap a
rich and golden harvest'. By 1847, Gautier had arrived at an
estimation of Corot which once more anticipates Zola's
famous cry of solidarity with Pissarro. 'He has the eye of a
painter without the hand . . . this incompetent achieves
astonishing results . . . everything is . . . seen, observed,
and felt; nothing is given over to convention or method, yet
even such complete awkwardness as this has its strengths and
resources: straightforwardness, good nature, rustic
simplicity . . .'[59]

(b) INTIMACY

Penetration of the 'sens intime', of the underlying human
content of painting, was for Gautier a means of constantly
renewing his own mental landscape. It was being able to
evoke a particular temperament and thus see nature through
another's eyes. It could mean sharing a feeling; Ernest

Hébert, a painter who excelled at invoking an atmosphere of poetic meditation, stimulated this kind of critical pleasure; his *La Mal'aria* inspired a poem as well as a long verbal reverie in *Les Beaux-Arts en Europe*.[60]

> J'aime cette Italie adorablement pâle,
> Doux reflect de ton coeur, mélancolique Hébert!

('I love your adorably pale Italy, that sweet reflection of your heart, melancholy Hébert!')[61]

It could also simply mean absorption in a milieu. Gautier found praise for any artist who allowed this imaginative penetration to take place, who showed, like Brion in his *Mariage protestant en Alsace* at the Salon of 1869, 'an intimate understanding of his subject and a profound sympathy for it'.[62]

Looking at pictures was an essentially intimate experience, and *intime* is a key word which occurs in Gautier's criticism almost as frequently as the word *beau* itself. The experience of art was akin to the satisfactions of that withdrawn, contemplative, and cosy domestic life which features in his biography, and which, from his early existence *en famille* in the Place Royale to his cat-filled retreat in secluded Neuilly, looms large in contemporary memoirs of him and in his own autobiographical sketches (in the prefaces to *Albertus* and *Les Jeunes-France*, and in his *Ménagerie intime*, which is about domestic pets he has known; in Bergerat's reminiscences and the Goncourt diaries, for example). Further ramifications of this theme remain to be explored; as the image of a tranquil, 'admiring' and receptive state of mind it naturally finds its sharpest focus in Gautier's responses to domestic genre scenes. Israëls's *Une Maison tranquille* at the Salon of 1861 was especially appealing because it contained a cat: 'the cat is the familiar spirit of the home, its *genius loci*; it likes order, cleanliness, and calm, all the little comforts of a well-run household'. Above all, this atmosphere of bourgeois order, cleanliness, and calm was conducive to dreaming: 'This picture by M. Israëls has a secret charm, a mysterious appeal; you stand and day-dream in front of it for a long time.'[63]

The acknowledged master of the field was Meissonier, and of all artists he allowed Gautier the fullest abandonment to this state of calm, absorbed day-dreaming. 'Clear-sighted, clean, precise, and careful', he was a typically Gautierian extension of his art; even his seventeenth-century-Dutch-style house in Poissy, Gautier remarked, could be signed like one of his canvases.[64] Preferring Ponsard and Augier to Hugo and Musset, Meissonier had nothing in common with the Romantic school; but, Gautier continues, do not think him cold and passionless. He is moved 'by careful perceptions of the particular'. He actually paints a day-dreaming state of mind: 'How conducive to meditation this solitude is; what calm, what a studious atmosphere prevails in this good old room hung with faded tapestries, into which the daylight filters so discreetly...It would be good to read Horace, Boileau, Nicole, and Pascal in this sequestered and peaceful study, in which you can smell the passing of the years as on opening a room closed since the death of a grandfather or great-uncle', Gautier wrote of the *Jeune homme écrivant* at the Salon of 1853[65] (*plate 7*). But it is through his talent for making 'careful perceptions of the particular', his love of visible detail, and attention to 'the physiognomy of facts', that Meissonier really wins Gautier's full attention and allows free rein to his desire to contemplate, to be absorbed and transported, to transcend time and space. Thus the critic could proclaim at the Salon of 1857 that 'M. Meissonier is, perhaps, of all our artists, the one who adheres most closely to the conditions which used to apply to what is called painting'. That is to say: 'To paint superlatively, on boards the size of a human hand, one or two figures, three at most, who are doing little more than being alive, engaged in some not particularly dramatic activity like smoking, or drinking beer, reading, looking out of the window, or painting . . . or even less'.[66] *Le Fumeur* engaged Gautier for a whole hour simply by 'the verisimilitude of the drawing, the choice of pose, the delicate marriage of colours, the arrangement of the details, and the intimate feeling of life—the very things that constitute composition in painting'.[67]

The delicacy of the painter's observation was enough on its own to fascinate and absorb the spectator; everything in

Meissonier's tiny canvases was communicative, even the backgrounds;[68] incidental details of décor, of costume, pose, or facial expression emerged to give meaning to the overall compositions, to make them psychologically complete *mises-en-scène*, worlds of reassuringly familiar everyday actions but which were nevertheless apart and self-contained. They could be totally convincing historical recreations;[69] it was enough that they were self-contained. 'Is it not a complete resurrection of days gone by?' Gautier wrote of the *Joueurs d'échecs* at the Salon of 1841;[70] he finished listing its evocative details by observing of the players: 'The destruction of the universe would not disturb them; they would continue their game on the ruins of the world'. The spectator could become as absorbed in them as they were in their game: Gautier can indeed be imagined 'on the ruins of the world', undisturbed and engrossed in a work of art.

Sufficient to themselves with their coherently associated details, Meissonier's pictures provided all that Gautier needed to be transported, to dream, to let his imagination and pen wander. This figure counting money, he mused in 1862, is 'a worthy man without any doubt . . . An inner satisfaction beams from his face'; you could trust him with your savings.[71] This was just the 'satisfaction intime', the sense of unassailable security which art could offer; if it provided a convincing enough platform, painting could allow the spectator simply to escape into a world of private thoughts and associations.

(c) PORTRAITS

The connoisseur of painting, the man with the painter's eye, 'sees through to a thousand little interior beauties of which he enjoys exclusive possession; he revels in the inner beauty of the picture', Gautier wrote in 1836.[72] He occupies the painter's dream like a man exploring a strangely familiar but newly constituted world, savouring its separate facets and putting them together again for himself. He becomes a spectator at long-past historical events, the contemporary of Cleopatra or Richelieu, a witness at moments of natural cataclysm or human violence; he is ever ready to be convinced that he is a Spaniard or a Turk in a Spanish or Turkish environment; he stands transfixed in front of portraits sharing the half-life of the sitters and dreaming of their milieux.

In 1859 he outlined his conception of the aims of portrait painting in terms which remind us that it was a genre in which, for Gautier, Ingres excelled: 'To interpret the human physiognomy in itself, without incidental subject-matter or action, to render it in its individuality and its characteristic details, to reveal the soul beneath the skin . . . , to come to grips with the thoughts behind the features and sometimes to sum up a whole age and a whole class in a mere head standing out against a vague background'. Once more the outer form is seen as inseparable from the inner life, and if the inner person is not to be read word for word from the surface, as in Lavater or Gall's popular theories, it is only because Gautier wishes to be able to dream more mysterious and poetically thrilling dreams. An unknown head, painted by the hand of a master, can inspire future generations to contemplate 'the still-youthful image of vanished beauty' and to experience 'a bizarre retrospective love';[73] Gautier wished to be able to commune with physically attractive enigmas. A sense of physical presence as Holbein or Ingres and his followers could achieve it was all important, and could be interesting enough on its own. Yet it was even more compelling when such robust material presences let slip unspoken or veiled messages, as did Ingres's *Madame Devauçay*. A portrait by Flandrin at the Salon of 1859, *La Jeune fille à l'œillet*, did this and more. 'There is something strange, mysterious, and disturbing in her beauty . . . a sphinx-like malice in her eyes; the line of her serious mouth betrays a barely perceptible smile . . . In front of this figure as with certain of Leonardo da Vinci's canvases, you feel somewhat ill at ease; she seems to belong in another sphere.' (*plate 8*)

If Gautier found himself 'somewhat ill at ease', his feeling was more than the discomfort of a materialist faced with the immaterial; it was an experience he was able to relish, for he went on, with typical hyperbole, to proclaim Flandrin's picture to be one of the most 'eternally alive' portraits ever painted, on a par with the *Mona Lisa*—eternally mysterious, eternally beckoning. If Flandrin's creature seemed about to cast off her thin mantle of flesh in order to re-enter the world of pure spirit, Leonardo's female figures already belonged there. They were the most mysterious and enigmatic of all, and the *Mona Lisa* in particular contained all the material for reverie that painting could offer. 'Leonardo's figures', Gautier wrote in *L'Artiste* in 1857,[74]* in an evocation which cannot but invite comparison with Walter Pater's famous purple passage of twelve years later,[75]

seem to know what men do not know; it is as if, before coming to admire their reflections in the canvas, they have lived on higher, unknown planes . . . it seems as if the arc of [the *Mona Lisa*'s] lips is about to let loose some divine sarcasm, some celestial irony, some angelic jibe; an inner joy, whose secret is beyond us, gives these lips their inexplicable curve . . . beneath the form *expressed* you sense there is a vague, infinite *inexpressible* thought, something akin to a musical idea . . . images you have seen somewhere before pass before your mind's eye, voices whose sounds you seem to recognize whisper languid confidences in your ear; repressed desires, hopes that drove you to despair stir painfully in some shadowy area of the mind in which light yet glimmers, and you realize that your melancholies spring from the fact that three hundred years ago, La Gioconda responded to your declaration of love with that same mocking smile which is still on her lips today.

Leonardo seemed to paint 'with the colours of a dream';[76] in a single figure he embodied all that Gautier's concept of artistic intuition could contain: 'images seen somewhere before . . . the sound of voices you seem to recognize . . . repressed desires'. Like Delacroix, who revealed what Gautier seemed to know was already there, as if in recollection of some previous or alternative existence, the *Mona Lisa* awakened deep memories. Yet Gautier's evocation of the painting's thrilling power is finally narrower, less mystical, and more literal than Pater's. For Pater, the *Mona Lisa* embodied 'All the thoughts and experience of the world . . . ' and represented 'The fancy of an eternal life, sweeping together ten thousand experiences . . . '; so far Gautier might have put the words into Pater's mouth. But where Pater sums up the effect of the picture in terms of the breadth of the associations it suggests—' . . . the animalism of Greece, the lust of Rome, the mysticism of the middle age with its spiritual ambition and imaginative loves, the return of the Pagan world, the sins of the Borgias . . . '⁷⁷—Gautier finally concentrates it in a single idea; its strange workings on his spirit could be put down to 'the fact that three hundred years ago, La Gioconda responded to your declaration of love with that same mocking smile which is still on her lips today'. For Pater the *Mona Lisa* was ' . . . expressive of what in the ways of a thousand years men had come to desire . . . '; for Gautier she was an actual object of unrequited love, and even here it is as it was with some of Ingres's figures: Gautier's emotion is finally that of a man who sees a field of amorous conquest placed tantalizingly beyond his reach.

In 1847 he had entertained the readers of *La Presse*⁷⁸ with the confession that he was still in love with Titian's daughter, and had twice travelled to Spain to kiss her half-opened lips. Unfortunately, he went on, her arms are too busy holding John the Baptist's head on a silver platter, so she has not been able to throw them around our neck; you can tell by her eyes that this is what she would like to do. Once more we confront the limits of Gautier's idealism. However mystical and other-worldly his dreams may sometimes seem, they always attach themselves to the physical, and ultimately demand physical fulfilment.

(d) VIOLENCE

The paintings of Decamps were never touched with Leonardo's mysticism; yet just as Leonardo's figures exuded a mysterious, living quality, so did Decamps's painting have that inestimable property 'la vie', and this was similarly rooted in a kind of sublimated physical response on the part of the critic. Decamps's pictures were 'victoriously scored by the lion's claw', an apt image, for never was this quality of 'la vie' to be felt more keenly than in scenes of violence.

Decamps's nature was a kind of super-nature in which almost anything was possible (monkeys might paint). His pictures could offer heightened experience, like halluci-nations; they were typically full extensions of the possible, parallel realizations in art of that 'indéfini du possible' which had, in 1830, always seemed to be just about to define itself in real life. *La Bataille des Cimbres* at the Salon of 1834[79] was a vision of violence that allowed full release to those violent, virile aspects of Gautier's mythic autobiography. It was violence and horror with no holds barred and which Gautier could relish whole-heartedly; it was taking place in an alternative universe, in a fantastic yet convincing world, a world of sublimated instincts. That it was a specifically artistic experience Gautier suggests with the art-historical superlatives at the beginning of his evocation. 'No *Selve Selvagge* by Salvator Rosa ever looked more rugged, arid, and desolate than this . . .; no sky painted by John Martin could conceal more lightning and tempest behind its clouds . . . it is as if you have been transported . . . into a world of carnage and destruction, whose streams are streams of blood, whose clouds are flocks of crows, whose mountains are heaps of corpses . . .' Decamps is completely the master of his means and stops at no half-measures; hallucinatory 'vie' also manifests itself in the painting's aptly violent execution, characterized by Gautier in terms of its savagery and ferocity.

This theme of violence runs through Gautier's criticism like a powerful leitmotif. In 1851, Gautier informs us, the animal sculptor Barye introduced a rare human figure into his sculpture:[80] 'man, that is, mind'. He read Barye's *Thésée* as 'the triumph of the spirit over the material . . . brute strength is vanquished! Victory belongs to the idea!' Once more, the human form impressed itself upon the critic as nature's supreme creation. Yet Barye's representations of pure animal instinct were irresistible; his *Jaguar dévorant un lièvre*, unanimously praised at the Salon of 1850–1 (*plate 9*), had Gautier completely involved and elicited his unrestrained verbal collaboration:

A poor hare, a predestined victim, has been taken by surprise, in spite of its nervous speed, in spite of the sharp hearing of its long, ever alert ears, by a jaguar crouched in ambush on a branch or a rock. There he is, his eyes staring lifelessly, his nostrils dilated, trying a sudden supreme leap from the jaws of the monster whose fangs are breaking his back. The jaguar purses his lips, half-closes his eyes. The papillae of his rough tongue are already savouring the blood and the marrow; he seems drunk on the breath of life which is being exhaled beneath his bite; his warm prey will still be palpitating in the depths of his entrails. And see how anxious he is not to let go of it, how his steel muscles contract to hold on to or dispute it. His whole body quivers. Voluptuous shivers run along his sinuous spine, which is arched like the back of a cat being stroked. There is more here than the appeasement of hunger; it is the exultation of the successful hunter and the atrocious pleasure of the vicious attacker who kills without risk to himself.[81]*

Gautier sympathizes with the victim and at the same time empathizes with the jaguar's excitement; he also experiences a voyeur's fascination at nature's uncontrollable, unselfconscious, and perpetual violence, an experience akin to that of the Sublime, man's confrontation with forces over which he has no control and in front of which his conscious and moral understanding of things seems dwarfed. For once, art does not rival nature; Gautier admits he was sceptical about the amount of effort Barye's jaguar seemed to be expending in so simple an action as eating a hare, but, he goes on, a visit to M. Huguet de Massilia's menagerie at feeding time convinced him of the 'nervous and orgasmic convulsions' of wild animals with meat.

Like the erotic, the violent in art represented an extreme, an outermost limit of that realm of human instinct and passion which art could embody and exteriorize. It is significant that sculpture, the supreme art, the most austere and the least Romantic, was able to concede a special place to violence as it did to the erotic. Auguste Préault, who exhibited a *Tuerie* and an *Ophélie* at the Salon of 1850–1, was the leading exponent in this area; like Rousseau and others of Gautier's specifically Romantic heroes, he was considered threatening enough to be long refused admission to the Salons. He was sculpture's Delacroix: 'Préault's figures weep, sob, scream, smile, embrace, or tear at each other with plethoric life and unimaginable exuberance and vigour.'[82]

Where sex and violence were combined in rich sensual mixture in a single figure, Gautier was led to heights of verbal abandon. Glaize's *La Mort du Précurseur* at the Salon of 1848 produced a starkly dramatic evocation in which Salomé herself is familiarly addressed. In construction and tone Gautier's passage finds echo less in the sombre, austere exoticism of his friend Flaubert's *Hérodias* than in the psychic midnight of Isidore Ducasse, Comte de Lautréamont, whose *Chants de Maldoror*, first published in 1869, were to become a major source of inspiration for André Breton and the Surrealists. The untamed forces of the irrational are here as much to be experienced within, to be recognized as forces within the mind of the beholder, as they are to be confronted in the harsh world outside; it is experience which, along with everything else and transcending notions of good and evil, Gautier is ready to accept whole. If his tone is accusing, it is so the more closely to enumerate and celebrate the physical and visual splendours surrounding the crime:

> Oh lovely Herodias, false and lascivious dancer, you really have been very modest, only asking the tyrant for one head, just one, that of a poor, bearded, and sun-burnt saint. He would have given you fifty in exchange for one more smile, a thousand for one of those undulations of the hips which make your robes of gold brocade throw out such brilliant sparks beneath the lamps of the orgy. But you only wanted one, capricious creature! so that painters might portray you superb and exultant for eternity, with your insidious gracefulness, your diabolically innocent eyes, and your blood-red smile, portray you, in a rich antithesis of fascination and horror, holding on the salver sullied with thick clots of blood the ghastly, grimacing head, its eyes rolled upwards in its final spasm, its mouth twisted, its neck of dark purple showing the white patches of broken vertebrae and sliced arteries.[83]*

3 Outside the sphere of art

Gautier looks at his world of art as if it were a broad panorama contained in a fish-eye lens, a horizon whose individual features achieve greater or lesser prominence according to the direction in which the lens is pointed but whose peripheral limits persistently defy definition. The imagery of spheres and prisms is Gautier's own; yet in speaking of art as a sphere he admits a concept of that which is simply 'outside the sphere of art'. A brief examination of what he considered to be outside the sphere of art should enable us to arrive, negatively, at a limiting definition of his vision, to determine the fundamental qualities that he demanded of art. For, dogged by Gautier's image of the sphere, we find that we have already been driven, in a circular argument, to a preliminary conclusion: all that which was outside the sphere of art was that which limited his capacity for admiration and identification, which placed barriers in front of his powers of empathy.

'The sight of the Parthenon cured me of the Gothic disease,' he wrote in his autobiographical sketch for *L'Illustration* in 1867.[84] He did not catch his first glimpse of the Parthenon until 1852, yet he was already declaring in 1836 that the Greeks were 'masters in everything'.[85] Medieval statues with their 'inordinate length' could not stand comparison with antique sculpture, for all their fashionable and Romantic appeal following Hugo's *Notre-Dame de Paris*, for all the master's polemic on behalf of the modern grotesque and melancholic in the preface to *Cromwell*, and for all Gautier's own early love for the bold vernacular of Villon and Rabelais. Gothic sculptural figures 'hardly bear serious examination any better than Chinese porcelain or Japanese grotesques', Gautier continued in 1836; 'you must be mad, or German, to prefer the gaunt cut-outs of Ghirlandaio or Bizzamano to Corregio's Dianas and Ledas. The former are merely laughable barbarities, valuable as curiosities, like the tomahawks or the loin-cloths of savages, while the latter are masterpieces of genius, observation, and science'.

To abandon or ignore the lessons of the Greeks and of the Renaissance was worthless affectation; to disregard their achievements of observation and science was a kind of heresy, an evasion of responsibility to history. Lehmann's *Sainte Catherine* at the Salon of 1840, for instance, only just avoided condemnation as an affected and mawkish curiosity; unforgivably, it had dispensed with modelling, and seemed on the point of abandoning perspective too. In the most infantile and ignorant Gothic pictures you can see the artist 'doing his best to copy nature, lacking not the will but the means'. But when a man of the nineteenth century and of Lehmann's talent returns to the first fumblings of art, it is like a 'jeune cavalier', bearded and moustachioed, saying ' "I want to go bye-byes. Give me sweeties" '.[86] Giotto and Cimabue, Gautier concluded, owed their faults to their epoch; the nineteenth century possesses the means to a fuller celebration of man and nature, and whether or not to make use of them is not, for Gautier, among the choices that an artist has at his disposal.

The pagan spirit that underlay Gautier's antiquity and Renaissance manifested itself above all in a celebration and idealization of the human form; studied attention to imperfection and physical ugliness was desecration; it led to the production of mutations, of deviations from the ideal norm, and resulted only in disgust. There was no conceivable justification for Biard and Pigal's immensely popular caricatures at the Salon of 1837: 'painting must avoid trivial imitation of ridiculous figures or of deformity',[87] for the disgust it inspired was simply an unacceptable reaction. Unrelieved ugliness was a reproduction of the chaotic and inexplicably 'coarse reality of things'.[88] 'Never let it be forgotten that the beautiful is as real, if not even more real than the ugly, for the ugly is merely an accidental deviation from the archetype', he wrote in 1866,[89] noting 'a certain bias towards ugliness, under the pretext of realism', at the Salon. The naked human figure embodied man's highest conception of beauty: 'it is forbidden to dream of anything beyond it, lest monsters and chimeras result.'[90] Thus to say that Millet's peasant at the Salon of 1863[91] 'looks more like a sloth laboriously heaving along its poorly articulated limbs, than a creature made in God's image', was already criticism enough. He even reprimanded Muller for his weeping Irish girls at the Salon of 1859:[92] 'Redden the eyes if you wish, but the nose, never!' Since the ugly was a deviation from the all-investing archetype, to cultivate it was as much affectation and deliberate mannerism as was self-conscious primitivism; this was the crux of Gautier's argument against Courbet and Realism.

The importance and complexity of the issue were heightened in the case of Courbet's *Enterrement à Ornans* at the Salon of 1850–1,[93] because of the scale of the picture's apparent pretensions. It offended Gautier on every level. Firstly, it could not be said to exist within any traditional view of the artist's relationship to patron and public. Where was it to hang? Certainly not in a church, nor in a palace, public building, or private house. For given its massive dimensions, it should contain more general interest; it should be an exposition of broad, universal concerns, in the manner of the Renaissance. The subject of a burial, moreover, offers just this resource to a painter; Gautier explains how it could present allegorically its pathetic and profoundly moving theme, 'for, having accompanied others, everyone must in turn be accompanied on that inevitable pilgrimage . . ., must come to that little garden which is watered with tears . . .' But a burial at such-and-such a place becomes mere anecdote and does not justify treatment on a vast scale. A woman mourning her child is a subject that symbolizes an eternal human fact, 'the collective representation of maternal grief'; but a bourgeois 'Mme Baboulard bewailing the loss of Dodolphe' on an epic scale is individualism taken to ridiculous extremes. Certainly, Gautier continues, generality can be found in particularity, if the spectator is allowed to make a mental transference, if not too many details are filled in to limit the play of his imagination. What do a few touches of local colour matter if the theme is universal, if it could just as well be taking place in Montmartre cemetery as in the Père Lachaise? But Courbet has made this extension of the subject impossible, 'by accentuating the characteristic features of his figures in an effort to make each an individual portrait, and ending up by producing what are virtually caricatures'. He has depicted not generalized Weeping Relatives or an archetypal Consoling Priest, but recognizably contemporary and individual members of the Franc-Comtois bourgeoisie. Not, Gautier the lover of the *mot propre* qualifies, that we want exclusively conventionalized heads; but 'there is a big difference between free study of nature, nature intepreted to accord with the overall meaning of the scene to be rendered, and the juxtaposition of portraits which in no way contribute to the expression and seem to isolate themselves through their very likeness'. Courbet's painting is an unsuitable treatment of its subject; the major criticism against it is that it thus transgresses the terms of the Renaissance tradition. Gautier refers to the Old Masters as final unshakeable witnesses for the prosecution: they sometimes introduced portraits of particular individuals into their compositions, he writes, but they always reserved the centre for the ideal.

Courbet's other and equally serious crime is that he is guilty of blindly following a system, ignoring that Romantic code of 1834 which had asserted the artist's right, if not his need, to be pragmatic and irrational. Courbet's grandiose ambition is to see his 'figures from real life in the company of prophets, gods, and heroes'. It is an inverse idealism, which, for consistency's sake, demands a corresponding brutality and laxity of execution. Proof that his manner is a manner and not simply honest ineptitude can be found in his earlier self-portrait, where he has had the coquetry not to apply his system to his own person. He is paradoxically as much of a mannerist as Boucher: 'Both overshoot the mark, for a manner is a kind of ideal gone wrong'.

'Is the ugly alone true?' Gautier asked in a summing-up of his feelings in 1853.[94] 'Cabbages are real, but roses are not unreal.' 'Does not M. Courbet affect ugliness just as Boucher affected elegance?' he explained again in 1859; 'does he not paint things to look dirtier, muddier, and more brutal than they are when he sees them, and is it not permissible to believe that when nature does not appear repulsive enough to him he flatters it inversely, overemphasizing its coarser aspects, in order to make it fit in with his system? When he happens to come across elegance, he must reject it, just as an idealist would suppress the trivial.' Courbet placed himself outside Gautier's Romantic art-historical continuity above all by refusing to commit himself to his instincts, which would inevitably have led him towards the ideal. To be fair to Courbet, Gautier declared his own obvious preference in the quarrel between 'love of the ideal and love of truth': 'We prefer artists who take the choicest forms offered by nature, in order to express their inner dreams . . . but this does not prevent us from liking the exact reproduction of things without arrangement or flattery of any kind, assuming, that is, that such imitation has ever been possible. The artist is implicated in his work whether he likes it or not and puts into it something of his own particular ideal.'[95]

Ribera, who saw himself as the 'head of the naturalists' school' in seventeenth-century Spain, is called in as an example; his ugliness and horror, like that of other Spanish and Flemish masters, was acceptable because his instinct for idealization led him to introduce redeeming qualities of beauty-in-itself into his painting. 'The ugly can only be part of painting when redeemed by colour and fantasy, that charming pair of liars who are almost always so truthful', Gautier had written in 1838 apropos of Biard's cheaply sensational 'caricatures';[96] the corollary of this argument applied to Breton, the painter of peasants, in 1859.[97] His *Plantation d'un calvaire*, although it was not the deliberate exploitation of a subject in order to 'indulge in ugliness', was criticized for its 'dirty, earthy, rancid, tired, and commonplace colours, unpleasant in themselves'. Breton's *Le Lundi*, also at the Salon of 1859, represented 'a mean village pothouse completely devoid of picturesque effect'; here once more was 'the coarse reality of things' unredeemed by any higher intervention on the part of the artist. To bring such a subject into the sphere of art would have required 'the magical flamboyance of Rubens, the powerful sensuality of Jordaëns, or the irresistible joviality of Jan Steen'.

Of all contemporary realists it was Manet who made the most radical departures from the flamboyance, sensuality, and conviviality of Gautier's Renaissance and Baroque. Like Courbet, who 'maintains that he receives a direct impression from objects and borrows nothing from his precursors' knowledge',[98] Manet too 'departs from the rules recognized by the logic of centuries past'.[99] He simply ignores 'the orthography of painting'.[100] *Olympia*, at the Salon of 1865 (Gautier is not known to have paid any attention to the 1863 Salon des refusés), offered the critic nothing.

Olympia, whose title calls to mind that great Roman courtesan with whom the Renaissance was infatuated, cannot be explained from any point of view, even if you take her for what she is, a skinny model stretched out on a sheet. The flesh tones are dirty, the modelling non-existent. The shadows are sketched in with more or less broad streaks of boot-polish. What is there to say about the Negress who is bringing a bouquet wrapped in a piece of paper, and the black cat which is leaving its muddy paw prints on her bed? We could still just about forgive the ugliness if it were lifelike, well observed, and redeemed by some splendid effect of colour. Even the least pretty woman has bones, muscles, a skin, forms, and a colour of some kind. Here there is nothing, it angers us to say, but the desire to attract attention at any price.[101]*

Not only did the picture fail to provide Gautier with any opportunity for sensual or emotional identification; in recalling 'that great courtesan with whom the Renaissance was infatuated' it presented itself to him as a deliberate travesty, a childish outrage; this was the only explanation for its apparently wilful lack of redeeming features.

The essential qualities that Gautier demanded of art, whatever its kind, here reveal themselves by their very absence. If Olympia was only an undernourished studio model such as the one that had disappointed the 'jeune rapin' at Rioult's studio and such as he must frequently have encountered subsequently on visits to friends' studios, and if her cat, showing an unusual lack of fastidiousness with its grubby paws, was hardly the ideal of a cat, there was little compensatory beauty-in-itself or verve of execution to be found in the muddy flesh tones and shadows, nor in any splendid effect of colour. Art was 'a dream borrowing the forms of reality in order to make itself manifest',[102] and there was no dream, but what was completely unforgivable was that even the forms of reality were treated with nonchalant lack of respect. There was no modelling, no anatomy, no structure; this was Manet's unpardonable offence, and one for which, we have heard, even Delacroix was censured.

Here lies the substance of Gautier's most persistent and fundamental criticism, and it can be seen to stand as the direct and logical corollary of his love of sculpture and of sculptural, three-dimensional form in painting. Objects in art must be palpable; they must ultimately be seen to exist in the round and in space. An absence of modelling and perspective had caused him to criticize Lehmann in 1840, and it had explained the inferiority of medieval art; structure must be understood and explained or at least implicit. Together with emotional definition, clarity of intention, art must offer Gautier physical definition: the objects of the real world which it handles must be distinct from one another, and must finally provide the senses (especially the short-sighted eyes) with such evidence of their existence as they possess in the real world, or, indeed, with even greater evidence. If the identity of objects is compromised, then *vraisemblance*, emotional *justesse*, and the power to absorb and transport are as good as lost.

Thus both Courbet and Whistler were criticized for painting cardboard cut-outs. Courbet's *Demoiselles de la Seine* at the Salon of 1857[103] was 'a landscape from the realms of high fantasy like those you see on the wall-papers of provincial inns', with leaves 'cut out of green paper'. In one of Courbet's 'two bulky creatures' Gautier discerned 'no forms swelling beneath the folds of her dress', and of Whistler's *La Princesse du pays de la porcelaine* at the Salon of 1865 he observed: 'It is nothing more than a figure from a folding screen cut out and pasted on to the canvas'.[104] If some figures from real life take similarly flat forms in Gautier's prose, figures from art must have correspondingly fuller presences. Flandrin demonstrated a lack of convincing solidity at the Salon of 1847;[105] his Napoleon was 'stiff . . . lifeless and colourless, without modelling', and seemed to bear no kinship to any earthly phenomenon. 'In what world is this taking place? Is it on Saturn or Mercury?' (This was an example of the influence of Ingres at its most dangerous. If the Master's own Napoleon in the Hôtel de Ville was hardly human, it was because it lived the perfect life of sculpture, inhabiting the superior world of *Idea*; Flandrin's was just a strange extra-terrestrial.)

Where in Courbet Gautier objected to the rigid application of a system which deprived his creatures of life and solidity, it was especially because Courbet of all artists—Zola's 'creator of flesh'—possessed the virile temperament by which to create the most sensually compelling milieux; of *La Curée du chevreuil*, for instance, at the Salon of 1857,[106] Gautier wrote that 'materialist painting could not be taken further' and reminded us that 'we are not one of those people who scorn this kind of painting'. Courbet lacked 'composition . . . drawing . . . and style', but this was a less fundamental failing than that of Hamon, whose exhibits at the Exposition Universelle of 1855 were 'the shadow of a dream', so spiritualized and insipid as almost to disappear altogether. 'Beyond extreme sobriety there is nothingness', and this, we have seen, was to be shunned at all costs. 'It is fine to be delicate, but you must exist, even at the price of a little coarseness. When spirits want to make themselves visible, they are obliged to take on a material semblance.'[107] The same was remarked of Gérôme at the Salon of 1859:[108] 'his painting is so delicate it . . . evaporates and disappears . . . thought needs substance in order to manifest itself, especially in a plastic art'. Gautier never ceases reminding us of this fact through the example of his own solidly material imagery; he had made a similar statement of his aesthetic convictions in *Mademoiselle de Maupin*. He wanted 'brightness, solidity, colour . . . No fog or haze, nothing uncertain or irresolute'.[109]

His hostility to the early manifestations of Impressionism and his demand for a degree of finish in painting are predictable extensions of this need for substance, *vraisemblance*, and palpability, and further reflections of his implicit view that the artist should make sense and create his own apprehensible order out of the profusion of visual experience, that he should ward off the danger of perceptual anarchy and aesthetic anguish, of creating forms without meaning. Spontaneous and directly communicative as it can be, the sketch has its limits, Gautier wrote apropos of Haffner's *Passage du Rhin* at the Salon of 1848:[110] 'such canvases are like box roots, in which you can see anything you choose, a Turk smoking his pipe, a steamboat or the Emperor Napoleon'. Daubigny's *Vue des bords de la Seine* at the Salon of 1852[111] could have been a landscape-to-enter, a holiday for the imagination, a whole and definitive spatial and sensual experience, but for the lack of a few brush-strokes: 'then this tree-lined river would have been navigable for boats and provided refreshment for the eyes'.

Gautier does not need nor wish to be reminded that he is looking at artefacts of canvas and paint. A work of art was successful when it provided the means for imaginative excursions into alternative realms of experience, when it allowed the spectator to forget that he was sharing an illusion and let him temporarily be convinced that what he was experiencing was a figment of reality, as in a vivid dream. Only then did it become a picture. 'It is an excellent sketch', he wrote of an exhibit at the Salon of 1866,[112] 'but it is not yet a picture . . . a local colour, accurate as it may be, lying flat on the canvas within a smeared contour, does not constitute a figure.' Colour and line might be spoken of as beautiful in themselves, but always in relation to some motif; a brush-stroke remained incontrovertibly a brush-stroke. Gautier could never concede that it could have an intrinsic quality and interest of its own to rival that of a human figure or, as was the case with Monet's *Navires sortant des jetées du Havre* at the Salon of 1868,[113] that of a ship. Monet, Gautier condescended, told him less about ships than Eugène Isabey; his heavy and brutal manner was totally inappropriate for such finely proportioned and detailed objects. The ship, uniquely beautiful in itself, was the thing. 'The patch and the impression, big words in common use these days . . . are not enough. We do not want slick painting, but we must have painting that is finished.'

The mysterious and miraculous process of artistic creation, of materialization in plastic form, could not be simplified by any dogmatic, merely fashionable approach; the end in art might sometimes justify the means (as it did in Delacroix, whose 'faults' were finally seen as inevitable sacrifices to an irresistible vision), but the means could never justify the end. Landscape painters no longer know how to draw, Gautier wrote at the Salon of 1868,[114] with Daubigny in particular in mind. Most of the landscapes on show are mere sketches. You can't render every detail (see his criticism of the obsessively microscopic Delaberge in 1841[115]), but 'to limit oneself to the application of *patches*, as they say nowadays, which may be accurate but which only indicate the outside contours and the silhouettes of objects, is really an oversimplification of the artist's mission. That at first glance canvases thus treated produce an *impression* (another fashionable word), we agree, but they do not stand long examination'. They offered little to retain a hold on the imagination, few details to explore and no lasting 'satisfaction intime'; they seemed finally to deal in clichés. 'There are *clichés* for every season and every time of day.' It was all too easy; Gautier missed Corot's naïvety and sincerity, the signs of a struggle for realization in paint, and he missed Cabat's simple devotion to the unpromising scene before him. Landscape painting was better in 1830, the critic concluded regretfully; the only remedy is long and patient study of nature, a return to Old Crome and Théodore Rousseau, to the values of the *mot propre* and, for the spectator, to the feeling that a corner of nature was being perceived and understood as if for the first time, revealed to and through fresh and unprejudiced eyes.

Where freshness of response in front of the motif, and pure vision uncoloured by literary preconception were just the claims that were to be made on behalf of Monet and the landscape Impressionists, Gautier could see nothing but the dogmatic application of a brutalizing and trivializing system. Even Corot at his most hazy and diaphanous (as he appeared at the Salon of 1868,[116] where he was welcomed by Gautier with the proviso that his example could lead younger painters into trouble) always indicated 'the armature of things', whatever his vagaries. The criticism that Gautier had offered to Daubigny in 1861[117] may sum up his feelings about painters who used 'patches' to obtain 'impressions'. 'We are not insisting that he should paint in all the veins on a leaf in the background; but trees need to be rooted in the ground, their branches need to be fixed to a trunk and to form a distinct silhouette against the sky or the horizon, especially when they are in the foreground. Trees are neither ostrich feathers nor wisps of smoke . . . Every object is delineated by a contour, apparent or real, and M. Daubigny's landscapes offer only juxtaposed patches of colour.' Gautier concluded by admitting that he preferred the neat and polished landscapes of one Kuwasseg to such 'pretentious negligence'.

Criticism of lack of distinctness, definition, and structure, of offhand treatment of the forms of reality was fundamental criticism of lack of *vraisemblance*. Poorly realized or degraded motifs curbed Gautier's ever pressing desire to abandon himself to a painter's vision, and made him wary of entrusting himself to the principles of that painter's world. And with this we are led straight back to Paul Delaroche, the contemporary painter who aroused some of Gautier's earliest and most vehement antagonism.

Delaroche could never be accused of lack of finish; but, like Monet, he confused means with ends: he seemed to treat technique as an end in itself. He was not, Gautier insisted, a born painter; his talents were those of a *metteur-en-scène*, of a dramatist. 'He will be to painting what Casimir Delavigne is to poetry' was Gautier's final verdict in his review of Delaroche's posthumous retrospective in 1857.[118] Yet he failed in Gautier's eyes even to produce dramatically convincing milieux. In his long 1857 article on Delaroche Gautier was scrupulously fair, even typically generous to the painter whose popular success he had so begrudged during the '30s; if in 1857 he found 'a good deal of skill' in Delaroche's *La Mort de Jane Grey* (*plate 10*), twenty years previously, in 1837, this skill had itself been found to be at fault.[119] It distracted from the drama of an execution scene that might in theory have held Gautier's whole attention: 'you are concerned not for the woman who is about to perish but for her beautiful, brand-new satin dress, with its stiff, straight folds which will get crumpled when she puts her head on that little block, which is ever so neatly made and looks like something from a fancy-goods shop'. Delaroche was a prettifier of potentially horrific subjects, and horror and violence were in Gautier's eyes the exclusive domain of Delacroix and Decamps, of the Romantic liberators of instinct and destroyers of the barriers of polite convention. Hence Delaroche's popularity among the bourgeois, those 'cowardly dreamers, effeminate drinkers of water'.[120] 'It is nice horror, horror everyone can understand . . . he has scrubbed, soaped, waxed, and polished horror so much that he has made it pretty; the most terrible scenes become pleasing to the eye, so daintily does he arrange all their grim details.'[121] Being concerned with surfaces and textures to deceive the eye, with dramatic and sentimental expression, his work did not finally bear long scrutiny, as that of a real painter like Decamps or Meissonier might. Thus at the first appearance of *La Mort de Jane Grey* in the place of honour at the Salon of 1834,[122] Gautier's invective had been made up of observations like: the green cushion is absurd because it does not give beneath Jane Grey's knees; whoever heard of erecting a scaffold by a column? He even found fault with it on grounds of historical accuracy, so passionate was his youthful loathing of the picture and his desire to find in it no redeeming features at all: people lay and did not kneel for execution in those days, as everyone knows, he remarked scornfully. A real painter would not have made such mistakes. It is significant, Gautier observed in 1837,[123] that Delaroche the so-called history painter has never exhibited a nude torso: it is because he merely paints costumes on dummies.

In his remark on Delaroche: 'you are concerned not for the woman who is about to perish but for her beautiful, brand-new dress', Gautier once more presents us with the curious phenomenon of criticism which seems finally to come home to an aspect of himself; for have we not heard him tell the Goncourts[124] that at the theatre he was more absorbed in the fold in an actress's costume than in the sentiments being put across by the characters? (His criticism of Pradier, who 'forgets that marbles should only be loved platonically', is a similar instance.) Yet there is no fundamental contradiction here. 'I am a *subjective* being', he also told the Goncourts. His apprehension of things was not reasoned or moral, and for Gautier in the theatre[125] as in painting true *vraisemblance* could only spring from a primary and almost exclusive attention to visible form. Alternative milieux, absorbing new harmonies, were to be constructed from the dictionary of the world's visible, material resources; the subject and its superficial accessories could never be the starting point for true painting. Apropos of Delaroche in 1837,[126] Gautier suggested that the subject in painting was so unimportant as to be a mere pretext or convention. 'Painting really only represents a certain quite limited number of actions and motifs; it needs subjects which are already fixed and established . . . and which everybody should easily be able to understand . . . form is eternal; subject and action are mere accidents.' This statement might seem to be an anticipation of the twentieth-century, formalist aesthetics of a Roger Fry; but the importance Gautier attached to visual experience was never, as we have seen, to lead him towards a concern with the purely abstract and non-figurative.

The previous year he had summed up his views in a little manifesto in *La Presse* entitled 'De la composition en peinture',[127] which ended with a sort of parable about artistic creation. This is how a picture is generally conceived: the painter amuses himself by making sketches, playing around with different poses; he has nothing else particularly in mind.

1. Théophile Gautier in 1854. Photo: Nadar

2. Auguste de Châtillon, *Portrait of Théophile Gautier*, 1839

3. Théophile Gautier in St. Petersburg in 1859. Photo: Richebourg
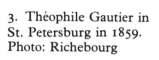

4. Théophile Gautier, sheet of pen and ink drawings,
reproduced in A. Houssaye, *Les Confessions*

5. Jean-Baptiste-Auguste Clésinger, *Femme piquée par un serpent*, 1847

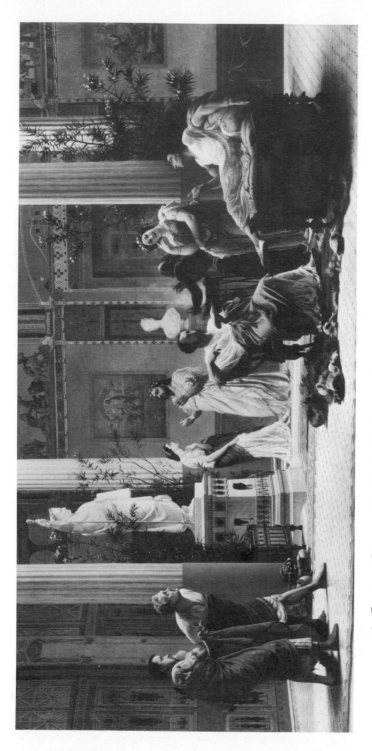

6. Gustave-Clarence-Rodolphe Boulanger, *Répétition du 'Joueur de flûte' chez S.A.I. le prince Napoléon, dans l'atrium de sa maison, avenue Montaigne*, 1861. Gautier is standing and declaiming in the centre background; the cast includes the Prince himself, the dramatist Émile Augier, and leading members of the Comédie Francaise.

8. Hippolyte-Jean Flandrin, *Portrait of Mlle Maison*, 'La Jeune Fille à l'œillet', 1859

7. Ernest Meissonier, *Jeune homme écrivant*, 1852

9. Antoine-Louis Barye, *Jaguar dévorant un lièvre*, 1850

10. Paul Delaroche, *La Mort de Jane Grey*, 1834

11. Alexandre-Henri-Georges Regnault, *Exécution sans jugement sous les rois maures de Grenade*, 1870

12. Paolo Veronese, *The Marriage at Cana*, 1562–3

All kinds of figures and objects (typically, we are treated to a list of these) emerge from the webs of line, and among these sketches there is one which looks better than the rest. This the painter works up into a more finished drawing. He then pesters one of his literary friends to come up with a nice, pompous title which will catch the public eye at the next exhibition; he can now get hold of the requisite props and attend to necessary details. 'For in their initial compositions painters do only entirely nude figures, which have no other significance beyond that of their physical attitude or their forms, and this, we can hardly stress it enough, is the chief purpose of painting, the subject being, as it were, an accident.'

Out of 'folâtrerie' and 'débauche', and without the artist's conscious intervention, emerges the human figure. No idea or system obtrudes; it is the artist's instinct which spontaneously creates out of meaningless forms, as out of nature's inscrutable chaos, a world in which the human figure dominates. This world is totally communicative, understandable, and hospitable, it is conceived on a human scale and in it human emotions and appetites can finally find reflection and extension. Here Gautier's whole pagan religion of art is summed up, and his Renaissance-based vision contained. (His parable of artistic creation recalls Leonardo's method of stimulating the imagination by studying random stains on a wall.) His theory of the artist who is profoundly in touch with indestructible form, who approaches nature with 'scrupulous sincerity . . . integrity . . . and perfect naïvety',[128] and thus allows his unique instincts and temperament unconstrained play, enabled Gautier to accept within the sphere of what could be called art the largest possible variety of communicative embodiments and figurative milieux. That which was outside the sphere of art was always and exclusively that which used the non-visual as a point of departure, from the doctrines of Realism and Catholicism to the desire to stimulate the laughter and applause of a public which liked vaudeville and waxworks.

4 Plenitude

A man for whom the visible world exists, Gautier himself

sometimes hardly seems to exist at all outside the world of his own perceptions. The perceptions define the man, or rather allow him to elude definition, for in his pagan dream of sensual plenitude and repletion (his version of Winckelmann's *sufficienza*), personal identity is transcended. He wishes to be able to seize universal correspondences, to grasp some divine harmony by becoming an ego-less part of it. Depending no doubt upon the mood in which he is read, he can be felt to be sharing that 'monumental slumber of high noon' with which David Piper has characterized Albert Moore's High Victorian Roman maidens,[129] and which for the Goncourts was the key to his nature; or worse, he can seem to exist in an Oblomov-like state of mindlessly comfortable oblivion, acquiescing in the 'stupefying well-being' for which he longed and of which he felt ashamed when faced with Ingres's sustained fertility in 1862.[130] His highest aspirations, and the assessment he would perhaps most have envied for himself, are contained in his own evocation of the spirit of Paolo Veronese (*plate 12*):

People who only see the surface of things and who are moved to shed tears of tenderness by Romantic sentimentalities have sometimes accused Paolo Veronese of being cold, of having no heart, no passion, of lacking ideas and purpose, of delighting exclusively in the marvels of his stupendous technique. Yet no painter ever had a higher ideal. That eternal feast celebrated in his pictures has a profound meaning; his banquets are all symbolic, for scarcely anything is eaten at them, and it is not drunkenness that brightens and animates the brown eyes of those fine groups of men and women, but a sense of universal joy and divine harmony.[131]*

Veronese was one of Gautier's four or five first names in painting; he was a typical Gautier artist, a dispassionate creator of milieux like Decamps and Meissonier, and of magical harmonies like Delacroix and Rembrandt. Like Delacroix, he reflects the best of Gautier. This is the Renaissance out of which the critic's dream of a new, Romantic Renaissance sprang; it is finally a poetic dream of an unsurpassably serene sensual paradise, a hallucinatory vision of flowers, gold, marble, and silks, of what Aldous Huxley has called 'praetersignificant form':[132] intensified and other-worldly colours, patterns, glows, and sheens. It is a world in which all the senses find balanced acquiescence at their highest pitch of receptivity. Around Veronese's ever-laden table

. . . men easily rediscover felicities more intoxicating than those shared by the solitary couple in old Eden. Do they not have women, flowers, perfumes, gold, marble, silk, wine, music, poetry, art, that flower of the mind? The exchange of ideas or feelings with a being similar to yet different from oneself; variety in harmony; admiration, that spiritual love, and love, that admiration from the heart which both exalts and prostrates you; the consciousness of belonging to that perpetual, collective man with whom God converses, in the silence of creation, in order to pass the time of eternity!

Glory then to Paolo Veronese, who brings the elements of happiness that divine benevolence has placed at our disposal shining before our eyes! An earth on which there are more than twenty thousand kinds of flower and plant purely for ornament, where the decoration of sunsets is changed every evening, where splendid form is so superbly clothed in colour, cannot be a vale of tears. Yes, if people wanted it, the water of *The Marriage at Cana* could turn into wine perpetually, and the harlot's perfumes into heavenly fragrances![133]*

Such was the insight, first elaborated in the preface to *Mademoiselle de Maupin*, that Gautier's pagan religion of art was to nurture. His evocation of Veronese draws on the sense of plenitude that he took from his experience of art itself. It is his vindication of form as of his own stance; it embodies his dream of personal apotheosis, and his definitive message to the century.

VII Journalist and Contemporary

I Introduction

Gautier was a world traveller, in Europe, Asia, and North Africa as well as abroad in the large world of art. He was a European figure, a stature he had achieved by at least the middle of the Second Empire, less through the impact of his poetry, which remained essentially and artistically Parisian, than through his ubiquitous physical presence outside Imperial France as artistic ambassador extraordinary, with a massive portfolio of briefs and credentials. After the public and private disasters of 1848 he had quickly sought to re-establish a fashionable and cosmopolitan life-style, which, to all outward appearances, was soon to reflect the bravely new and confident style of the Empire: by 1849 he had a new mistress, the elegant, intelligent, and Italian Marie Mattei, whom he shortly followed to Venice; in the same year he was to be seen at Ascot and later among the crowd of fashionable neophiliacs that perused the Chinese junk moored in St. Katherine's Docks; he was at the Madeleine for Chopin's funeral and in Bilbao in time for the bullfights. In the year of *Les Beaux-Arts en Europe* he was invited to dinner by Delacroix; in London for the World's Fair of 1862 he dined with Thackeray.

Recognized by the State and by *Le Moniteur universel* for the usefulness of his limitless descriptive powers, he was tailor-made as the representative of the Arts, in that collaborative fraternity of Industry, Science, and Agriculture that was presided over by Peace and Progress hand-in-hand with the Emperor Napoleon III. Gautier was forever being dispatched from Paris in brand-new trains, on scientific or military expeditions abroad, from which he was expected to return with literary daguerreotypes as evidence, for the newspaper-reading public, of the ever expanding benignity of the Imperial figurehead. His role in the monumentally serious and elaborate Allegory that was the basis of the Second Empire's internal peacetime propaganda was clearly fixed (had he not intimated, ironically, that he wished to be part of a permanent *tableau vivant?*); Louis-Napoléon, always aware of the weight of his historical antecedents, was seeking definitively to affirm Paris's place as the capital of Europe and to brighten her lustre as the art-capital of the world, to establish artistic as well as economic and dashingly military dominance, just like his shrewd uncle Bonaparte who had appended artists and intellectuals to his Egyptian campaign. Gautier's greatest contemporary triumph, as the author of *Les Beaux-Arts en Europe* and the man best qualified to represent the Empire of Art and embody its diverse qualities, should have been *Les Trésors de l'art de la Russie ancienne et moderne*, a heavyweight and glittering attempt symbolically to glorify mutual sympathy between the peace-loving empires of France and of Russia, united in pursuit of the high ideals of Brotherhood, Progress, Trade, etc., all presided over by smiling Art. This *de luxe* project, for which he signed a 30,000 francs contract in 1857 for a prospective two months in Russia, which was to be illustrated by 200 Richebourg photographs, published in an expensive limited edition under the direct personal patronage of Alexander II and dedicated to the Czarina Maria Alexandrovna, was never properly completed; like the Second Empire itself, it foundered under the weight of other insupportably grand commitments.

Gautier may have tended to view Russia and Turkey, Greece and Algeria as, if they were all framed on the walls of some macrocosmic Exposition Universelle; certainly, as the Second Empire's sub-empire of Art conscientiously pushed its frontiers outwards towards new territories of subject-matter, so did Gautier's range of sympathy and admiration expand, or at least his most banal official excursions into the real world had so prepared his prose to behave like a camera as to make it appear so. As a professional cosmopolitan and eclectic, and as a critic who claimed to have visited all the galleries in the world,[1] he was able to turn his pen, in 1855, to welcome to the artistic capital of the universe virtually every living artist of note in the Northern hemisphere, from Millais and Hunt to the Norwegian Lunderen (for 'art is a hardy plant which flourishes everywhere, even in places where there is only lichen beneath the snow upon which for the reindeer to browse'[2]), not to mention a large collection of Chinese art, which received twelve pages. All this, and more, was apart from very detailed studies of French art in all its manifestations, from Ingres to Chabal-Dessurgey.

Gautier is the perfect guide to mid-nineteenth-century French art because he tacitly assimilates and embodies so many salient nineteenth-century attitudes. Trained by his Romantic youth as a sensitively perceiving organism, un-prejudiced and impartial in his use of the *mot propre*, he also produced in himself a faculty for broad, rich, and accurate reflection. By conscientiously keeping his options open, by rejecting systems and relying on intuitive judgements, he had prepared himself to be receptive to more contemporary currents and moods than perhaps even he was aware. He was a reflecting as well as a perceiving organism; as a man who, locked in perception, lost himself in the object and became a Spaniard in Spain, he was a participator, an actor as well as a spectator. He always dressed the part. He is like a chameleon; for all his impassioned attempts to emancipate himself from what he discerned as most drab and negative about his own time, he increasingly seems to disappear against the background of its larger preoccupations. This was perhaps his great qualification and success as a journalist: he was able spontaneously to reflect and fulfil contemporary demands, and slip without apparent effort into this role. Also like an actor, he is often only as interesting as his material; for much of his career as a professional journalist, he emerges not only as a critic of his age but also as a spontaneously responsive move-by-move commentator, as both a man with a message and a reflector of prevailing moods and tastes.

2 Art journalism up to 1848

(a) LA PRESSE

Émile de Girardin's *La Presse*, the context in which Gautier was first forced to make a tacit definition of his role as a journalist, was itself a direct response to a new market, arising out of the needs and reflecting the values of the middle-class revolution which had found its symbolic embodiment in the person of Louis-Philippe. The professional newspaper industry that Théophile entered in 1836 by way of Madame de Girardin's literary salon was indeed a brand-new one, and one that Girardin was in the process of creating virtually single-handed; through the aggressive but shrewd genius of its enterprising proprietor, *La Presse* was to bring far-reaching and irreversible changes to newspaper production. It had been launched on 1 July 1836, only weeks before the young Gautier began his long and fruitful collaboration; he was thus almost in on its founding, and played his part in determining its style.

Girardin himself, the nineteenth-century Citizen Kane, elsewhere described as 'the Napoleon of the press' (in his own lifetime), or simply 'the father of the modern press' (René Mazedier), may have been daunting as an employer, but he was certainly a man likely to appeal to a Jeune-France imagination, at least from a distance. There was nothing mythical about his early biography. He had been born in 1806, and was thus only just outside Théophile's immediate age group; he was the illegitimate son of the Comte Alexandre de Girardin and of Adélaïde-Marie Dupuy, a lawyer's wife whose portrait by Greuze had appeared at the Salon of 1800 as *Jeune fille à la colombe*. Having hit upon journalism as a means of satisfying his large personal and above all political ambitions, he had resigned from a post at the Inspectorat des Beaux-Arts in 1828 to found *Le Voleur*, a monthly review of the arts and sciences, which was followed in 1831 by a *Journal des connaissances utiles*; these titles suggest the all-grasping range of his interests and energies, among which the arts occupied a large place, at least for their potential as a point of access to life in the public eye and as a source of profitable exploitation. By 1834 he was a young member of parliament for Bourganeuf, yet the establishment of a solidly respectable reputation was to remain beyond even his powers; doubts about his nationality, for instance, founded on his shady birth, were temporarily to exclude him from the Chambre in 1839. But that he was always a force to be reckoned with, a man not to suffer differences of opinion easily, he had personally demonstrated on 22 July 1836, by killing Armand Carrel, the rival editor of *Le National*, in a duel; this was a matter of weeks before Gautier was enlisted to add his sparkle to the pages of *La Presse*.

Girardin's first and most decisive act in founding the newspaper on which his subsequent fame rests was to halve, at a stroke, the fixed and universal annual rate of subscription. Newspapers, under the Restoration and Constitutional Monarchy, could not be bought singly on the street, only by subscription at the high rate of 80 francs a year; by reducing the annual subscription to *La Presse* to 40 francs, Girardin played a major part in turning the newspaper into a mass medium, a change whose beginnings were reflected in the rise of subscriptions to Parisian newspapers from around 47,000 in 1824 to 70,000 in 1836 and 200,000 ten years later. [3] *La Presse* was produced on a sound commercial basis; linotype and the rotary press enabled large editions to be printed quickly and relatively cheaply, and Girardin's motto—'sell cheaply to sell a lot'—was made financially feasible by the novel realization of the full commercial possibilities of advertisements, the revenue from which enabled the subscription to be kept low, thus attracting more readers, and thus in turn more advertisers. It was a sound formula for expansion: by October 1836 *La Presse* had a circulation of 10,000,[4] and subscriptions rose from 13,500 in 1840 to 23,000 in 1845[5] and 70,000 in 1848.[6]

The implications of this process of commercialization and democratization that Girardin brought to bear on the press go further. 'We do not intend to do all over again what the old press has done, but to do something else in another way', he wrote in his editorial prospectus for *La Presse*'s first number.[7] Daily newspapers under Napoleon and the Restoration were concerned very largely with transcribing parliamentary debates, with political news and comment; expensive and often densely unreadable, by Girardin's and modern standards, they were primarily a feature of the cafés, which, with their particular political allegiances, remained the centres of informed discussion for the educated and relatively leisurely professional middle-classes (see Stendhal, for instance, on changing his café in 1830, in *Souvenirs d'égotisme*). The café was the place in which to pore, collectively, over a single copy of a newspaper, the subscription for which was perhaps raised among the customers, or which was provided by the establishment as part of its service. *La Presse* was aimed at a new and wider market, and intended to be consumed in a different setting. The lower subscription rate meant that the lower, mercantile bourgeois could have his own newspaper to himself in the comfort of his own home. It was designed to be accessible and satisfying to the individual, and to the individual perhaps with a limited or recent background of information and education; it did not need further elucidation through collective street-level discussion. Parliamentary debates were printed, but in précis form, and Girardin's editorial comments were meant to make sense of complex issues and reports; the number of section headings was increased, and short, abrupt, instantly digestible news items began to appear on the inside pages (*La Presse* generally consisted of four pages). These *Nouvelles et faits divers* contained, as well as announcements about the movements and health of the royal family, members of the government, regiments, and foreign dignitaries, more homely and sensational pieces: interesting suicides, unusual murders, and, an example from 27 November 1839, the news that a girl in Bordeaux had given birth to a child with three heads. 'Sensation prevails over explanation and appearance, often, over reality', comments a historian.[8]

Above all, *La Presse* claimed to be impartial; it was to be unaffiliated to any political ideology, above all coteries, as Girardin promised on 1 July 1836. This claim was an essential and well-considered means of reaching and pleasing a wide readership, and was no doubt especially attractive to the idealistically pragmatic young Gautier. *La Presse* was to present itself as a disinterested observer, as an informed commentator on events of importance or interest to the reading public at large. In practice, this was to mean that the newspaper, in other words its editor, would usually follow and reflect the fluctuations of prevailing public opinion in its political ideas; Girardin is justly summed up in the authoritatively opaque language of the *Encyclopaedia Britannica* as 'a middle-class conservative who occasionally showed progressive tendencies', a not inapt if over-general description of the regime under which he rose to notoriety. The tone of *La Presse* was pleasantly instructive; the newspaper sold itself less as a report, document, or manifesto than as serious, informative, and often anecdotal conversation. This change of tone in relation to that of longer-established, denser newspapers, like *Le Moniteur universel* or *Le Journal des Débats*, has been characterized thus: before Girardin, newspapers were aimed at the upper levels of society; ' "For 80 francs a year" ', they said, ' "you will have my opinion on the political systems of our times" . . . Girardin: "For 40 francs a year I will inform and at the same time instruct you" '.[9] Another historian of the press definitively pinpoints Girardin's readership as 'the ordinary middle classes, the comfortably off tradesman, and those people who, without owning a fortune, were nevertheless willing to add forty-odd francs to their annual budgets in order to keep up with politics, to be in the know'.[10]

La Presse ensured its large circulation among the new bourgeoisie, the 'comfortably off tradesmen', by remaining unchallenging and undemanding, if often sensational and apparently hard-hitting; it was essentially reassuring. Girardin had gauged his market cleverly; perhaps his single most telling and characteristic innovation was the use he made of the feuilleton, the new emphasis he placed on the non-political, cultural, or 'general interest' section of the newspaper. *La Presse*'s feuilleton, which regularly occupied the whole of the bottom third of the front page, and usually the same areas of the second and third pages as well, concerned itself with such varied 'connaissances utiles' as Girardin had presumably wished to exploit in his earlier *Journal*: with, for example, fashionable *physiologies*, like A. Deschamps's 'Physiology of the dancer', or with topical titles like 'Corsets and hygiene'; it was a platform for publicity, enabling Girardin to explain at length the advantages to advertisers of *La Presse*'s typographical style, for instance,[11] as it was for Gautier's theatre and art-critical bulletins. Most successfully and significantly of all, the feuilleton was turned into the *roman-feuilleton*, the serial novel.

For nearly a century and a half the small-circulation periodical had been the focal point of Parisian literary and cultural life, with a place in every cultivated salon; with its feuilletons and particularly with the serial novel *La Presse* became the first newspaper to assume the role of popular dispenser of culture (as well as of dispenser of popular culture), making a key contribution to the rise of the newspaper over the periodical as an indicator of and organ for Parisian literary activity. Along with Madame de Girardin herself, who wrote under the *nom de plume* 'la Vicomtesse de Launay', Balzac, Dumas, and Scribe were among those first enlisted to contribute instalments of original and previously unpublished fiction; such names, along with those of Hugo, le Bibliophile Jacob, and Gustave Planche, now became the common property not just of the artistic salon, the exclusive periodical and the bookshop but also of the domesticated bourgeois, increasingly confident in his relative affluence and eager for a degree of cultural refinement, or at least for the kind of entertainment that would befit his aspirations towards social gentility.

La Presse was also essentially and perhaps ironically a by-product of the Romanticism that had been the background accompaniment of the Revolution of 1830, reflecting a widely disseminated belief in the possibility of a new and universal artistic language or of a popular, psychologically relevant art; further, it was a product of that desire for escape to some ideal milieu which had been a key feature of the Petit Cénacle's utterances. Newspapers of longer standing had of course printed art, theatre and literary criticism, archeological and scientific reports, under the headings *Variétés* or *Faits divers* to distinguish them from the political material in which they appeared as buried afterthoughts; Girardin not only gave broad contemporary culture a new prominence and integration in his newspaper by placing it on the front page; he also introduced, with the serial novel that he juxtaposed with the serious news, a note of pure escapism, something harmlessly to fill the leisure hours of the bourgeois and satisfy the more romantic tastes of his female dependants. Hence there was a proliferation of 'feminine' serial novel titles (a mode most richly exploited by Balzac), such as Charlotte de Sorr's 'The

Happiest Woman in the World';[12] for the head of the household himself, there was S. Henry Berthoud's 'Sidelights on the history of the nineteenth century',[13] or the *physiologies*, of the mason, the huntsman, or the sailor perhaps, to reassure him of his secure place in the social order of things. Thus Vigny could write in his *Carnets* in 1839: 'The Parisian bourgeois is a king who every morning, at his levee, finds a flatterer on hand to tell him any number of stories. This inexpensive parasite is none other than his newspaper.'[14]

For the first time, the world was brought into the bourgeois home, and not only the world of foreign and domestic politics, finance, and high culture, but also that of fantasy. Like much post-1830 Romantic literature and painting, the newspaper after Girardin had worked his transformations provided surrogate experience, the illusion of broad liberal culture and of first-hand knowledge and insight, an illusion which the growing, newly self-important and increasingly affluent bourgeoisie welcomed, needing to feel that it had established some cultural and intellectual tradition for itself to match that of the lettered nobility (hence the appeal of the Vicomtesse de Launay, of *de* Balzac). The move of the newspaper, through Girardin's profitable democratization, away from the café and street-level (where experience was indeed still to be confronted full-on, as Baudelaire later discerned) and into the middle-class home met a new social emphasis on domesticity and domestic virtues: on the family, on motherhood, on saving and thrift, on a stabilized and regularized life-style, but above all on the home as castle: that is, not only as a safe retreat and haven, but also as the outward symbol of the prestige, wealth, and taste of the bread-winner. This new emphasis, exploited and echoed by *La Presse*, is the background against which to explore Gautier's early and persisting functions as a critic; it is directly reflected in some of the themes of his early writing, and, what is more, has a bearing on the history of *l'art pour l'art* itself.

(b) ARMCHAIR ESCAPISM

Gautier cherished the intimacy of his own home background and continually exteriorized it in his writing. Had he not described himself in 1832 in the preface to *Albertus* as 'a sickly young man who feels the cold and spends his life in the bosom of his family'? 'A space a few feet square in which it is less cold than anywhere else', he continued, 'is his universe . . . the mantelpiece is his horizon . . . He prefers to be sitting down rather than standing up, and lying down to sitting.'[15] The hyperbolic language of the preface to *Les Jeunes-France* offers the same insights: 'I take the Oriental view: only dogs or Frenchmen galavant about the streets when they could be sitting comfortably at home.'[16] In the same preface we are reminded that we are already dealing with a writer who prefers art to life: 'I prefer pictures to the objects they represent';[17] it thus comes as no surprise to find, in the story *Celle-ci et celle-là*, a fuller exposition of the theme of surrogate experience. It is transformed into the highest poetic ideality, and inextricably linked, as ever, to the theme of domestic intimacy and to its always imminently possible antithesis, travel. Albert, who represents 'genuine reason, the bosom friend of true poetry', is giving sound advice to Rodolphe, 'the human soul in its youth and inexperience':[18] ' "Oh my friend! you must be quite mad to want to leave home in the hope of running into poetry" ', he has been heard to say. ' "Poetry is no more here than there: it is within us." '[19] He goes on to present Gautier's youthful intuitions of the home, the room, as a microcosm, as an image and concretization of the being of its occupant, into which all experience is welcomed; the room also comes to represent experience itself.

Poetry is everywhere: this room is as poetic as the Gulf of Baya . . . or as anywhere else that is supposed to be poetic . . . look, the best part of your life has been spent within these walls; you have dreamt your most beautiful dreams here and had your most golden visions. Long acquaintance has made the most secret corners familiar to you; . . . like a snail, you are perfectly encased in your shell. These walls know and love you, and echo your voice or your footsteps more faithfully than anything else could; this furniture and you are of the same substance. When you enter, the armchair lovingly holds out its arms, and is dying to embrace you, the clock goes wild and its overjoyed hands gallop full tilt to strike the hour whose sound is worth all the music of the heavens to you, that of dinner- or lunch-time. Your bed smiles discreetly at you from deep in the alcove, and, blushing coyly between its purple curtains, seems to be telling you that you are twenty years old and that your mistress is beautiful . . . The house is a body of which you are the soul and to which you give life: you are the centre of this microcosm. So why wish to uproot yourself and put yourself in the wings, when you can command the whole stage?[20]

With this last opinion the bourgeois householder comfortable with his daily *Presse* might have heartily concurred.

Gautier establishes domestic décor and furniture as experience itself. His kissing armchair and galloping clock are as animate as the steam-driven, stove-pipe people invented by his contemporary the satirical draughtsman Grandville; they are bizarre images of a materially minded age. They are set in open opposition to first-hand experience of nature: the inorganic and man-made against the organic, art against life. The preface to *Les Jeunes-France* contains a hyperbolic tirade against nature which anticipates Oscar Wilde's similar outburst (in his essay 'The Decay of Lying'). Thoroughly Parisian Théophile has been invited to a picnic:

Dinner was taken on the grass . . . I wished I were somewhere else. Daddy-long-legs strode up and down the plates on their spindly feet without so much as a by-your-leave, flies fell into our glasses, caterpillars climbed up our legs. I was wearing a superb pair of white duck trousers; I got up with an indecent green patch on my behind . . . The murmur of streams, the chirping of birds, the whole orchestra of the eclogue and the idyll give me no pleasure whatsoever; I would gladly say, like Debureau to the nightingale: Shut up, horrible beast.[21]

He sums up his attitude: 'I cannot see what rustic pleasure can equal that of looking at the caricatures in Martinet or Susse's window, and I don't find the sun much better than gas light'.[22]

In 1833 Gautier had hardly travelled beyond the rural environs of Paris, as he had been at witty pains to point out in his preface; but he was to continue to dwell on domestic intimacy, on the room and its décor as an image of its occupant and as a snug capsule for comfortable, trouble-free and infinite mental travel, even after his momentous journey to Spain in 1840 had fully awakened his insatiable need for physical displacement. René Jasinski has compared the long poem *Albertus* to a Romantic gallery; from the Impasse du Doyenné onwards, Gautier's interiors, in real life as in his fiction, are filled with artefacts that are endowed with the power to transport, with pictures, tapestries, suits of armour, antique furniture, or carpets; descriptions of imaginary décor are to be found in the early story *La Cafetière*, in *Le Capitaine Fracasse*, and in the stories *Militona*, *Jean et Jeanette*, and *Avatar*, for example. Such decorative schemes, along with those that feature in Balzac's novels and biography and along with the earlier Orientalist décor invented by Hugo (now to be seen in his house in the place des Vosges), belong to a distinguished family of dandified interiors which includes Baudelaire's rooms in the Hôtel Lauzun and Edmond de Goncourt's *Maison d'un artiste*, and whose final overbred progeny were the hermetic creations of Comte Robert de Montesquiou-Fezensac and of Huysmans's Des Esseintes. If Gautier filled his home with exotica from his travels, souvenirs from the real world, his writing, especially passages like those quoted above, but above all his writing on art, prepares the ground for Des Esseintes's total glorification of surrogate experience, for that view of décor as experience itself that absolved the hero of *A Rebours*, in the English bar in the rue d'Amsterdam, of the need to carry out his projected journey to London.

Just as *La Presse* was bringing outside experience into the middle-class home, so were artists under Louis-Philippe beginning to respond to this new social demand for apartment-sized illusion. Art, like information and literature, was democratizing itself. There were the large-scale, popular, and dramatic historical fantasies of Delaroche, and Vernet's massive crowd-pulling battle panoramas; but more significantly, there was also a growing market for oil-painting on a smaller scale and intended for private ownership. From the beginning of Gautier's writing career, landscape painting devoid of historical or mythical allusion and of intimate, unhistorical proportion had established itself as a distinct genre in the Salons, and as vogues for seventeenth-century Dutch and eighteenth-century French painting made themselves felt, artists responded with small-scale domestic, rural, and historical genre scenes (this market was soon to be dominated by the expensive works of Meissonier), and with intimate and carefree visions of aristocratic idylls, of *bonheur* and *far niente* (Winterhalter and later Diaz were the exemplary masters here). Gautier did not fail to remark upon this need to create art for the private living-room; huge canvases are too big for the restricted and precious space of modern urban apartments, he commented in the opening lines of his *Salon of 1842* for *Le Cabinet de l'amateur et de l'antiquaire* (a review with a title to appeal to the middle-class connoisseur: it might almost have appeared in one of Meissonier's book-lined studies).[23] In an article on 'L'Art en miniature' in *La Presse* in 1839 he described the 'Lilliputian statues' contained in his own room: female figures by Pradier and Châtillon and a larger-than-life Turk's head, among other things.[24] At the Salon of 1848 he once more noted the impracticalities and redundancy of large-scale history painting, remarking that pictures of such size were anachronistic and impractical, unless destined for a particular site.[25] He distinguished two great technical divisions in painting: monumental painting, commissioned work in the grand style which should be executed on the walls of the building to be decorated; and easel painting, which was of manageable size and was broadly characterized by its fantasy and caprice, its high finish, its *élan* and originality. Contemporary easel painting is summed up with the telling epithet: 'it is painting for painting's sake, art for art's sake'.

With his hyperbolic, satirically complex, but none the less openly stated emphasis on the home as a sanctuary for imaginative and illusionary experience, in direct opposition to any confrontation with the uncomfortable and inconvenient real world, Gautier reflected and demonstrated his deep and intuitive collusion with the underlying values of *La Presse*. But it was above all with his view of the work of art designed to take its place in a domestic context, as a means by which the spectator might be transported to different, unfamiliar, and ultimately better worlds, that he can truly be seen to subscribe to and satisfy that need for illusion and second-hand experience in the home which *La Presse* had so successfully set out to meet. Every picture or sculpture that was successful for Gautier was a trip into an alternative nature; to say he had been 'transported' was his commonest expression of critical pleasure. 'You feel you have been transported into an unheard-of, impossible yet somehow real world' he wrote of Goya's *Caprichos* in *La Presse* in 1838;[26] 'You feel you have been transported into an alternative nature', had been his reaction to Decamps's *Paysage turc* at the Salon of 1833,[27] and to Decamps's world the following year: 'You feel you have been transported . . . into a world of carnage and destruction'.[28] Boulanger, with his *Enfant prodigue* at the Salon of 1838, offered a staircase by which Gautier could climb away from his troubles: 'this staircase . . . makes you want to step into the picture, to put your hand on the banister and climb two at a time . . . it looks as if it can only lead to pleasure';[29] Adolphe Leleux at the Salon of 1845 painted ground Gautier could walk on, landscapes he could feel himself physically entering.[30] Decamps, who of all artists possessed 'the secret of genius', provided some of Gautier's most convincing escapist experiences. 'It is like a window opening on to an unknown land, bathed in light', he had written of a Decamps at the Salon of 1839; 'you are transported a thousand leagues and three thousand years away from reality.'[31]

Pictures were escape; they were aids to larger visionary experience than nature on her own could offer. Like the unseen top of Boulanger's staircase, they promised to be the realizations of dreams. A poem inspired by the landscape painters Bertin, Aligny, and Corot, which took the place of a Salon article for *La Presse* in 1839, sums up the views that linked Gautier to his readers and to their need for instant illusion.[32] First he wins the identification of the tedium-bound bourgeois by proclaiming himself to be a similarly bored slave of his profession:

> . . . nous, hommes de critique,
> Qui, le collier au cou comme l'esclave antique,
> Sans trêve et sans repos, dans le moulin banal,
> Tournons aveuglément la meule du journal;

('. . . we critics, collars around our necks like the slaves of antiquity, who, in the common mill, blindly and unceasingly turn the grindstone of journalism;')

But thanks to the landscape painters, we are reminded of other possibilities; through art, the urban interior is made to drop its threats of claustrophobia, and is transformed into a vehicle for journeys, a theatre for visionary experience:

> Sans sortir, avec vous nous faisons des voyages,
> Nous errons, à Paris, dans mille paysages;
> . . .
> Vos tableaux, faisant une trouée au mur
> Sont pour nous comme autant de fenêtres ouvertes
> Par où nous regardons les grandes plaines vertes,
> . . .
> Les horizons sans borne et le ciel infini
> . . .

('Without going out of doors we go on journeys with you, wandering, while yet in Paris, through a thousand landscapes . . . Your pictures, making holes in the wall, are like so many open windows for us, through which we can look out over the great, green plains . . . the limitless horizons and the infinite sky . . .')

But here we are back in Paris,

> Ne voyant plus au lieu de ces beaux horizons
> Que des angles de mur ou des toits de maisons
> . . . .

('Seeing only roof tops and the corners of houses instead of those fine views . . .')

This desire for escape from drabness and monotony and from the confusion and conflicts of real life, provided by pictures no larger than the windows of modern town-dwellings but which offer more tantalizing views, is the essence of Gautier's rapport with *La Presse*'s readers. Here he is a true reflector of broad popular needs. Yet he remains a self-conscious 'artist'; he is no mere bored journalist, but glorifies and hyperbolizes himself into a slave from pagan antiquity, the collar around his neck, as if he were himself a figment of some Michelangelesque imagination. As such, he gives the popular needs that he reflects the stamp of cultural approval. He imbues them with idealism, and moulds them into an aesthetic. His views are rooted in and inseparable from that common need for instant second-hand experience among the domesticated and self-confident bourgeoisie, to which *La Presse* was a response. They are the product not only of the Romantic idealist, in love with the distant and colourful in time and space, but also of a journalist who shares, spontaneously reflects and fulfils the needs of his public.

(c) RAPPORT WITH READERS

La Presse established Gautier as a household name. It was an instant and popular guide to world events, and as its regular art critic, Gautier performed the task of a travel guide around the Salons. His writing manifests the same variety and sharpness of juxtaposition, and he makes similar claims to impartiality as his newspaper. The later experienced world-traveller is from the beginning of his career an experienced traveller from inside a self-contained world of art, and description, evocation, and transcription remain the basic fulfilments of his role as a journalist, as of his role as a real travel writer. The tone in which *La Presse* addressed itself to its readers has been encapsulated in the phrase 'I inform and at the same time instruct you'; Gautier's first duty as an art critic was to be informative, simply to describe what was there. Reproductions of works of contemporary art were of course not widely available; the topographical, descriptive style of Gautier's Salon reviews provided second-hand experience of contemporary art even to those provincials, the subscribers to *La Presse*'s *Édition des départements*, who might not see the exhibitions at all.

Description, verbal attention to visible facts, was an affirmation of Gautier's fundamental faith in the articulacy of the visible world; he believed, as he put it in 1837, in the communicative power of 'the physiognomy of things',[33] in vision as the key to all true knowledge. Where Delacroix, as Gautier's model Romantic, transcribed the inner visions of his microcosm, Gautier was concerned with transcribing his experience of the visible world; yet for all his attention to the outside 'physiognomy of things', Gautier is no more impersonal than Delacroix. He is above all a subjective guide. There was no contradiction here with his desire to be impartial; his impartiality was that of the Romantic artist he always considered himself to be, a poet rather than a schoolmaster, who referred for selective judgement to no outside doctrine, but only to his own sensual and emotional responses. And there was no refuting the logic of his early challenge: 'What would you think . . . . of a host who took you straight to the latrines?' Thus he fulfilled the second of the unspoken functions that have been ascribed to *La Presse* in the phrase 'I inform and at the same time instruct you'. He was informative because he dwelt on the physical facts before him and contained them in his ever adaptable prose; he was instructive simply in what he chose to dwell upon, and in his insistence on the subjective quality of his responses. Writing as an artist, he guaranteed his success as a journalist; in his criticism up to 1848 he is pragmatic, direct, sensual, impassioned, contradictory, elusive, and hostile to anything that might blur his perception of 'the physiognomy of things'. He provided his readers with an unselfconscious, week-by-week live performance.

An introductory article to the *Salon of 1837*,[34] entitled 'Topographie du Salon', demonstrates the spirit in which Gautier embarked upon his task. It carried all compromise and confusion before it with the force of its hyperbole. He compelled his readers to take note of 'the physiognomy of things'; he encouraged them to share the immediacy and intimacy of his sense impressions. The spectacle was, as he had predicted from past form, indeed confusing. 'Scumbled surfaces sparkle like mirrors, dazzling highlights emit sparks as you pass, freshly gilded frames flash to left and right, an alcoholic vapour from varnishes and oils which are hardly yet dry and are melting in the heat permeates the whole hall, and you are overcome with a dull vertigo which prevents you from discerning much of anything in this painted confusion of figures and costumes from every age and every land.' He had little objection to drunkenness, but had he not promised himself 'neither torrents nor cataracts', clarity, well-defined and contrasting sensual experiences? Thus his first point was to insist that pictures should be hung in some order, by genre or according to their lightness or darkness. As it was, they were placed at random, and the *livret* did not say where particular paintings were to be found; here Gautier discerned his professional role. 'Taking a turn around the Salon is thus a real voyage of discovery, as fraught with risks as a trip to the North Pole': his art critic's job in 1837 was as exciting as O'Neddy had said the inner life was, 'as adventurous . . . as the life of Arab tribes in their wildernesses'. An inhabitant of this unfamiliar world, Gautier was preparing 'a kind of . . . itinerary' for his disoriented readers, 'which will enable them to steer clear of all the perils of this pictorial voyage'. The perils were apparent from embarkation; he packed his public straight off to Delacroix, Boulanger, Roqueplan, Scheffer, Winterhalter, Aligny, Corot, and Marilhat, preserving it from Montvoisin, Caminade, Franquelin, Roëhn, Destouches, Dubufe, and Biard. Don't look up at the Abel de Pujol ceiling, he cautioned; look at the architecture instead, if you're an architect; if not, you needn't bother . . . the article continues in this cursory, peripatetic vein. At last we've finished the long gallery, he sums up some hundreds of words later; let's sit down and get our breath back . . .

The article is a reconnaissance with the odd skirmish; it is conducted by an expert, a virtuoso guide, and boyish wit. Its confidentially direct tone suggests that the guide really does have his readers' best interests at heart (we shall have frequent occasion over the next thirty-five years to heave a sigh of relief and slip away with the long-suffering critic to smoke a cigar in the deserted sculpture gallery); with Delacroix and Ingres as signposts, Gautier will continue thus to present *La Presse*'s bourgeois subscribers with an annual travelogue. 'Do us a feuilleton!' Feydeau would ask him at the literary gatherings of the Second Empire; his Salon articles for *La Presse* have the charm of fluent, anecdotal, and informed conversation. His pragmatic and entertaining tours were intended to give his readers an inside view, privileged glimpses into the unfamiliar and often esoteric world of art, brought to them, like other new insights and informative material, by their daily *Presse*. In those journalistic live performances, Théophile the facile young virtuoso of the feuilleton offered what amounted to pleasant courses in instant connoisseurship, coining epithets, drawing distinctions, and making wittily paradoxical characterizations that were no doubt destined to find their marks over Parisian dinner-tables or in provincial drawing-rooms.[35] John Martin, for instance, is 'the poet of immensity', suffering 'the nightmare of the infinite';[36] Ary Scheffer paints 'the poetry of consumption':[37] he is 'the Novalis of painting', while Corot is a 'Theocritus in paint';[38] Gavarni is a 'painter-reporter', 'like a mushroom sprouting from the cracks in the Parisian streets'.[39] Gautier can evoke and contain a work's atmosphere in a few lines; one of Goya's *Caprichos*, for example, inspires in him 'the same disgust as when you tread on the soft belly of a toad'.[40]

His readers become acquainted with the specialist language of the studio in the same way they would if they were overhearing Gautier talking to his artist friends. He is the witty and provocative Jeune-France and carefree gipsy of the Impasse du Doyenné, throwing out hyperbolic challenges. 'There have only been about ten or twelve first-class sculptors since the beginning of the world, counting God and Prometheus', he revealed in a very early article for *La Presse*;[41] Soufflot is described as 'the creator of that unsuccessful spongecake they call the Panthéon'.[42] He amuses the bourgeois by remaining truculently anti-bourgeois: 'A vast crowd partly composed of bourgeois and national guardsmen looking for their portraits' congested the Louvre on the opening day of the Salon of 1838,[43] which he would explore for the benefit of these same bourgeois; the previous year the mediocrity of certain historical landscape paintings was associated with the staidest bourgeois qualities: 'your trees', he wrote directly to the artists concerned, high-handedly talking over the heads of his readers, 'look like . . . national guardsmen's plumes which have done ten years' service'.[44] He could be mercilessly mocking and dismissive in his early criticism of artists; of Bridoux's drawing, exhibited among other efforts by students from the school in Rome in 1836,

Gautier wrote that a child could do better. 'Infinitely better drawings are used every day to light studio stoves.' The sculptures, meanwhile, were 'beyond the bounds of the ridiculous and the mediocre'.[45] The young Simart's bas-relief, for example, had one fault: 'that of existing'. In 1838 Gautier resolved to take a more lenient attitude; students should not be criticized as masters, genius grows in silence, and a word out of place can ruin it; but since we are obliged to criticize: 'nothing could possibly be worse than this first bas-relief. Everything about it is awkward, flabby, incorrect, and unpleasant'.[46]

If he grew gradually mellower and more tolerant, less wittily damning in his criticism and less eager to outrage, he maintained his humour and sense of irony, and this contributed much to the tone and no doubt to the success of his art-critical contribution to *La Presse* up to 1848; above all, humour and irony enabled him to fulfil his function as a journalist who was obliged to give comprehensive coverage to the art of the Salons, while at the same time allowing him to stand aloof, to maintain a private identity in the face of art with which he could not whole-heartedly identify and yet which was not so offensive as to merit serious criticism. 'With me, you've got to read between the lines', he was to tell Saint-Victor, who told the Goncourts, in 1868;[47] armed with this general proviso, the perceptive reader might, for instance, have been prepared to expect no pictorial miracles of Adrien Guignet's *Le Gaulois* having read Gautier's summary of the picture in 1847. It represents, we learn, a pre-Christian Parisian crossing the Place Royale. 'This, moreover, is how we would still be today if Julius Caesar had not conquered the Gauls. We also like the forest and the landscape.'[48] At worst, this is the stuff of fatuous, pen-pushing journalism. 'Oh sweet idleness! Oh tender words spoken beneath the arbours! Oh sweet declarations! Oh long kisses beneath the silvery moon! Oh passion! Oh youth! This canvas makes you think of all that.'[49] If this evocation of Baron's *Soirée d'été* is ironical in intention, the irony is so subtle as to disappear from view. At best, this game of ambivalent meanings enables Gautier to be tantalizingly elusive. 'There is also a play at the Palais-Royal which we dare not review in case some harm should come to us', he wrote in a theatre feuilleton in 1841;[50] 'we are speaking of *Le Jettator*. We tremble to write this terrible word; even the little coral hand in the shape of a pair of horns and the holy medallions which are hanging around our neck scarcely reassure us, for we ourselves have been pursued by a *jettatura* of the most terrible kind, which has been the cause of as many disasters in Paris as the cholera itself. We admire the courage of the authors, and shall not emulate it.' There is no more; other feelings Gautier might have had about the production are not to be found outside this pert and isolated paragraph. Is it a hyperbolic trick to avoid discussing a tedious play, while giving it routine publicity and perhaps implying its exaggerated sensationalism? At the same time, we know that his superstition was deep and genuine, that he did indeed wear charms and religious medals around his neck, and through quasi-mystical belief in the power of visual form, trust in the power of their configurations: the passage could thus also be read with perfect candour.

Gautier is not to be pinned down, and this is how he confirmed his identity as an artist, as one emancipated from the demands of reason and consistency. His irony and elusiveness were further reflections and tacit acknowledgements of the complexity of the world of art and of the irrationality of his responses to it; as art's representative, Gautier was to embody its irrational qualities. This elusiveness, a natural product of his spontaneity and pragmatism, was an essential part of his appeal as a journalist; by casting a tantalizing cloak of mystery and awe around some of his opinions, and by presenting himself as a visitor from the magical and mysterious world of art, Gautier the verbal alchemist was sure to maintain his readers' interest and curiosity. He never gave too much away; indeed, early in his career he did all that he could to spread positive mystification. The satirical complexity of *Les Jeunes-France* has been hinted at; a series of articles for the *Figaro* in 1837, 'Soirées d'artistes', 'Excès d'artistes', and 'Chambres d'artistes', is another satire on Bohemia that also contains strong elements of self-parody. Here Gautier attempts to elude identification even as an 'artist', let alone as a member of any other social category. 'The hero of the novel you are reading is an artist suffering artists' sufferings, which are recounted by another artist in the most artistic way possible.' 'The grocer no longer exists. It is the artist who has killed him', begins the satire; it ends with the plea: 'Lord, Lord, give me back my grocers!'[51]

Yet for all their frequent humour and irony, Gautier's articles for *La Presse* finally treat art and artists with unquestioning seriousness. In that view of the artistic personality which we have seen emerge from Gautier's writing, the artist is presented as a superior being; as an 'organisation d'élite', he is always a figure to be looked up to. The artist is sublimely indifferent to the world: hence his superiority. This, and the separateness and impartiality of art itself, were articles of faith which were fundamental to Gautier's Romanticism, to the whole doctrine of *l'art pour l'art*, and were consistently stressed, by direct or indirect means, from his earliest writings onwards. His Salons were travelogues which described the exhibitions as if they were foreign lands; paintings were different worlds, alternatives to everyday life; his irony, elusiveness, and mystifications presented even the critic himself as a separate being.

Separateness and impartiality were also, of course, qualities prized by Girardin: the separateness of the daily news from immediate experience, and the impartiality of the editor. On a certain level, Gautier's idealism itself was as much a reflection, albeit a less conscious one, of a new social ethos, as was the more calculatingly responsive newspaper in whose columns he set about propagating his ideals; it similarly met the need of a middle-class audience for a culture that was self-contained, self-defining, and above politics, apparently outside the influence of any political coterie. '*L'art pour l'art*', it has been further observed, was 'partly the expression of the division of labour which advances hand in hand with industrialization';[52] Gautier's *l'art pour l'art* indeed presents art as a wholly separate, specialized activity, the superior one, of course, but otherwise just as specialized as most other pursuits in a growing, metropolitan society. Where the artist was concerned, what Gautier was offering his readers was the equivalent of a long and sophisticated *physiologie*. Giving instant and exclusive insights into the separate world of art, Gautier came to resemble Vigny's 'flatterer . . . who tells any number of stories', providing his audience with the reassuring feeling that it was gaining something like inside knowledge. On such grounds *l'art pour l'art*, so recently a movement of rebelliously youthful 'outsiders', was assimilated by the public of the 1830s, and Gautier's critical writing in *La Presse* met with its obvious and rapid success.

But if Gautier's *l'art pour l'art* was a reflection and satisfaction of new societal needs, it was only this in part. Born out of the Petit Cénacle and Gautier's Romantic youth, it remained first and foremost a rebellion, part of a radical movement with a genuine and unprecedently passionate faith in the redeeming and liberating power of art. The hide-and-seek tone with which Gautier established his winning and deep-rooted rapport with his readers, and the idea of chaperoned but perilous family excursions to the beauty spots of art, could thus readily be dropped, as more immediately serious matters arose; in their place came direct and impassioned polemic, and the broadcast to his age of messages that were very much Gautier's own.

(d) CAMPAIGNING ROMANTIC

A fashionable and successful young man in the mid-1830s, Gautier in his twenties was self-consciously modern. He was 'modern' in a double meaning of the word which his generation was possibly the first to establish, and which we have inherited: modern as being both profoundly, if not actively collusive with contemporary social changes and values, as well as being self-consciously rebellious against much in contemporary life. Gautier's undoubted sense of his own modernity was compounded of these two apparently contradictory aspects.

Fresh from the experience of a carefree milieu that saw itself as an exclusively 'artistic' island in a sea of squalid and mundane concerns, he had been blessed with an idea of what could be; he was as prepared to be optimistic about the possibility of a fuller realization of his ideals as he was uncompromisingly 'artistic' in their defence against threats of repression, misunderstanding, and compromise. Such threats came less from the relatively easy-going bourgeois, than from the guardians of art as it had been, who were more despotic in the exercise of their judgements. The 'grisâtre' had reappeared as a target in the shape of the Salon jury; a new Renaissance would truly have begun, 'if it were not for the debris of the older generation blocking the way for the younger one'. The jury had refused Delacroix, Rousseau, and Préault, among others. 'This is sheer madness . . . what do you know about art, mes chers Seigneurs?' Gautier demanded. 'Not accepting your judgement, we shall review the pictures and statues refused by you as if they were in the Salon where they should be, and hung in the best places.' So he mounted, in 1839, a verbal Salon des refusés, celebrating the rich inventory of an imaginary Impasse du Doyenné.[53]

It was the same story in 1840. The landscapist Cabat was rejected, Gautier was sorry to announce,[54] and Delacroix's *Trajan* was only finally accepted by a majority vote of one. Gigoux and Chassériau were among promising younger artists refused, and so, as usual, was Rousseau. Préault's entire entry was rejected, along with works by the sculptors Foyatier, Etex, and the Dantans senior and junior. 'When will there be an end to this scandalous state of affairs? . . . let there be room for everybody.' His *Salon of 1845* opened with an apology: 'It is boring to keep saying the same thing, but since things are still the same, the same things still need to be said'.[55] (Baudelaire too noted that to inveigh against the Salon jury had become a commonplace, and in the interests of maintaining his cool independence, resolved that his criticism would not echo the general clamour.[56]) Delacroix was once more among those refused; in the face of such an 'inane and shameful action', Gautier's passionate identification with the artist knew no bounds. 'Don't you breathe the same air as we do?' he belaboured the jury; when Delacroix sends a painting to the Salon, 'it is because there is something in that painting. What satisfies him may certainly satisfy you. Don't be more watchful over his glory than he is himself'.

The usual complaints, and apologies for the monotony of his polemic, preceded the Salons of 1846 and 1847;[57] and the monotony of his complaints, Gautier would have agreed, seemed to be growing in proportion to a level of tedium and

mediocrity in the Salons themselves. Such was the effect of
the jury's repression of 'the ardent, studious younger
generation',[58] of 'gerontocracy trying to suppress youth'. If
Delacroix is too dangerously Romantic, Gautier asked the
jury in 1845, what about sober and severe Chassériau?
'Passion shocks you, you don't like style . . . What does
please you? Alas, that which meets with so much success these
days: mediocrity.'[59] In 1837 and 1839 mediocrity had
concentrated and readily identified itself in the works of
Delaroche, Biard, and Pigal; by 1845 it had become a more
diffuse threat. 'Criticism's task is difficult this year. If there
are a few works which are out of the ordinary, there is a sum
total of extreme talent. Anyone who did a little better than
everyone elso would really have done very well indeed.'[60]
Ruskin, who happened to be passing through Paris in April
1845 and managed to catch a disinterested glimpse of the
Salon, made similar observations on its general tenor:

> . . . my first impression was, of immense *pains taken*, and immense
> knowledge possessed, and all coming short of a good end, for want
> of innate purity of feeling . . . There is much that is execrable,
> much that is coarse, vulgar and wrong, but comparatively little of
> what is weak. The labour is enormous. Five or six complete
> panoramas of battles, ten or twenty yards long, every figure painted
> in with the greatest possible care. Shipwrecks with elaborated
> crowds of five hundred men, and forest pieces with all the leaves put
> on numerically . . .[61]

It was a Salon in which, as Gautier informed his out-of-town
readers, almost all the works on show were battle or religious
pictures;[62] faced with the neat and polished execution of
Vernet's massive *Prise de la Smala* (bigger than Veronese's
Marriage at Cana), Gautier could not begrudge the picture's
popular success, but only wished it would not distract
attention from more serious art. It lacked the qualities that
Gautier expected to find in a battle picture: 'We would like it
to have been dripping with gold and precious stones, with
costumes of shining velvet, strange, barbarous weapons,
maddened chargers steaming with sweat, their pupils and
nostrils full of fire . . . naked Negroes fighting tooth and
nail'[63]—qualities of Romantic bizarrerie and Oriental

savagery. The religious pictures, he remarked,[64] generally lacked only one thing: 'religious sentiment'. The previous year he had complained of the same emotional and sensual poverty; Delacroix, Scheffer, Decamps, Roqueplan, Meissonier, and others had followed the example of Ingres by refusing to exhibit, in protest at the harshness of the jury, and Gautier found little in what remained to console him for this desertion of the cause of Art. He sensed that everyone was on his best behaviour, noting that there was no bright colour, owing to the misused influence of Ingres, and that there were no nudes, due to fashionable neo-Christian ideas and 'English cant'; a great deal of technical competence was evident, but so were a lack of imagination and a monotony in the choice of subjects.[65] His similar general summary of the Salon of 1840 has already been heard: 'It is all perfectly beautiful and perfectly boring . . . we have said that these canvases lack genius: they also lack faults'.[66]

(e) WHAT COULD BE

This negative praise in 1840 was directly complementary to his enthusiasm for Delacroix's *La Justice de Trajan*; in all his criticism of bland mediocrity and in all his invective against the 'old men', 'mastodons', and 'gerontocracy' of the Salon juries, he was armed with an idea of the power of liberated genius, of the possibility of a continuing artistic revolution latent in the energies of youth. The younger generation was still Gautier's own generation; on its behalf he directed his efforts at winning the sympathy and understanding of his readers. Yet his task as a critic was as much to instil a greater receptivity to sensual enjoyment in the *épiciers* as it was to represent to them the artists who provided its visual key. The Romantic Renaissance which fired the young Gautier's enthusiasm was to permeate the whole of society, finding visual manifestation in every private and public artefact. For this revolution to take place, artists needed enlightened support and patronage from the public just as, in principle, they should not be ashamed of descending from their ivory towers to transform objects of everyday usage.

At the beginning of his *Salon of 1841* for *La Revue de Paris* he remarked upon the negative aspect of this separation between artist and the rest: 'In the French school we are presented with the strange phenomenon of an art developing under its own impetus and without a public, except that of artists themselves'.[67] Hence his efforts to make the public see artists' problems from an artist's point of view. In his *Salon of 1847*, for instance, he explained the sculptor's financial and physical hardships in full detail, from the expense of materials and studio space to the very blisters on his hands and sweat on his face; the very gratuitousness of the effort involved contributed to make sculpture 'the supreme art form'.[68] In his invective against the Salon jury in 1845 he made another typical appeal for public identification and collaboration.[69] Unlike other arts, he pointed out, painting does not have the whole year and the whole town with which to commend itself to the public; the Salon is the artist's only outlet. Artists moreover need 'instruction from the crowd'; the bourgeois with his 'rough and ready common sense' can provide as valuable a lesson as the theorist. With a sensitive and perceptive public, and free entry to the Salons, true quality will emerge spontaneously, unconstrained youthful talent will find its natural application; pictures of mixed merit hung together will tacitly criticize each other. This argument was to be extended to breaking point at the Salon of 1848.

If Gautier finally seems to have been unable wholly to convince himself on the subject, his fundamental opinion remains: artists learn from enlightened public response to their work and should remain open to it, just as Romantic genius, as represented by Delacroix, mixed in the turmoil of modern life and was touched by its fevers. Reciprocally, artists are educators of public taste and sensitivity, custodians of everything that touches on the quality of everyday visual experience. They should take matters in hand, Gautier wrote in *La Presse* in 1837 in an article entitled 'Du Costume moderne'[70] deploring the impracticalities of the stove-pipe hat, the low-cut waistcoat, and the stiff collar, and the ridiculous figure cut by the modern-dress Napoleon on top of his new column, 'a gigantic walking-stick topped with a grotesque'. The ideal that artists should pursue to improve all this was, as ever, to be found in the Renaissance; the idea of a new Renaissance and how to achieve it had been treated with a seriousness that went beyond 'jeune rapin' 's enthusiasm for picturesque trappings, in two very early articles for *La Presse* in 1836: 'De l'application de l'art à la vie usuelle' and 'Applications de l'art'.[71]

The first of these two articles puts the notion of genius, of the 'organisation d'élite', into some perspective; it confirms that Gautier's conception of the artist during this highly idealistic period was not always such an exclusive one as it may sometimes seem. Art was a separate and distinct activity; it nevertheless belonged within a broader vision of things, and if the artistic genius was made to occupy the elevated centre of this vision, this was very different to having him inevitably consigned to Sainte-Beuve's ivory tower. Artists, Gautier wrote, were indeed too willing to shut themselves away in some 'ideal abstraction', and this was the result of a fallacious attitude separating bourgeois from poet. The usual bourgeois attitude to the poet, the journalist generalized, consisted in an idea of 'some temperamental, dreaming creature who does nothing except on inspiration from on high'—an idea which elsewhere, of course, Gautier did little to discourage. The bourgeois, he had to admit, did not care much for art: 'that passionate love of perfection which characterizes members of the élite is unknown to him'. But the bourgeois would become more sensitive if his environment became more 'artistic'; then, Gautier concluded, the new Renaissance would truly begin.

The article which follows—'Applications de l'art'—contains theoretical and practical suggestions for a modern domestic architecture. All useful and reasonable things have been with us since the beginning of the world, Gautier grandly states; it would be absurd to try to invent a new architecture. Gothic, Greek, and Roman are discussed for their merits and defects, but the answer is a flexible, vernacular French Renaissance style—the architectural equivalent to the language of Villon and Rabelais and Gautier's other pet 'grotesques'. A detailed verbal sketch of a three-storey dwelling completes the article; Gautier's model house is an integrated scheme of sculptural motifs, painted walls and ceilings, and Renaissance-style furniture. Here, he wrote, was enough to keep two sculptors in work for a year.

If the fifteenth- and sixteenth-century Renaissance was to provide its forms, Gautier's dream of a new Renaissance was of course founded in a rose-tinted view of antiquity, a time when 'art did not scorn to come down to an everyday level'.[72] Yet in the nineteenth century 'artists think they would be demeaning themselves if they descended to the practical'. There were of course exceptions to this rule; one was Ziegler, who, in 1842, had just opened a potter's establishment. Here was a contemporary artist who had understood that an important part of his mission was to 'impart to man-made objects a beauty of form which will bring them into harmony with the phenomena of natural creation'. Ziegler felt 'those vague filiations of ideas which link art to nature'; his vases echoed the shapes of fruits, birds and open flowers. 'It takes more than . . . a common workman to grasp these distant connections, these vague similarities . . . it takes all the musing of a poet and an artist in love with line.' Where Ruskin promised to make artists out of workmen, Gautier's artistically integrated society was to be created by artists. It took the uncommon sensibility of an 'organisation d'élite', after all, to seize that elusive tissue of correspondences out of which art was born; to create forms like those of Ziegler's vases, to ennoble and harmonize objects of everyday utility, required a special, exclusively artistic receptivity to nature, for 'every form that does not have its model in nature . . . lacks consistency and charm'.

Ruskin would have endorsed this last view; but Gautier's ideas on the place of art and artists in society never achieve, finally, the depth and comprehensiveness of Ruskin's. In all his broadest idealism, in his most practical visions of a new Renaissance, he remains an artist himself, caught up in his own immediate sensations; for all the passion of the arguments supporting it, Gautier's new Renaissance, with its happily façade-chiselling sculptors and the patronage of its enlightened and hedonistic general public, remains a personal and poetic dream. His final evocations of Ziegler's vases read less as the work of an educator of public awareness, than as the vague ruminations of a sensitive and cultured man of leisure; Gautier the poet can never resist displaying the fruits of his own exquisite sense of correspondences. One vase calls up 'the vague idea of a faun or a wood-nymph putting its head through the foliage'; another reminds him of 'a wild flower . . . embellishing an antique urn in an Etruscan tomb with its leaves'.

In his criticism up to 1848 Gautier might have defined his role as that of a mediator between artist and bourgeois in the cause of a new visual 'quality of life', of an artistic utopia based on the experience of his Romantic youth, had he been less eager to be carried away by the experience of the moment and less quixotic, less immediate in his sensual reactions. For all his broad, and largely consistent statements of ideological yearning, his sympathies always came to rest, sooner or later, in individual works of art, and were temporarily focused and absorbed in them; his sense of what could be, founded in his immediate experience, was tempered by what stood immediately before him, and tended to adjust itself to it. Such immediacy and frankness of response were, after all, qualities he generally missed in the art of the Constitutional Monarchy, and for which he tirelessly pleaded.

(f) INSTINCT

'Properly speaking, there is no such thing as a subject in painting, only a thousand different ways of feeling',[73] Gautier wrote at the Salon of 1847, where, thanks to Mme de Girardin's new tragedy *Judith*, which had created a vogue for biblical 'Judith' subjects, he was able to observe that no two artists painted the same subject in the same way. The previous year, in his *Salon of 1846*, Baudelaire had made a similar statement: 'Romanticism does not exactly consist in choice of subjects nor in the faithful reproduction of appearances, but in a way of feeling'.[74] Both statements have their roots in Stendhal's formulation, quoted by Baudelaire a few lines later: 'There are as many kinds of beauty as there are habitual ways of seeking happiness'. For all their common ground in Stendhal's straightforward and liberating insistence on following the dictates of feeling, on beauty as emotional truth, Baudelaire and Gautier, as art critics during the latter years of the Constitutional Monarchy, offer significantly divergent visions of the future.

Baudelaire did not belong to the generation of 1830. New to the critical scene in 1845 and writing on his own initiative, outside the framework of the professional newspaper, he takes a distant and well-measured stance ('the newspapers would not dare to print what we have to say. Are we then going to be very cruel and insolent? No, the contrary: impartial'),[75] in an attempt at redefining Romanticism from scratch. His 'manière de sentir' is a feeling exclusive to the age, for, as he goes on to say in the *Salon of 1846*, Romanticism consists in 'a conception analogous to the moral climate of the century'.[76] His conclusions are presented in sentences which have the pristine clarity of equations. He came away from the Salons of the 1840s with the same impressions as Gautier and Ruskin: 'let us confirm the fact that everyone is painting better and better, which is a terrible pity in our opinion; but as for inventiveness, ideas, and temperament, there is no more of that than before',[77] he wrote in 1845, and in 1846 of 'this interminable Salon, within which differences are less discernible than ever and in which everyone can paint and draw a little, but not enough even to deserve classification'.[78] What he demanded to supersede this uncertainty, fatuous technical facility and mediocrity was dictated by reasoning based upon his subjective apprehensions (he was 'reasonable and impassioned');[79] it was 'the advent of the *new*'. 'To the wind that will blow tomorrow, no one is turning an ear; yet the heroism of *modern life* surrounds and is crowding in upon us. We suffocate enough on our true feelings to be able to recognize them.'[80] He demanded a brand-new painter 'who will be able to wrest away from contemporary life its epic side, and make us see and understand . . . how great and poetic we are in our cravats and patent-leather boots'. Baudelaire's Romantic future was to be a new and apt painting that would echo and correspond to, his experience of the present, and whose emotional necessity was susceptible to dialectical demonstration.

Gautier's 'thousand ways of feeling' are the product of the Romanticism of the Petit Cénacle, of that yearning for an ever greater plenitude of experience that had underlain its passion for the *mot propre*, for the distant and unfamiliar, for the violent, the macabre, and the ecstatic. Gautier was not intent, in his *Salon of 1847*, on working out any new critical formulation; his comment about 'ways of feeling' was made purely apropos of different treatments of the same 'Judith' subject, one by Ziegler and another by Horace Vernet. In 1845 Vernet had driven Gautier to plead for 'naked Negroes fighting tooth and nail'; in 1847 Gautier underwent similar reactions. For an atrocity picture, Vernet's *Judith* was not atrocious enough by half: 'rip open breasts with both hands, unleash cascades of entrails and let blood flow in streams . . . paint cut-off heads with their white vertebrae . . . just get on and be violent, be ferocious and terrible, overcome your disgust with fear . . . but for God's sake no mealy-mouthed horror, no butchery for the sweet of tooth, no clots of blood made of currant jelly. The executioner should appreciate your decapitations!'[81] The passage is characteristic of Gautier's response to that mediocrity, eclecticism, and lack of feeling and conviction which he had not been alone in discerning; it demands direct confrontation with the *mot propre*—no clichés, no euphemisms, real blood instead of redcurrant jelly—and it does this with schoolboy relish; it dwells upon the imagery of violence as a means to liberation from polite and stultifying constraint, just as Victor Hugo and his band of young supporters had used the hyperbolized violence of the first night of *Hernani* as a focus and an image of the Romantic struggle in 1830. Where Baudelaire contemplated the mediocrity before him and was able to perceive the need for a celebration of the totally new, Gautier faced with the same mediocrity turned back to the ideals of the early 1830s, which he saw being prostituted in the hands of men like Vernet and countless successful imitators. His vision of the future was a continuing cultivation of 'ways of feeling', an ever expanding plenitude of convincingly expressed experience; and the key to this future, the liberating magic word, remained Instinct, to whose demands Gautier exhorted artists to bend with all the violence and passion that he could muster.

'Be violent and absolute! Eclecticism may be good for philosophy, but it is fatal where art is concerned. Have the courage of your talent . . . and if you were a Romantic in 1828 or 1830, carry on being a Romantic.'[82] Gautier was

witnessing in 1844 the sad decline of his old comrade-in-arms
Eugène Devéria, who provided other painters with a lesson:
don't repudiate your youthful instincts; don't be ashamed of
the bright colours of your first sketches. Louis Boulanger, for
instance, another member of Gautier's Romantic generation,
should value and preserve his natural 'restlessness, his search
for new effects, his continual experimentation', for 'it is better
to overexcite than to restrain oneself, to overshoot the mark
than not to reach it at all'.[83] 'Young painters, young
artists . . . give your chargers their heads, sink the rowels of
your spurs into their panting flanks, launch yourselves on a
space-devouring flight',[84] he wrote further on in his *Salon of
1844*, using the high Romantic imagery which he was still to
be calling upon in order to evoke Delacroix's world-devour-
ing temperament thirteen years later. Artists should simply
know themselves; Gautier could encourage them to no higher
aim than that of self-realization. 'M. Gigoux has treated his
composition much too soberly, and has not abandoned
himself enough to himself', he wrote of a massively ambitious
Cléopâtre at the Salon of 1838;[85] 'a little daring, a little
genius, a little hell-fire would not do any harm; without losing
your respect for tradition, try to be yourself, M. Rogier' was
all that he asked of the too tentatively respectful Rogier at the
Salon of 1840.[86] Artistic temperaments should speak in their
own *mots propres*; the violence of Gautier's exhortations was
intended to blast away the debris of preconception, timidity,
systematised vision, received ideas and blinkered perception,
to allow a quietly spontaneous, mysterious and organic
process to take place: 'Let us calmly produce what we have
within us, like roses, which do not try to make blue flowers' he
concluded his *Salon of 1845*.[87] Like Decamps in 1839, who
was 'like the sun' and Devéria who 'paints in the same way as
he walks or speaks',[88] and like Pradier, who produced statues
as an orange-tree produces oranges,[89] artists might create as
spontaneously and unselfconsciously as nature; like the poet-
critic, in abandoning themselves to instinct, they should
become ego-less but articulate beings, profoundly in touch
with the perceptible world around them. 'Let us commit
ourselves to the unknown', he wrote in the astonishing prose
celebration of artistic genius that follows his article on

Töpffer's treatise in 1847.[90] This 'inconnu' has been seen to become a concrete entity in certain of Gautier's ghost stories (see the *Jeunes-France* story *Onuphrius Wphly*, and other fictionalized instances of the devil guiding the artist's gestures); as such it is an image of instinctual powers that are beyond the artist's conscious control, and of the incommunicable vortex of the spectator's aesthetic experience. Thus the landscapist Cabat is advised in 1840: 'Don't be so suspicious, young painter, of your own genius. Why so much work and anxiety? . . . Leave more to chance than to will, and do not keep such a close watch on yourself. Let that stranger who comes to visit great artists and works in their place without their noticing it take your brushes sometimes. This stranger has made the most beautiful things in the world; Homer himself was only his secretary, and Raphael the man who sharpened his pencils.'[91*]

No aesthetic programme or systematic doctrine is of any use to the artist in his courtship of the 'inconnu'; no intellectual structure of critical criteria will help the critic or spectator to grasp the full range of pleasure and experience to be gleaned from the world of art. Thus the critic too should cultivate his instinctual and sensual responses. This is not to say that Gautier's writing up to 1848 is devoid of real and overt criticism, but it is criticism that is always based on close feeling for a particular artist's strengths and temperament, for what Gautier sees as his particular potential. Even when he is talking about artists whose work is simply 'outside the sphere of art', he is always painstakingly pragmatic. Flers, at the Salon of 1840, should mistrust his painterly facility, while Marilhat, who is losing his spontaneity, should forget about draughtsmanship and return to Egypt to recapture his fluent first manner.[92] Poussin is good for Gleyre, Gautier remarks at the Salon of 1845; he suits Gleyre's philosophical nature, while his effect on Decamps is likely to be entirely negative.[93] In 1848 he had been troubled to see Diaz spoiling his natural talent by concerning himself with style and design, and was dismayed to feel that he may even have been the cause of the trouble himself, through some critical remarks he had made at the previous exhibition. 'You put together such a scholarly argument that the artist, half convinced, sets about trying to lose his genius'; in a personal address to Diaz, he pleads with him to forget whatever stupidly rational advice he may have been offered.[94]

Gautier bent over backwards to avoid falsifying his artists' intentions or invading their integrity with notions of his own. In his criticism he did little more than suggest and point to further possibilities; he saw his own role as a necessarily limited one, that of encouraging and helping artists to a fuller grasp of their own inherent strengths, to a realization of their whole selves. In 1844 he summed up his attitude. 'Beware of temperate advice. Where art is concerned, nothing is more insidious than common sense. Madness is worth a thousand times as much: mad El Greco made pictures which pass for Titians!'[95]

Such was the urgent message to artists his criticism embodied; it was to remain the key to his hopes. In view of the increasing conformity of the Salons, it was a message which certainly needed spreading; yet one senses, from the very vigour of Gautier's exhortations, that there were fewer and fewer ears to hear it.

This message was occasionally still transmitted in the terms of the Romanticism of the late 1820s and early 1830s, and these, by the 1840s, must have begun to sound distinctly old-fashioned. Balzac had remarked as long ago even as 1831 that Romanticism was a thing of the past: the public was tired of the Orient and Spain, of 'l'histoire de France walter-scottée', he had written in the preface to the first edition of *La Peau de chagrin*.[96] Gautier, by the late 1840s, could indeed have seemed in danger of becoming something of a solitary Romantic die-hard; the world victory to which he continued to look forward was that of the warriors of Romanticism on their panting chargers, led by battle-scarred Delacroix. This victory, the victory of instinct over the mediocre hordes, was, in the 1840s, to be proclaimed and celebrated in some Parisian Salon of the future, which would comprehend every shade of livable experience.

What Gautier wished above all was to be held in awe by the rich and varied spectacle which would thus be offered him; yet his vision of the future was to be no more, essentially, than an expansion of the sum of his past and immediate experience, for in practice, we have seen, he had difficulty in detaching himself from that experience. He was a man with a powerful faith and a vital insight; but he was no natural theorist. Thus where Baudelaire was able to translate his vivid apprehensions about the present into the proposal of an art which might come to terms with that present, Gautier's vision of the future grew increasingly blurred. From the mid-40s, his criticism is characterized by a gradually escalating internal conflict, between an eminently sane but ever less fashionable Romanticism, and the concrete evidence of his moment-to-moment perceptions and responses.

(g) THE SALON OF THE FUTURE

Disappointed at the imaginative and sensual redundancies of the Salon of 1844, Gautier went on to outline the kind of Salon he would like to see in a passage which is probably the last of its kind directly to express his true feelings. 'Painting is not only the imitation of real objects—indeed this is one of the least of its merits; it is a means of expressing the secret ideal of the soul, and of portraying not what is but things as we would wish them to be . . . Art is a desire!'⁹⁷ Painting should be an exposition of every conceivable 'way of feeling'; it makes tangible the desires of the imagination. 'Thus we should like to see modern painting less concerned with the exact representation of a patent-leather boot, a gaiter button, or some rough old bit of wall, than with seeking to realize that which does not exist, dreams of beauty and splendour, poetic scenes, gods and heroes in their true characters.' The suggestions that Gautier makes as to the range to which this 'desire' may be extended do not limit themselves to dreams of the impossible; art should make use of new archaeological discoveries; 'the whole of Olympia is to be redone' with new local colour; *Faust Part Two* and the legends of the Nibelungs come to his mind as unexploited sources of imagery; the Orient is open, providing material for biblical scenes just as they must have looked, and India is unexplored.

In 1846 he gave a further airing to this idea of the Salon as a cathedral or pantheon, which might reflect and celebrate the whole of creation; this time the steamship and the locomotive were enlisted to help art satisfy its desires.

The glorification of man and the beauties of nature, such would seem to be the aim of art in the future. The great painter who will arise—for every age produces the geniuses who are necessary to it—will be able to colour his ideal with all the shades of humanity, from the alabaster of the Norwegian virgin to the ebony of the daughter of Damanhur . . . The task of poets, painters, and sculptors is to write the commentary of creation; the time has come to study nature directly; in a few years from now, the Salon should be a panorama of the world . . . From the discovery of steam will date a new era in poetry . . . The modern Pegasus will be a locomotive![98]

This more positivistic and, for 1846, more commonplace vision, in marked contrast to the mystical and idealistic role given to painting in the dream of 1844, is possibly an echo of Baudelaire's plea in 1845 for a painting of modern life; it is a reflection of the same publicly expressed optimism, on Gautier's part, that the Salons would fulfil their promise to become unified world-experiences. In 1848, as the material and social world outside demonstrated its instability and imperfection, Gautier's call to the realization of great desires through abandonment to the 'inconnu', to the recreation of the world in art, reached its passionate apogee. 'Let everyone translate his dream into reality, express his thoughts, pour out his feelings, satisfy his tastes, and fulfil his fantasies, bizarre or insane as these may be, without fear, without false shame, with the frankness of the free man; for no one can have complete consciousness of his own idea . . . Artists! Never has there been a finer moment! . . . The universe is yours, the visible and inner worlds, religions, poetries, and histories, the civilizations of the past, present and future: everything of which the mind can dream or conceive.'[99]

Young artists, he cries without pause for breath, as if inciting the mob from the top of a barricade, 'let yourselves be carried away by your daring, your impetuousness, enthusiasm, and love!' The nineteenth century is the most glorious of all; man is taking full possession of his planet with the railway and the steamship; soon it will hold no secrets from us: we shall erect 'towers of harmony'—there is a Fourierist note here. Brand-new fields of subject-matter are opening up, the sensual paradises of the Orient, Tahiti, America . . . etc. Not only is the visible world richer than before; all the ancient myths are to be redone, with a view to creating a vast new mythology to correspond to the ideas and needs of the age. Thus Gautier heralded the age of the encyclopaedic Salon and the Exposition Universelle. Underlying the best of his criticism up to 1848 was a massive confidence that he could operate a personal synthesis of all the experience the world had to offer; it was waiting for his embrace, or bear-hug. With the aid of instinct, whole-hearted abandonment to the 'inconnu', to passion and lusty sensuality, he was just, but only just, able to synthesize his own potentially fragmented roles as Romantic artist and working middle-class journalist, even as the basis for that synthesis, the particular cultural requirements of the audience of the 1830s, began to slip away. In an attempt, no doubt, to confirm his sense of his continuing modernity, he had even enlisted the railway into his vision; but the image of the iron-clad Pegasus inevitably clashed with the terms of medieval battle in which Instinct was typically clothed. The year 1848 was, for Gautier as for Baudelaire, a genuine trauma and a watershed; if it drove Baudelaire to a further awakening of his powers, it struck a decisive blow to Gautier's confidence in his own modernity. The Salon of 1848, meanwhile, remained to be explored; it consisted of 5,180 separate works.

3 1848–1872

(a) JOURNALISTIC EXPEDIENCY

As a polemicist after 1848 Gautier is not entirely convincing. His virtuosity with 'sentences that fall on their feet like cats' finds its full application; his general announcements can read more and more like bland propaganda, and the expression of his real opinions seems to become increasingly obscure. He is ever elusive, a two-dimensional public figure who indeed demands reading between the lines, but whose burgeoning prose is still frequently pierced with crystal-clear insights. The Goncourts, having sensed a certain absence and vacancy behind Gautier's solid physical presence in 1857, were subsequently struck by this corresponding lucidity; beneath the often impenetrable public image of the successful man of letters in mid-career, they discerned the almost boundless benevolence and ever passionate commitment to art that underlay all his writing.

Gautier, the stylist dressed in red, as far as the bourgeois is concerned; the most astonishing good sense in literary matters, the sanest judgement, a terrible lucidity flashing forth in quite simple little sentences, in a voice like the lightest of caresses. This man, who, on first acquaintance, seems closed and somehow entombed deep within himself, decidedly has great charm, and is sympathetic to the highest degree. He says that when he has wanted to do something good, he has always started it in verse, because there is always an uncertainty as to the form of prose, while a verse, if it is a good one, is a thing struck like a medal; but that the exigencies of life have turned many a short story started in verse into a story in prose.[100]

The contradictions and shifting emphases within Gautier's art criticism are partly to be accounted for by this 'uncertainty as to the form of prose'. 'An article, a page is something you get right first time', he had already told the Goncourts;[101] a spontaneous process, his prose writing reflected the contradictions and shifting emphases within the man. Furthermore, he did not consider his journalism to be of lasting importance: 'I am not after the best'.[102] He was obsessed with permanence, with creating and communing with monuments, and his forms were sculpture and verse that is 'struck like a medal'; this preoccupation towers over other passing concerns on which his later art criticism touches. Confronted with the works of Ingres, he was to speak of his own massive journalistic output as 'a few thousand frivolous lines cast to the four winds of journalism',[103] for the instant daily experience that Girardin had put on sale in 1836 was also instantly discardable; Gautier did not expect nor intend his pragmatic art-critical bulletins to be examined as a whole, as his work as a poet might be. It did not matter what he wrote in newspapers, as long as it did not betray the cause of art, as long as it served the best interests of artists, and as long as it was fluent and expedient; with this realization, the man behind the prose could withdraw. Even his irony, with which in his earlier criticism he had kept us in tenuous touch with the complexity of his private motives and reactions, is more frequently absent.

His introductory article for the *Salon of 1848* in *La Presse*[104] establishes an uncomfortable tone: it is an unhappy mixture of the imagery of sculpted verse and of grandiose polemic in the style of a Romantic manifesto. The scale and frenzy of the arguments, from a close observer who had wished to court 'neither torrents, nor cataracts' and who valued the intimacy of his own sense impressions, suggest that Gautier had no alternative but to be carried blindly along by the tide of events; he had no desire to participate in them either for or against, only to complete his verbal quota. Art is his only cause, but as an artist he once more becomes a semi-conscious reflector of broader public life and upheavals. 'No one can have complete consciousness of his own idea'; open to any experience, he exhorts artists to be the same: 'let yourselves be carried away', and see what happens. Thus he is able to justify a stance of supreme and tactful acquiescence, safe inside the serene and trouble-free world of art.

'What do the uproar in the streets and the terrors of the bourgeois matter? Art, leaning on its elbows, looks on as in a dream, and from time to time interrupts its meditations to take up the pen, the brush, or chisel . . .' The authentic Gautier speaks; but the incendiary language of the anti-jury polemic that follows strikes a false note. For all his conviction on the subject, his revolutionary-style invective, it has been remarked, reads as expedient space-filling, particularly since the jury in 1848 had already been abolished: '. . . let the people judge for itself! A jury, even one elected by artists, would be worthless. Don't worry, everyone will get strictly his fair share, count on it'.[105]

Gautier's argument in favour of free access to the Salons only just bears reading twice. It is rhetoric which could almost as easily be turned into an argument in favour of a jury. Does this Salon differ strikingly from previous ones which have undergone enforced purification? he asks. 'Not in the least. The general impression is the same as ever, apart from a few barbaric or laughable canvases which don't number more than a dozen.' The authors of these ludicrous pieces will see the folly of their ways when they are exhibited in public; if refused by a jury, they would persist in self-dramatization and assume martyred attitudes. The hilarity of

the public in front of their canvases provides 'a cruel but
salutary corrective, and this may encourage those with head-
strong but too impatient senses of vocation to work harder'.
(What guarantees that the public might not like these 'pieces
of burlesque'? It liked Biard and Delaroche, after all; and
might not its unkind peals of laughter also induce a martyred
attitude in the recalcitrant artist?) The author of one of these
'eccentric paintings', Gautier goes on to inform us, went so
far as to beg M. le Directeur, on bended knee and with
wringing hands, to let him remove his canvas from public
mockery; this is an object lesson in humility, Gautier concludes. In advocating this process of natural selection, he
seems to be in real danger of undermining his role as a critic
and educator altogether; his argument merely provides expedient verbal décor, words to echo. the resonance of the
moment.

In *La Charte de 1830* in 1837 he had praised the Constitutional Monarchy as a generous patron of the arts, by
proclaiming the king to be 'one of the greatest artists of the
epoch', and himself a true friend of 'order and of the laws that
have brought peace and wealth to our country'.[106] Under a
nascent Republic in July 1848, Gautier wrote of a 'Republic
of the Future'[107] whose constitution could offend nobody;
the authorities might rest assured, the poet could continue to
earn his living unmolested, and a persistent poetic desire for a
new Renaissance or Athens could again find expression:

The Republic as we understand it is opulent, sumptuous, witty, and
refined . . . The titles of nobility have been suppressed; we would
have preferred it if every French citizen had been declared a
gentleman . . .
    There will always be an aristocracy among men that no republic
will suppress, that of poets . . . The conqueror, the artist, the
legislator, and the scholar are poets when they have discovered an
idea, a form, a truth, a fact . . .
    The republican, thanks to his steam-powered slaves, will have
the time to cultivate his field and his mind. Anyone who is not an
artist will be a farmer . . . We firmly desire this fine Athenian
republic . . . which will place beneath every foot flights of white
marble steps; the pediments of its palaces and temples will stand out
against a serene blue sky.

If it had been possible, a decade and a half earlier, in an age in which utopias proliferated, passionately to believe in a new awakening, hopes born inside the Petit Cénacle and the Impasse du Doyenné were beginning to fade. Behind the hollow rhetoric of this improbable dream of a republic of the future the same fundamental faith still shines through, faith in the power of the artist to create new worlds and in the superiority of his calling; but it is now expressed in such immutably poetic terms, those of the serene marble temples and palaces of Art, as irrevocably to divorce it from any semantic bearing on larger contemporary realities.

Gautier was to continue to insist upon art's place in society, as, for example, he did once more in 1848, calling upon the painter and the sculptor to complete the work of the engineer.[108] In 1862 he remarked of the London Exhibition Palace, 'of that architectural order we shall call mechanical', that it was 'evidently in this direction that artists of the future must look in order to find the new architecture';[109] but he merely noticed such developments as part of his reporter's job; he did not campaign for the realization of an artistic utopia in steel and glass, and he is never to be regarded as a critical herald of twentieth-century modernism.[110] If he was able to see the beauty of the modern world in its activity and constant flux, and demand a similarly realistic awareness from artists, the 'serene reverie' of the antique world always remained closer to his sympathies. What emerges from his criticism after 1848 is a view of art less as a desire than as a retreat: in the static image of the serene temple, art is established as consolation for the contemporary confusion of values that Gautier was instinctively and professionally bound to reflect.

(b) CHAOS

Gautier's criticism up to 1848 had been enlivened by a sense of struggle; he wrote as a dauntless campaigner for the values of his Romantic youth. The Salons were marked by two strongly contrasting tendencies, personified in Ingres and Delacroix, antitheses that Gautier was joyfully able to reconcile; such contrasts enriched and vitalized the world of art. At the Salon of 1846 he had been struck by a 'confused

pantheism . . . a vague eclecticism', [111] but he had been able
to evince from this a vision of a more splendid age. Only
three years later, such great hopes had disappeared from the
language of Gautier's general public pronouncements. Re-
gretting the absence of Ingres, Decamps, Chassériau,
Ziegler, and many others from the Salon of 1849, he wrote of
art as in direct opposition to the world's other concerns. 'It
should have been a matter of pride for these lofty
intelligences . . . to show that the passing disturbances in the
forum or the street had no effect whatsoever upon their ideal
serenity.' [112] (He can only just bring himself to call a street a
street; 'forum', which sounds more distant, suits his purpose
better.)

By the Salon of 1850–1 the active questing of the 'modern
Pegasus' seemed already to have fulfilled its aim. [113] Any
optimism or sense of future is now absent; there are few
great experiences with which to be carried away; the exhibition presents itself in his account as static and definitive.
Art seemed to be consolidating and stabilizing itself. The
existence of two fruitful schools had been very noticeable up
to 1848, he writes; the exhibition of that year was 'a real
Saturnalia of forms and colour', while this one, one of the
biggest ever, has a distinct character and physiognomy of
its own. Ingres and Delacroix have paid off their troops.
'Individualism reigns', and 'talent is democratizing itself' (it
is still the Republic). No single work emerges as outstanding.
Historical painting has almost disappeared; religious pictures
are few and mostly mediocre. 'A vaguely pantheistic feeling
seems to inspire these so very varied and contrasting works;
everything is given the same importance, man, animals,
landscape, flowers, still-life. Subject-matter, which people
used to be so anxious about, has lost its importance; pure and
simple representation of nature seems to be theme enough.'
As well as 'pantheistic', the Salon of 1850–1 was 'vagabond';
it displayed 'the most charming and unexpected diversity'.
Were these the polite terms in which Gautier's all-embracing
world-experience was to be welcomed? His appeals for a
liberation of instinct also seem to have met with a sober and
pedestrian response: 'each artist believes in the nature of his
talent'. If there were fewer 'folies' and 'extravagances', the

Salon was characterized by a higher level of technical competence than ever before: the Old Masters were studied, not
for the spirit of their works, but as if they were 'recipe books
for pictures'.

The following year the world-containing cathedral had
become a Babel.[114] 'Taken as a whole, the Salon is very
confused and very diverse; behind a great deal of talent one
senses a great uncertainty of spirit.' Landscape painting, once
a means to intimate contact with the visible world—to
identification with it, instilling it with an ordering *idea*—now
seemed to evoke in Gautier a sense of nature's underlying
chaos; much in evidence in 1852, it seemed to embody less a
reverential pantheism than a mindless anarchy of inarticulate
forms: it was 'a sanctuary for societies without beliefs, which
take refuge in the bosom of mute, impassive nature in order
not to have to formulate a *credo*'. There was a lack of doctrine
and direction which Gautier could no longer embrace. He
could diagnose the problem very accurately, but he could no
longer propose a miraculous cure or so easily envisage that
vague future synthesis to which instinct had been the key.
'Art no longer has at its disposal anything but dead ideas and
formulae which no longer correspond to its needs. Hence this
anxiety, this vagueness, this diffusion, this ease of transition
from one extreme to another, this eclecticism and cosmo-
politanism, this journey into all the worlds of the possible,
from the Byzantine to the daguerreotype, from studied
mannerism to wilful brutality. There is a strong feeling in the
air that something is to be done—but what? Is it a laundress
or a dryad, a wash-basin or a hero?' The rift is widening
between the conclusions to which Gautier's observations lead
him, and the compensations he instinctively seeks. 'What
makes the uncertainty worse', he goes on, 'is that art no longer
has any real purpose nowadays; it remains in a state of simple
dilettantism; it skirts life without mixing in it.' What about
the ideal world apart, the serene temple of art, which, it is
true, was not to be constructed by dilettantes, but which
might well 'skirt life without mixing in it'?

Art, Gautier had written in 1844, was a desire, for an ideal
nature of 'belles formes, bèlles idées'. In a theatre feuilleton
for *La Presse* of 11 February 1850, he phrased this idealism

differently, in a statement that marks the shift in his thinking and which is fundamental to any reading of his later criticism: 'art, like love, is just an effort of the soul that longs to escape death'. The article offers a crucial bearing on Gautier's craving for permanence; it was prompted by a special performance in memory of the bass Alizard. There is no need to be jealous of the amounts earned by live performers, Gautier reassured his fellow poets.

Our verses remain, their songs are carried off in the wind . . . Of the poet, the painter, and the sculptor, only the clay exterior disappears; his thought survives whole. In love, without your realizing it, the secret motive inspiring you is that of escaping nullity and passing on the torch of life to another before the cold breath of death extinguishes it in your hands. Every man worthy of the name seeks to assure his own immortality of body and soul, and this is the reason why nothing is real in this world except art and love, the only two things which create.

Nature reproduces itself indiscriminately; art and love create, because they reproduce an ordering 'pensée', an idea: 'the thought survives whole'. In simply reproducing nature's chaos, in reflecting human confusion in front of nature as the Salon of 1852 did, art must have seemed to Gautier to be in danger of losing its identity. It was his mission as a critic to nurture and instil an ordering 'pensée', in an effort towards which he was to underline art's separation from chaotic life; what better image of order and permanence than a classical temple? His whole critical career is open to examination in terms of how he ordered his Salons, of how he attempted to extract patterns from profusion and blinding chaos (see the introductory article to his *Salon of 1837*, with its description of literally dazzling gilt and varnish), just as the sculptor and the poet brought forth order and thought from formless, inarticulate stone and from the indiscriminate profusion of the dictionary.

'The nineteenth century, the climactic age of humanity, is seeking the formula of the generations of the future, and it will find it. Meanwhile everyone is bringing his own individuality to light; for lack of idea ('à défaut de pensée'), dreams come into being; people are experimenting, groping, appropriating the techniques of the past and inventing new ones.'[115] Gautier needed models upon which to base his vision of the future, just as he had needed Delacroix and Decamps through whom fully to formulate a conception of the artist. In the absence of new and towering indicators of what could be, he was left with his heroes of the past and with the present spectacle of artists 'trying to seize hold of the nineteenth century's elusive ideal'; the realization that this elusive ideal might reside in the very diffusiveness and eclecticism of the Salons themselves, in their very 'défaut de pensée', was inadmissible. The less the Salons held Gautier's full interest, the more purely did his writing, in his absence, as it were, come simply to reflect and share the Salons' general characteristics.

(c) 'SENTENCES THAT FALL ON THEIR FEET'

At the beginning of 1854 Gautier began to contribute to *Le Moniteur universel*, now the official organ of the one-year-old Empire. He finally left *La Presse* in April 1855; as if to mark the end of an optimistic, eager, and idealistic period, Madame de Girardin, the Romantic muse who had grown obese, died in June. For the Empire's official art and theatre critic, he was the perfect choice: the poet of *l'art pour l'art* was the very embodiment of art in its highest, nineteenth-century sense. His fifty-two articles on the Exposition Universelle of 1855 are his most monumental and enduring celebration of the separate and distinct world of art; they were almost all collected in two volumes and subsequently bound into one compact hand-book or bible-like edition, as *Les Beaux-Arts en Europe*. As a genuinely representative world-experience, the Exposition Universelle was rich in those contrasts of response, relationship and viewpoint which Gautier had sought in his real travels, but here they were heightened and enlivened by juxtaposition: 'those numerous pilgrimages, which have turned us into a sort of Wandering Jew of art, are easily surpassed by a cab ride to the avenue Montaigne; you can learn more about art in four hours than we have done in fifteen years'.[116] The contrasts were certainly large: 'the exhibition divides itself into four distinct areas: . . . England represents individuality, Belgium *savoir-faire*, Germany

ideas, and France eclecticism'.[117] All his inspiring heroes and
most of his contemporaries were there in full strength,
awaiting verbal apotheosis: Ingres, Delacroix, Decamps,
Louis Boulanger, Camille Roqueplan (dead), Aligny, Corot,
Rousseau.

Where the Salons could no longer hold his whole attention,
it was because such contrasts, passions, and loyalties were
absent. The Second Empire was bringing art more closely
under its official wing. By means of extensive, if only loosely
co-ordinated state patronage, and a proliferation of councils
and committees with special responsibility for the Fine Arts,
the administration sought to turn art into something resemb-
ling a public institution, to bring it into line with a whole
programme of industrial and educational improvements. The
artist's public image necessarily underwent a corresponding
change: if Gautier's readers in the 1830s had been prepared to
accept the notion of the artist as a member of an élite, with
special gifts of instinct and impartiality which were well
beyond the experience of the common herd, the middle-class
public of the Second Empire was evidently not. The image of
the artist which was emerging was a more down-to-earth one:
that of a public educator and guardian of taste. A new
conscientiousness, as Gautier was quick to note, made itself
felt in a general and sober attention to detail: to finish and
technique, to research into geographical and historical accuracy. The crucial *poetic* element in Gautier's original vision
was thus considerably devalued; he sensed this change with a
kind of despair, but it was finally beyond his understanding.
All he could do was reflect it, and this, indeed, was all that he
was called upon to do.

The younger artists who were rising to prominence were,
what is more, men Gautier did not always know personally,
and who had not influenced or shared the hopes of 1830. He
could not maintain with artists such as Baudry, Bouguereau,
Cabanel, or Puvis de Chavannes the fighting polemic stance
with which he had declared his identification with Delacroix,
Rousseau, and Pradier. He had no more 'grands refusés' to
support; all the great names of Louis-Philippe's reign, including Courbet, had arrived at their mature styles by the
beginning of the Second Empire, and almost all were either

integrated, or, like Ingres, deliberately absent from the Salons, or dead; with Delacroix, Ingres, and Decamps in pride of place at the Exposition Universelle, and Rousseau himself achieving some popularity, even Gautier could hardly remain combative on their behalves indefinitely. Neither could the Salon jury any longer reasonably be seen as the enemy; it had been reinstated in 1852, but under conditions which allowed artists themselves a louder voice: half of its members were elected by previous exhibitors. In 1857 the Académie des Beaux-Arts was once more allowed to supply the whole jury, but after the further reforms of 1863, Gautier was to find himself one of its members.

It was perhaps necessary, therefore, for the critic to restate and re-emphasize his impartiality, in order to cover his sense of distance from events. In the face of a lack of interior definition in the Salons, his rhetorical question in the *L'Artiste* prospectus of 1856, 'why limit oneself, why not take ample pleasure in everything?',[118] assumes more urgent overtones. What else can a conscientious critic do when he is confronted with a situation that offers him so few emotional footholds, so few solid platforms from which to focus his vision on what could or should be?

In 1857 he once more noted this mediocre eclecticism and lack of recognizable schools[119] and could only acquiesce in the situation. But individualism taken to extremes led to mindless chaos, and finally in full circle to that emptiness, that lack of contrasting experiences that has been seen to be Gautier's particular anguish. 'Anarchy and Individualism . . .', he wrote in 1857, 'subdivide art to infinity.'[120] By 1861 eclecticism seemed to him virtually to have arrived at uniformity; Gautier expressed his disillusion at the absence of causes and contrasts in terms of nostalgia. Think of the passions the Salons aroused in the old days, the colourful crowds clamouring for entrance on the first day, the mutual hostility of the eccentrically dressed partisans of line and colour, which only just stopped short of actual blows. But artists have changed: 'they studiously avoid any fashion which is a bit conspicuous or bizarre. They eschew originality of appearance just as, in the old days, they used to cultivate it'. Art too has changed; there are no more 'violent antitheses

. . . no doubt you can discern something like groups of similar talents here and there, but it is only a conformity of temperament which throws them together by chance . . . Any general formula which you might try to apply to contemporary art is subject to so many exceptions that you must soon abandon it. Classification, even by genre, is no longer possible'. The organizers of the massive Salon of 1861 had indeed opted to hang the exhibits in alphabetical order, but so as to avoid complaints about obscure positioning from artists; this in itself would of course have contributed to a sense of stylistic confusion. Gautier followed this order too, and in spite of the homogeneity given to his account by its appearance in book form, in time to meet the occasion, the *Abécédaire du Salon de 1861* is less a celebration than a catalogue, this for all its elegance and wit, qualities which the Salon visitor had come to expect from the fashionable critic's charming and fluent peregrinations. With no possibility of classification, of making sharp distinctions between experiences whose very separateness should heighten awareness of the scale and richness of a potential unity, there was little interest for the observer who wished to be rapt, fascinated, and transported: the twenty-three articles that first appeared in *Le Moniteur universel* were largely written, Joanna Richardson has suggested, by his son Toto.[121]

Gautier reconciled himself to the situation by his absence. His journalism fills with repetitive statements and space-filling digressions which indeed suggest the presence of ghost-writers who were skilled in parody. The very syntax of his later criticism reflects and demonstrates 'that ease of transition from one extreme to the other . . . that journey into every world of the possible' which he had noted at the Salon of 1852;[122] his prose often leaves the same impression as that which he took away with him from the Salon of 1864: 'It is all so bright that splendours disappear in the general radiance',[123] such was the strength of his rhetorical and journalistic empathy. The Goncourts report a scene at the offices of *L'Artiste* in 1857, in which Charles Blanc, a fellow-contributor, reproaches Gautier for putting 'everything in the foreground in his articles, of not giving the reader a chance to rest, not putting in any neutral passages, making everything sparkle'. The Gautier of the Goncourt diaries retorts characteristically. 'I'm fed up. Everything seems neutral to me. My most highly coloured articles just seem grey in the end. They are like blotting-paper: I shove on red, yellow, and gold, I daub away like a man possessed, and they still don't seem colourful. And what makes me really unhappy is that in art, I love line and Ingres.'[124] Gautier echoed the encyclopaedic bent of the age by writing as if for a thesaurus. An article on Gustave Doré published in 1856[125] illustrates the kind of rhetorical overkill in which the critic indulged himself.

Typically, he makes a very general opening remark. Some artists are not classical or official history painters, but are blessed with instincts of their own. He narrows down this observation: 'These artists do not sniff at the task offered and demanded of them by the epoch in which they live'. He paraphrases and illustrates this: 'They accept its ideas, costumes, fashions, and crazes . . . they are modern, imbued with the spirit of their age . . .' Next, some examples are provided. 'Among these artists one may mention Charlet, Tony Johannot, Raffet, Gavarni, Daumier, G. Doré . . .' Now the specific topic for discussion is introduced, '. . . Gustave Doré, the youngest, the latest arrival, and perhaps the most astonishing'. Doré's most striking characteristics are summed up in more precise terms: 'G. Doré is hardly twenty-three or -four and has already produced enough work to fill the life of a centenarian. The Latins had an epithet—*portentosus*—for which we have no exact equivalent and which means abnormal, excessive, prodigious: you could not find a better word to characterize Doré's talent . . .' Adjectives and metaphors appear in force to underline the point: 'He has endless reserves of inexhaustible fertility, which bubble and overflow from some deep spring whose gushing energy nothing could staunch. Newspapers, albums, books: Doré is ready for anything . . .' The article is a progression by near-paraphrase; meanings overlap so that there are no gaps, and the writing thus acquires a very dense quality, an overall richness of detail and texture like that of a Second Empire drawing-room, festooned with decoration.

(Another familiar image comes to mind: Doré also seems to wear his attributes as if they were an impenetrable suit of embossed and knotty armour, made of small interlocking and overlapping pieces.) The reader is carried along by this interior dialectic without pause for breath. A new idea is introduced almost as a rhetorical question; there are no sharp transitions. 'Such labour would seem great enough to bring the most robust constitution to its knees.' (How does Doré do it? we may well ask.) The answer confirms what we already know about Doré's excessive, prodigious, and abnormal nature: 'Doré sustains it easily, effortlessly and untiringly . . .' The point is illustrated: 'not a single line scores his white forehead', and this piece of visual evidence is supported by others: 'no bruise-like halos ring his clear eyes; his cheeks are ever full and rosy . . .', and, as final crushing proof of Doré's *abnormal* and *excessive* nature, it is revealed that 'he brushes in canvases of twenty feet in a week, for recreation, and sketches out subjects containing twenty or thirty life-sized figures . . .'

This is the introduction; the ground is prepared for more detailed exploration. 'The young artist's highly original talent consists in two quite distinct veins, which intertwine without touching each other . . . like the milky spirals in the stem of a Venetian glass.' An aptly long simile adds richness to our image of Doré's temperament; Gautier's spirals gently lead us more deeply into his world. Here once more we confront those mysterious labyrinths of intuitions and correspondences referred to in *L'Histoire du romantisme*, in which ideas are said to meander 'through the convolutions of the brain'.[126] 'G. Doré is both a realist and visionary'; this key statement is paraphrased, elaborated, and illustrated according to pattern. 'He has powers both of observation and of intuition . . .' Now Gautier gives his own poetic associations free rein, and his images home in ever more closely on the contents of Doré's prodigious imagination: 'Although in broad daylight he confronts nature face to face, with boldness and resolution, as soon as the black, membraneous silhouettes of the bats begin to flit through the paling dusk, as soon as the crows flap to roost in the skeletons of the trees, then he sees with that visionary eye spoken of by Victor Hugo when he

addressed himself to the old Albrecht Dürer'. Mention of
Hugo and Dürer, who evoke their own associations, provides
a more definite set of co-ordinates with which to place Doré;
more grotesque and Gothic evocation follows: 'the clouds
stretch out like crocodiles climbing over the horizon on their
misshapen elbows . . .'; this is one example from a series of
gem-like images linked by semicolons, translations of actual
or typical Doré motifs. Then comes a more objective
summing-up: 'The whole of the Middle Ages is here as the
Romanticism of 1830 dreamed of it . . . but with something
still more bizarre, something more fantastic and something
wilder, which is further spiced with a note of humour and
caricature!' But this is only a short respite; the listing
continues, and by means of repetition the reader is almost
hypnotized or browbeaten into sharing Doré's bizarre visions
and identifying with his temperament.

And now the realist side; the torrent of sentences has not
released us yet. 'But this is only one aspect of his
talent . . . he is an unlikely mixture of Albrecht Dürer and
Courbet.' The reader is then swept up in a description of *Les
Lutteurs à la salle Montesquiou* and enveloped in a dense
verbal atmosphere of unrelentingly amassed details. 'The
spectators are as gross as hippopotamuses or as skinny as
lizards, hypertrophied or mummified through excess, red
with meat or green with absinthe . . .' The tension is
suddenly dropped in a new paragraph. 'Is it a good picture? Is
it a bad one? We would really find it very hard to say . . .'
Gautier retires fatigued from this furious *tour de force*.

He was never lost for words. Within his ever ready webs of
metaphor and his lists of adjacent meanings he assimilates
and transposes whatever experience is offered to him. Doré, it
is true, was an artist with much to commend him to Gautier's
verbal imagination; he had inherited a feeling for the Romantic grotesque with which the critic could easily sympathize,
and, like Delacroix, he possessed the revelatory power of a
visionary. Gautier's excessive prose is itself a perfect metaphor for Doré's excessive character. But he does no more than
explore and reflect; Doré is simply there before him, to be
absorbed; there is no comment on the quality of the experience he offers, beyond the degree of facility with which

the words flow from the critic's pen. Indeed, there is a positive refusal to make further qualitative comment; it is as if the question of the quality of Doré's work were for Gautier a matter of tired indifference.

Brilliant and enhancing as this evocation of Doré's world is, it leaves a shallow impression, a sense of empty virtuosity, the feeling that a well-tried rhetorical system has been applied and that we might be about to sweep on into another world which has been caught and immobilized in the same syntactical net. Such ease of transition, it could further be argued, was the essence of the experience of the daily newspaper, which could bring together riots in Madrid, Court engagements, new vaudevilles, and news of provincial crime in the same instantly digestible typographical format. Borel's savage and mysterious America was by 1866 linked by telegraphic cable to Europe (and in 0.32 of a second, we are informed by Jules Verne, who, as a representative of the new machine age in *Vingt Mille Lieues sous les mers*, was less interested in mysteries than in their technological solutions). With this new ease of world communication, with the newspaper, the telegraph, photography, the railway, and the steamship, information and experience were offered in unprecedented profusion; confronted with this, Gautier the official critic and traveller could hardly avoid evolving a technique to cope, a technique to distance himself. Thus his language can be seen as providing protective décor, in the sense that the bourgeois home with its newspaper provided protective décor; it was a comfortable alternative to the frightening and dangerous profusion of outside experience. Thus does Gautier seem to place his thesaurus-like language between himself (and us) and his experience, so that the experience comes to be seen through the words, just as nature could be seen through landscape painting.[127]

Yet in assimilating the diffuse experiences of contemporary art into his expediently evolved language, Gautier kept his dreaded chaos at bay. Words were the organs of 'la pensée', the means to involvement on a human scale; as long as he always had something to say, as long as he could claim to be able to describe anything, the overfull world could remain simply a full world, a spectacle to be watched from the outside. It was a chaos to whose each separate element, at least, Gautier was still able to ascribe an idea, if he could no longer discern an ordering 'pensée' in the whole.

(d) THE DESIRE FOR CONTINUITY

Gautier was finally obliged to reflect prevailing artistic standards and to accept almost anything into his prose, to record, for example, that M. Palizzi the goat specialist had gone over to sheep for the Salon of 1857, and was meeting with equal success.[128] He may have criticized Salon painters in general for their fatuous search for novelty in disregard of the deeper demands of art; yet novelty might be the only salient quality by which to note the presence of a particular work. Thus the visitor to the Salon of 1864, prompted by the undisputed artistic mentor of *Le Moniteur*, might have directed his steps towards M. Schreyer's exhibit:[129] 'A new effect in painting is a rare thing . . . but *Les chevaux de cosaques irréguliers, par un temps de neige*, by M. Schreyer, gives rise to precisely this very precious sensation of novelty. It has never been painted before'.[130] In 1868, he could no more ignore Leloir's anthropologically accurate savages of the Canary Islands[131] than he could neglect Lambron, a specialist in harlequins and undertakers;[132] and much as he disapproved of the comic and anecdotal in painting, he was unable to resist a smile at Saal's *Un Indiscret*, which represented a bear creeping up behind a mountain-landscape painter.[133] In *L'Artiste* in 1858 he had reviewed Gérôme's decorations of the new papal railway carriage,[134] and, in *Le Moniteur* in 1857, Didron's devotional objects.[135] Between his last article on the Salon of 1863 and a postscript covering a few deserving artists he had overlooked, he was to describe the fireworks at an Imperial birthday party;[136] ten years earlier, he had gone to elegant and tactful lengths to avoid committing art-critical *lèse-majesté* over Debufe's portrait of the Empress Eugénie:[137] 'It would be bad form indeed for us to discuss in the anatomical terms of ordinary criticism a face before which even the most impudent eyes are lowered'.

The Salon of 1852 had contained 1,757 works with a maximum three works per artist; the catalogue of the Salon of 1868 listed 4,213 items, with two works per artist: the critic was obliged to select works characteristic of a genre, or those which he deemed to be of original subject and execution. A supplement to the renamed *Moniteur* in 1869[138] (it had just become *Le Journal officiel de l'empire français*) reviewed the 'Progress of France under the Imperial Government, from Official Documents'; section XI, Fine Arts, revealed not only that new prizes had been offered for the Imperial School in Rome, and that 'Pupils, who have promptly become masters, have maintained during this period the renown of a school which is one of the glories of the nation', but also that the Empire had so far spent 16 million francs on commissions, among more than 2,000 artists.

For all this, Gautier was still usually able to bring his encyclopaedic scholarship to bear in detailed criticism of individual works; his interest in artists and his benevolence towards them individually was undiminished. As well as the steward of the Salons and a journalist of popular appeal, he remained an artist writing on behalf of artists. Of Puvis de Chavannes's 'enormous weaknesses' he wrote: 'a painter is being born here; let us not kill him off straight away. We shall leave him alone, and criticize him later—when he has only got qualities'.[139] With Courbet he could maintain a jovial benevolence: 'there is reason to declare that the master-painter of Ornans is making great progress. If one were to say to him, as before: Bonjour, M. Courbet, how are you keeping? he would have every right to reply: Very well'.[140] In 1851 he was indignant that Courbet had not received a decoration.[141] 'We have . . . looked among the unknown talents for those who show promise, and we have always tried, in our criticism, to see things from the artist's point of view', he wrote at the end of this Salon;[142] for all his personal disillusion and apprehensions, he was never to abandon this effort.

In his later attempts to identify with unfamiliar talents and to bring them closer to his own experience, the avatar was made full use of. Gautier had first come across Baudry in the 1853 Prix de Rome exhibition;[143] he was to measure his originality in 1857 by reference to his 'masters of the past': he was a rich mixture of Giorgione, Titian, Paris Bordone, and Barocci.[144] The manner of Puvis de Chavannes in 1859, 'with his great leaning towards the antique, mixed with a sort of medieval naïvety', was characterized by reference to the Mantegna cartoons at Hampton Court.[145] Such art-historical erudition was of course a reflection of the Second Empire's eclectic historical consciousness, of its tendency to use all the 'recipes of the past'; it was also a further symptom of Gautier's sense of distance. Yet it was proof above all of his continuing eagerness to belong, to collaborate with artists.

'Caramba! Here's a *Guitarrero* who is not straight out of the Opéra Comique', he wrote of Manet's exhibit at the Salon of 1861; 'Velazquez would greet him with a friendly little wink, and Goya would ask him for a light for his *papelito* . . . There is a lot of talent behind this stoutly painted, life-sized figure . . .'[146] But for all his protestations at the genuine and painterly talents of Courbet, Manet, and Fantin-Latour, he was finally unable to welcome them into his pantheon. Continuity was broken. 'You examine yourself with a sort of fear, you run your hand over your belly or your skull to see if you have not grown fat or gone bald and become incapable of understanding the daring of youth', he wrote in 1868 in a Salon article on Courbet, Manet, and Monet.

You say to yourself: 'Am I really an old fogey, a dotard, a mummy, an antediluvian fossil who no longer understands a thing about his century . . . ?' . . . and you think of the antipathy and horror aroused thirty-odd years ago, in people who lacked neither wit, talent, taste, nor breadth of ideas, by the first paintings of Delacroix, Boulanger, Scheffer, Corot, and Rousseau, so long banished from the Salons . . . Yet disgraced, reviled, and per-secuted as they were, these artists have become illustrious, univer-sally recognized masters, and they had just as much talent then as ever, perhaps even more, for they were giving the first flower of their genius. In the light of these striking examples, which are still close enough to us, scrupulous people may wonder if it really is im-possible to understand anything in art other than the works of one's own generation, that is, the generation with which one was twenty. The canvases of Courbet, Manet, Monet, and *tutti quanti* quite probably contain beauties which escape us veteran Romantics with our manes already streaked with silver . . . For our part, we have in all conscience done all we could to get used to this new painting, and when we had the honour to sit on the jury, we did not reject it. We have tried to be just towards what was repugnant to us . . .[147]*

This failure to comprehend, Gautier saw as a personal failure. There were compensations, above all in his 'discovery' at the Salon of 1869 of Henri Regnault, a young painter who was to be killed during the Siege of Paris in 1871, and the colour, solidity, and bloodthirsty exoticism of whose works seemed to place him in direct line of descent from the Romanticism of Devéria and Decamps (*plate 11*).[148] Regnault came closer than any other artist to filling the part of a final genius of the future; he was welcomed by the critic in a last blaze of sensuality and superlatives. If the critic's role too was to 'pass on to another the torch of life', Regnault might have been regarded as Gautier's natural and unplanned offspring. Otherwise there was little in the contemporary world to satisfy him.

'We were hardly counting on writing a Salon for 1872' he wrote in that final Salon. 'In spite of everything, one's thoughts come back to the eternal themes of life . . . Verse and marble have secret affinities . . . Sculpture and poetry constitute man's frail immortality.'[149] Gautier did not abandon his belief in the possibility of self-liberation, abandonment, and fulfilment during the Second Empire, but merely expressed it with a different emphasis: an emphasis on *le beau* and the permanence of art which echoed the period's own serious idealism, its faith in an idea of attainable perfection, and its preoccupation with establishing its own permanent monuments—exhibition palaces, opera houses, railway stations, and grand boulevards. Gautier's cult of *le beau* was partly a necessary shift of emphasis in his life's mission in order to accommodate new circumstances; it was also the reflection of a personal need. He would periodically revert to the Romantic imagery of unbridled gallops and knights in armour, particularly, of course, in the obituaries of artists of his generation which proliferate in his journalism after 1848 and darken its tone. That of Chassériau is typical in its pathos: 'A combatant withdraws, your dearest friend perhaps, his hand over his wound, and says to those in his rank: "Carry on, it is nothing. . . ."'[150] His love of the timeless, serene, and unblemished existed alongside and in tension with his nostalgia for the days when Romantic *poésie* had emerged as an intoxicating, world-changing cause; both became, in the end, expressions of his need for a sense of continuity.

This need for continuity made it hard for Gautier to see outside a Romantic framework, beyond the promises of his youth, which had itself been imbued with a strong sense of past, an art-historical self-consciousness. He wished to be able to bring all his experience of art into this continuity. *Le beau* was the means by which he embraced while attempting to transcend his age, and reaffirmed his sense of art's fundamental and undying quality. There was, of course, an alternative for the future, that heralded in the realism of Courbet and Manet; but this was an alternative which, for Gautier, was simply inconceivable as such, even though, in calling for large-scale painting of figures from modern life[151] and for sincerity and naïvety in front of nature,[152] he can seem to be among critics who unwittingly played a part in the rise of the new art.

He had been launched on his career as a popular journalist by a newspaper which was in many ways a product of the same ferment as that which had spawned his Romanticism; he was obliged to follow Romanticism in its myriad later ramifications as he was to remain a journalist. He indeed emerges as that 'Wandering Jew of art' as which he had described himself in 1855, carrying the burden of the weaknesses of the art of his time as he reflected its strengths. He is a contemporary, finally, who for all his studied disdain of his century was unable to transcend the broad limits of contemporary culture, and who survives as its most articulate, most faithful, and often its most ingenuous representative.

Conclusion

I Gautier's historical contribution

By the time of his death in 1872, and for a very large section of the reading public, Gautier's name had come to stand for criticism itself. Yet for this century it is Baudelaire rather than Gautier who towers over the field of mid-nineteenth-century art criticism in France, Baudelaire whose poetic insight and inexhaustibly fertile intellect provided Romanticism with a qualitative definition that would guarantee its future and his own. It is thus inevitably against Baudelaire that Gautier's value as an art critic must finally be weighed. For if in reading Baudelaire we seem miraculously to become the privileged operators of a two-way link between the nineteenth century and our own, Gautier seems correspondingly distant across time, uncomfortably bogged down or transfixed by his age. In this sense Baudelaire can be discovered as an essentially modern critic; Gautier, reciprocally, seems to be the culminating representative of an older type. Indeed he can seem in many ways to have more in common with his eighteenth-century precursor Diderot than he has with his younger contemporary Baudelaire. Gautier was ready and willing to acknowledge his debt to Diderot, whose art criticism, after all, was a widely shared nineteenth-century discovery: 'In his immortal Salons, Diderot . . . founded the criticism of painting', he declared categorically in 1854,[1] and Diderot had of course ranked high among the 'jeune rapin' 's historical 'flamboyants'. The less Gautier succeeds in striking Baudelaire's fiercely unmistakable modern chords, the more perhaps does his art-critical journalism appear as a simple continuation of Diderot's own similarly sweeping, open-handed, subjective, and pragmatic writing on the art of his century.

Yet the expressions of Baudelaire's admiration for Gautier remain with us, and ensure that he does not slip away from our attention altogether. There are two important articles,[2] and above all there is the resounding dedication of *Les Fleurs du mal*; Baudelaire's admiration is extended to Gautier the man, 'Maître et Ami', to Gautier the impeccable literary craftsman and verbal magician, to the poet blessed with a 'love of the Beautiful, a love that is immense, fruitful, and ceaselessly reawakened', and in whom Baudelaire, as an act of solidarity, was able to recognize his own 'immense and innate understanding of universal symbolism and correspondence'.[3] Like most of his contemporaries, Baudelaire did not doubt that Gautier's stature was somehow 'immense', whatever the personal reservations we know him to have had on the subject.

Baudelaire's admiration may certainly sometimes appear equivocal; Gautier's further opinions on Diderot are less problematic. As a lover of the exclusive and autonomous *beau*, Gautier emancipates himself from Diderot and the *philosophes* in quite predictable terms. For, as he wrote in 1861, 'Diderot misconstrued the real purpose of painting, in spite of his wit, his passion, his eloquence, and imagination. He failed to appreciate its autonomy . . . confusing philosophy with art . . . For a man who is a true artist, painting's only aim is itself, and that is quite enough'.[4] With this last judgement, Gautier makes a start on putting himself in historical perspective, for if Baudelaire admired him, it was above all in recognition of the fact that the 'parfait homme de lettres' approached everything, life as well as art, in the spirit of 'un homme vraiment artiste'; and this is the unspoken debt which binds Baudelaire to his older 'Maître et Ami'.

With the verbal anarchism of his dinner-table conversation, and as a benevolent and accessible *bon-vivant* and fashionable man-about-town, Gautier was undoubtedly an attractive father-figure to the young Baudelaire; this is hinted at, through veils of personal resentment, in Feydeau's memoirs.[5] As 'un homme vraiment artiste', Gautier shares with Delacroix the distinction of being Baudelaire's historical model. For both Gautier and Baudelaire the visual arts and the visible world were at the centre of their experience; each brought his deepest anxieties and apprehensions to bear in his thinking on art and artists. In the art criticism of both men is to be felt the presence of a poet of the *mal du siècle*, haunted by a yearning for complete and radical transformation and by a corresponding sense of impotence, of being in an unsympathetic milieu. Each manifested an imperative yearning for escape: Baudelaire's 'N'importe où hors du monde'[6] is Gautier's desire, frequently voiced in the columns of his art criticism, 'to flee into the steppes and abandon civilized life for ever'.[7] Both men often sought consolation outside actual events: a sense of excitement, of adrenalin flowing, or, in the truly nineteenth-century sense of the word, of poetry. They sought it 'Any where out of the world' (*sic*), in hashish or fantastic décor; their attention was often focused less on the world than on art. If the life of Stendhal's heroic, Napoleonic man of action was no longer possible, both followed the examples of Diderot and Stendhal in insisting that their own reactions to things, and to art-objects in particular, were as important if not more important than the things themselves; as art critics both saw themselves as artists, and art criticism as a creative effort.[8] Both expressed their commitment to art as a cult or a cause. Each manifested, at one time or another, a similar distrust of nature, which in Baudelaire's case could amount to positive revulsion and terror; both exalted the artificial in compensation. Baudelaire's concept of the 'surnaturel' is the direct cultural offspring of Gautier's tirades against nature and in favour of the artefact in *Les Jeunes-France*[9] and elsewhere; Baudelaire's 'Éloge du maquillage'[10] in *Le Peintre de la vie moderne*, for instance, is ultimately a pure extrapolation from Gautier's declaration that he found the sun not much better than gaslight, or women in the flesh decidedly inferior to their sculptural embodiments. The idealism of both is desperate in proportion to their sense of disillusion and *dépaysement*, and this sense is expressed metaphorically in their very life-styles. Gautier wore it with his red waistcoat, his flamboyant yellow babouches, and his permanently long hair, with that mythic and hyperbolically shocking public image, through which even today he is identified, incorrectly, as the one who took his alligator for walks in the Champs-Élysées; Baudelaire expressed it with his green hair and then with the sober costume of the Dandy, in a sartorial asceticism which was relieved only by the flash of red socks, *de rigueur* in the Baudelairean wardrobe. Both men invested a whole attitude to life in the world of appearances; for both the self-conscious cultivation and celebration of the artificial was a form of revolt, and provides the key to their respective historical personae; for both art criticism was thus the expression of a whole state of mind, and could engage them totally; it constituted a way of life.

Gautier's historical contribution to art criticism lies in his very life-style as a self-vaunted 'homme vraiment artiste'. This is a score upon which he deserves to be vindicated, and the treatment that his art criticism merits must thus of necessity be generously biographical and anecdotal ('the word *artist* justified everything' he wrote[11]). His criticism does not respond well to attempts at a purely conceptualizing, abstract, and academic assessment, for it is not in itself a primarily conceptual or intellectual exercise. Appraised as such, it loses in flavour and humanity; its impact is largely lost, and it is in this subjectively sensed impact that its originality is after all to be discovered, for it is the impact of the whole man.

In demanding this rounded treatment, Gautier and his immediate heir Baudelaire reveal themselves as unique among major contemporary art critics (with the exception of Gérard de Nerval, whose art criticism in any case occupies a relatively minor place in comparison). Pontus Grate has ably expounded the art-critical approaches of Gustave Planche and Théophile Thoré with a minimum of necessary biographical reference; Étienne Delécluze, Gautier's great predecessor from *Le Journal des Débats*, would respond happily to a similar treatment. These three great contemporaries, Delécluze, Planche, and Thoré, belong in a class that is as distinct from that of Gautier and Baudelaire as the art historian is from the working artist. Planche, the most rigorously detached, objective, and relentlessly analytical of the three, provides the clearest indication of their common position. If Gautier and Baudelaire applauded and upheld that tradition, represented by Diderot, of art criticism as an empathetic exercise, of the right of the informed man of letters to his subjective digressions in front of the work of art,

Planche deplored Diderot's influence for precisely the same reason: because it encouraged people to judge painting 'in terms of the thoughts it suggests rather than the thoughts it expresses'.[12] This is a statement that is anti-Romantic to the core; it echoes the feelings of Delécluze, who, if less misanthropic in the application of his critical rationalism (and who, for a critic of Gautier's despised Davidian generation, emerges over his long career as wiser, more flexible, and open-minded than Gautier might lead us to suppose), was nevertheless as concerned as was Planche with making historical assessments of contemporary painters from a detached and uncommitted expert or 'professional' stance, a stance as respectable as that of a doctor or lawyer. For the Romantic rebels Gautier and Baudelaire, art was experience itself, their own experience which they were inside and which was to be explored from the inside, subjectively, in terms of the feelings it engaged; Delécluze and Planche examined works of art from the outside, sought to determine their particular aims by a process of reasoning based on careful observations—not the thoughts suggested but the thoughts expressed—and thereafter made their judgements, with the ultimately postulated hope of being able to suggest or consolidate immutable criteria by which art could be assessed as historically great art, as minor art, or as not art at all.[13]

Unlike Delécluze and Planche, Théophile Thoré has a claim to be a true critic of the Romantic generation. But if he came to rely upon his subjective responses, on the associations painting, and particularly landscape painting, evoked, he too was finally concerned with evolving a comparative principle of superiority. His commitment was more broadly social and political than it was 'artistic'; as early as 1834 he was to be heard condemning a tendency towards 'l'art pour l'art' (a phrase, as Grate points out, that had become current critical jargon the previous year, in a similarly derogatory article by Hippolyte Fortoul)[14] and the artistic egotism that he quite rightly saw as accompanying it. In 1835 he discerned the major question in contemporary art as the choice between 'l'art pour l'art' and 'l'art social'.[15] The future resolution of this question was for Thoré 'L'ART POUR L'HOMME' (a concept usually proclaimed in triumphant capitals)[16], which he continued vigorously to oppose to 'l'art pour l'art'. As an intellectual formulation, and for all the vigour with which Thoré propounded it, 'l'art pour l'homme' is a little delicate. It is basically a demand for a subjectively apprehensible human element in painting, both in terms of underlying human presence on the part of the painter (and with this Thoré leads us forward to Zola's 'tempérament') but above all in that painting should express warm, identifiable, and common human feelings and preoccupations. In his great study of seventeenth-century Dutch art, *Les Musées de la Hollande*, this theme is overtly linked to liberal sentiment in politics, to a bourgeois democracy or republic, and made to stand against a repressive totalitarian monarchy or empire, the proper sphere, as Gautier the defender of 'royal and divine' sculpture would have agreed, for inhuman art for art's sake. In these extra-artistic concerns, Thoré too finally approaches art as a judge with history and dialectic on his side; for all his spontaneous identification with Delacroix and Rousseau, he was an outsider like Delécluze and Planche who assessed contemporary art within intellectual and historical terms: if he admitted the validity of his own reactions, he still wished to refer for final judgement to what art expressed.[17]

Gautier was never to check the rapacity of his vision, and seems, finally, almost to have grown simply unable to channel this psychic energy into intellectual or philosophical speculation, into the drawing of critical comparisons and conclusions. His energy was focused on his visual experience, so that his whole rapport with the outside world, his whole attitude to himself and his whole life-style assumed an essentially picturesque character. Such focusing of energy was an archetypally Romantic phenomenon; Nerval and Pétrus Borel are comparable examples of lives consumed in the pursuit of irresistible dreams, of particular and little explored aspects of experience. It was not in Gautier's robustly middle-class or humorously Gascon nature to be rapidly consumed physically or mentally; he was the first writer to bring such single-minded, self-conscious, and uncompromising focusing of energy to bear in widely read journalism. As such, he survived as the Romantic critic *par excellence*. Gautier's particular energy was infectious; it was transmitted to Baudelaire and through Baudelaire harnessed to produce its most powerful and resounding impact, but Baudelaire was not the only art critic to inherit it. Among Gautier's contemporaries, the Goncourt brothers stand out as perhaps his most direct and productive heirs.

In *L'Histoire du romantisme*, Gautier made a modest assessment of his literary contribution and that of the generation of 1830: 'This involvement of art in poetry has been and remains one of the characteristics of the new School . . . A host of objects, images, and comparisons which had been thought irreducible to words has entered the language and stayed there. The sphere of literature has expanded and now encompasses that of art in its immense orbit'.[18] 'Thus we began our careers,' Edmond de Goncourt likewise reminisced towards the end of his life, 'my brother under Jules Janin's influence and I under that of Théophile Gautier.'[19] Gautier's comparatively robust prose transcriptions and evocations of the visible world and of art were transformed or reduced by the Goncourts into that dense, febrile, and deeply neurotic *écriture artiste* which they applied to the works of Watteau and his successors, to Gavarni and Degas and to the more minor and digestible of their artist contemporaries. Gautier's dictum that a real writer should be able to find the words to describe anything was more than fulfilled by the brothers in their novels and *Journal*, in their tight-lipped, morbid, and spine-chilling excursions into worlds of decay and dissolution, to the mortuary and the dissecting table, and in the merciless descriptions with which they subsequently recorded the effects upon their tautened sensibilities. Patronizing, acrimonious, and snobbish as they almost invariably were in their relationships to their contemporaries, their corporate attitude to Gautier (which has relentlessly insinuated itself into the preceding chapters) was a relatively favourable one. Gautier may have been nerveless and '*vache*', but even the Goncourts seem finally to have been unable to help liking him. There is no doubt about their debt to him as writers; they certainly did not hesitate to record his compliments on their *Venise la nuit* in 1857, nor to accept his personal judgement: those who possess 'le sens *artiste*' and persist in a stylistic 'manière *artiste*', will, alas, ever be misunderstood, he assured them.[20] They were indeed the most persistent representatives of that self-consciously 'artistic' state of sensibility which Gautier had begun to make public.

Even Zola, in a sense, inherited the energy of this Romantic single-mindedness. He too was a lover of the *mot propre*, in his own prose and in the painting of Manet, Courbet, and Pissarro. In the footsteps of Stendhal, Gautier, and Baudelaire, he too vigorously reaffirmed the critic's right to his subjective responses, which, in an uncompromising campaign, he sought to codify, not in terms of vision or form, or of imagination, but in terms of 'tempérament', a solid human and humane presence that should communicate itself to the receptive, feeling spectator in works of art. Edmond de Goncourt amused himself with another literary-historical sequence in 1884, one that was based purely on the senses. 'In his effort to render nature', he wrote, 'Gautier had recourse only to his eyes',[21] and ever since, authors have been intent on exhausting every other sense: Fromentin, the ear (for the silence of the desert in his book *Un Été dans le Sahara*, much enthused over by Gautier at its first appearance);[22] Zola, 'the nose of a hunting dog'; and Pierre Loti, 'the nose of a sensuous Punchinello'. Zola's doggedly campaigning 'hunting dog's nose' finally points to social issues that had never engaged Gautier's 'œil rêveur' or his 'regard amoureux', and Zola's harsh criticism of Gautier's work as a whole comes as no surprise.[23] For although Gautier's prose, which after all embodies faithful and accurate *description* of appearances, simple transcription as well as subjective, empathetic, and digressive *evocation*, contains the seeds of that 'scientific', positivistic, documentary approach to description favoured by Zola and his recalcitrant pupil Huysmans (the prose of the Goncourts contains the same mixed seeds), it was for the aptness and wit of his more subjective, poetic responses to the visual world that Gautier seems to have been best remembered by his contemporaries. Who would have thought of dedicating a volume of poetry to Zola, and characterizing him as a magician? The real continuation of Gautier's effort as an art critic is thus to be sought less in the naturalist, descriptive documentation of modern life encouraged by Zola and his school and echoed in the painting of Manet and the Impressionists, than in the Nordic idealism and poetic mysticism of the Symbolist and Aesthetic movements, in a turning-away from life rather than in a documentation of its injustices or an analytical celebration of its compensations. It is finally to be sought less in France than among English-speaking critics.

In the light of hindsight much of Gautier's criticism seems to point forward to the French Symbolist movement in painting, with its emphasis on visionary experience, on transport to hermetic worlds-apart, on dreams and the Ideal, on dazzling jewel-encrusted surfaces, on the precious and eternal as on the fatal and the macabre. Gautier was a great admirer and early supporter of Gustave Moreau and Puvis de Chavannes, yet for all that he has in common here with Huysmans's Des Esseintes (the satirical function of whose character is not to be underestimated), Gautier's visionary yearnings are echoed far less clearly in the complex, varied, and problematic voice of Huysmans, than they are in the gem-like prose of Walter Pater. In Pater there is the same underlying pagan aspiration, a determined sublimation of questions of guilt and moral obligation through amoral art, and this, along with Pater's sensual, voluptuous, and theatrical High Anglicanism, distinguishes him from Huysmans if nothing else does. For Huysmans, conversion to Catholicism was to be undertaken with a profound seriousness; Pater's aestheticism amounted to a cult of amorality. Pater shares with Gautier a nostalgic preoccupation with an impossible past, and in particular with the Renaissance, and absorbs himself in it, almost literally shut away from the outside world in his Oxford rooms. He manifests Gautier's sensuality and yearning for plenitude, only in a more rarefied form, and indulges in the same rich prose evocation, which, if for Pater it has its place within a kind of poetically art-historical framework, is none the less as finely wrought as a verse from *Émaux et Camées,* and is primarily designed as an exquisite celebration of all the rarest and most tantalizing of *frissons.*

Also present within the circle of Gautier's heirs is that other great English-speaking critic of the *fin de siècle*, Henry James. James stands somewhat aloof from the Goncourts and from Pater, perhaps; but his art criticism nevertheless lies firmly within the same tradition. The tone of voice has changed; it is the tone of well-mannered, measured, and cultivated conversation, and recalls the monotonous unfolding of Gautier's own webs of syntax more than it does the high-pitched stylistic artistry of Pater or the Goncourts. Of all the critics so far mentioned, James is the one who speaks of Gautier with the most finely judged penetration: 'The beauty and variety of our present earth and the insatiability of our earthly temperament were his theme, and . . . he brought to this task a sort of pagan *bonhomie* . . . he was a sort of immeasurably lighter-handed Rabelais.'[24] Possessed of a cool and ever so slightly weary and sceptical worldly wisdom, James like Gautier was a thoroughly metropolitan and a truly cosmopolitan figure, at home in Paris as he was in London or Boston; his attention was drawn to French art and literature as much as it was to English. As a budding art critic in the late 1860s he was aware of a dearth of good English commentators on the fine arts; to turn from a critique in a London review to a critical feuilleton in a Parisian journal was, he wrote a decade later, 'like passing from a primitive to a very high civilization'.[25] He had thus recommended to himself 'the best French critics',[26] Stendhal, Planche, Vitet, and Taine, and if he does not mention Gautier in this catholic and broad-minded selection, Gautier was certainly a contemporary Parisian *feuilletoniste* with much to offer him. For James's major preoccupation too was 'the beauty and variety of our present earth'; less blatantly insatiable perhaps, he was as concerned as was Gautier with the description and evocation of this earth, its 'representation', in highly accomplished prose. He asked little more of painting, in his gentlemanly and untheoretical fashion, than that it should represent this earthly 'beauty and variety', that, to force a definition from him, it should be a 'vision of earthly harmonies'[27] (Gautier's more self-consciously and poetically phrased 'vague memory of Eden'[28]); its broad concern was 'the beautifying of existence, the conservation of enjoyment'.[29] Sharing

Gautier's traditionalism, James admired Delacroix and thought the Impressionists simply cynical. But it is above all in his fascination for 'the artist-life' that James the perfect man of letters confirms his rapport with Gautier, not only in his open enjoyment of the company and conversation of painters, but above all in his effort to live life itself as an art-form. 'If you are to be represented, if you are to be perpetrated, in short, it is nothing that you be great or good— it is everything that you be dressed', [30] he mildly satirized this attitude, in an observation that would serve as well beneath a photograph of the fur-coated Théophile as it would beneath a picture of James's own irreproachably frock-coated person. At the end of his life he wrote of himself in more determined and self-conscious terms: 'I am that queer monster, the artist, an obstinate finality, an inexhaustible sensibility'. [31] For James as for Gautier, the cultivation of the sensibilities towards an ever finer apprehension of the pleasurable, of beauty and variety, constituted a whole life's work, and a whole way of life. And both men were unequivocally conscious that it was a career that distinguished them from the metropolitan crowd.

Such was Gautier's original contribution and posterity: he prepared the ground for a self-consciously 'artistic' state of mind and approach to art criticism, a state of mind represented in some of its most typical extremes by critics such as the Goncourts, Pater, and Henry James: neurotic, exquisite, cultivated, and simply obstinate. These are his true heirs, critics for whom art stood for a reflection of all that was most agreeable in life, if it was not a critique of life, a turning-away from life, and a revolt against it, and for whom vision was a dominating and consoling passion. Historically, Gautier thus occupies a crucial position, between the heady, uncompromisingly rebellious passions of the Romanticism of 1830, and the exclusive sensibilities of the *fin de siècle*. He was the prophet of Art for Art's Sake in all its nineteenth-century manifestations, of that gradual erosion, tellingly reflected over his long writing career, of the ideals of Romanticism, and of their transformation into an idea of retreat into the hermetic and rarefied, or into the agreeable and safe.

2 A final assessment

Yet Gautier's contribution as 'un homme vraiment artiste' to
a continuing literary fashion for 'the artist-life', can still seem
to be a negative and passive one; his more immediate value as
a critic, to both his contemporary and his modern readers,
remains a vague quantity when seen against that of
Baudelaire. For unlike Baudelaire, and as Zola ruthlessly
observed, Gautier seems to hold out to the future no directly
or actively transforming insight; he was unable to sublimate
his nostalgia, *wanderlust*, and anxiety into something resemb-
ling a positive aesthetic stance, to transform those deepest
longings and apprehensions which, like Baudelaire, he allowed to permeate his art criticism, into an insight or
programme that would readily act upon the real world, that
might provide artists and readers of future generations with a
perspective on their own predicament. Baudelaire is characteristically ready with a possible explanation for Gautier's
failure to make this creative leap. It is an explanation that
points to the fundamental difference between the two men,
and which helps us towards a final and realistic appreciation
of Gautier's art-critical text.

'To repudiate the efforts of the preceding, Christian and
philosophical, society', Baudelaire wrote in 1852, 'is suicide;
it is to deny oneself the strength and the means for perfection.
To surround oneself exclusively with the seductions of a
purely physical art, is to create for oneself every chance of
perdition.'[32] He was thundering against 'the pagan school',
against that pseudo-classical, pseudo-pagan revivalism with
which Gautier was so closely in sympathy and which in 1852
was reaching a peak of popularity. Its current most typical
representative in painting was Jean-Léon Gérôme; along
with Théodore de Banville and Louis Ménard, Gautier was
justly identified with it in poetry (*Émaux et Camées* was to
appear in July). Baudelaire's words can indeed be read as a
harsh moral verdict on Théophile the amoral nineteenth-
century pagan himself: 'Frenzied passion for art is a canker
that devours everything else; and just as plain absence of the
right and the true from art amounts to absence of art, so does

the whole man disappear; the excessive specialization of one faculty leads to nothingness.'[33]

Baudelaire of course admitted to a similar passion: 'The glorification of the cult of images (my great, my unique, my primitive passion).'[34] But if the two poets have a 'great, unique, primitive passion' for the visual arts in common, an irreconcilable difference lies between them, for between Baudelaire's cryptic 'culte des images' and Gautier's worship of the plastic *beau*, his cult of all-revealing and all-consoling form, is all the difference between the outer world and the inner. Gautier is absorbed in the contemplation of exterior form and his whole attention simply distracted in the process; Baudelaire is a man whose whole moral and psychic being is embroiled in the inner life of the imagination.

For the profoundly Catholic Baudelaire, *le beau* was never a concept beneath which *le juste* and *le vrai* might be subsumed; he could even understand the furies of Muslims and iconoclasts against the painted image, he went on to declare in 'L'École païenne'.[35] The celebration of the artificial and the 'surnaturel' in which Baudelaire joined Gautier must thus, in Baudelaire's case, be seen within a larger moral structure. Baudelaire was obsessed with an idea of original sin, of the essential bestiality and destructiveness of man and nature; his cult of images was fundamentally a moral programme, and imagination, that 'queen of the faculties', fundamentally a moral faculty. If human nature was base and evil in itself, there was a corresponding and consoling possibility of bliss; and the means for perfecting himself, which Baudelaire declared the nineteenth-century pagan to be denying himself, could thus only be approached through artificial means, through the unnatural exercise of controlling, penetrating, and selective 'imagination' upon the world. The type of the man who led this redeeming inner life was the Dandy, with his disdainful, immaculate, immovable, and priest-like exterior; imagination found its proper and highest function, transcending and transforming the world, in the mind and hands of the artist and in the images he produced. Imposing the constraints of his own deepest inhibitions and anxieties upon his thinking on art and artists, Baudelaire operated between the crushing awareness of the possibility of perfection and the probability of damnation; he was a dandy and an artist himself, and his art criticism was a creative effort of the imagination towards what virtually amounted to the search for a definition of quality, a search for an artistic 'perfectionnement' which, far from contributing to any notion of art-historical 'progress', should consist in a direct correspondence to the quality of the present subjective moment, to Baudelaire's apprehension of the quality of this moment. His criticism was above all a process of refinement, selection, and penetration leading towards the proposal of an art which, in reflecting and transcending the real world, might make this real, familiar, and inherently evil world meaningful and hospitable. For if Baudelaire took refuge in art, it was more than mere escapism from unpleasant realities; art for Baudelaire was an urgent necessity, the resource without which life would not have been livable at all. Thus not only was his Romantic art intended to reveal the heroism of modern life, to show the nineteenth century how poetic it was in its cravat and patent-leather boots, as in 1845.[36] Reflecting the real world in all its mysterious chaos and complexity, art should enable the spectator to accept this world, by keeping him at one remove from it; to maintain a safe detachment from it while remaining a part of it all, like a man convalescing from a dangerous illness who watches the crowd from behind the glass of a café window. Such was the message of Baudelaire's culminating art-critical text, *Le Peintre de la vie moderne*.[37] His qualitative definition of Romanticism in terms of a painting of modern life, a modern art corresponding to pressing modern needs, was an argument in favour of art as a moral and emotional necessity, not merely as an agency for escape and consolation. This, together with his insistence that the artist should act on the conditions of the society he lives in—that he cannot, like the nineteenth-century pagan, finally deny these conditions without risking a kind of oblivion—has proved of incalculable importance to subsequent thinkers and artists.

Gautier's promiscuous approach to art criticism could not seem more alien to Baudelaire's rigorous and passionate effort to discern where the future lay. 'Lucky man! Man worthy of our envy! He has loved only the Beautiful, and sought only the Beautiful', was the equivocal cry with which Baudelaire expressed his sense of the unbridgeable distance between them.[38] Shortly before Baudelaire poured out his moral indignation at the amoral pagan school, Gautier had assimilated the Salon of 1850–1 with the grand declaration: 'Everything that is beautiful is moral'.[39] Gautier's pronouncement ultimately stands in line of descent from Stendhal's liberating emphasis on the vital connection between beauty and happiness; its underlying philosophical basis, unacknowledged by the unintellectual Gautier, is Victor Cousin's famous doctrine of the autonomy of beauty of thirty years earlier.[40] Gautier licensed himself and his readers once and for all to take their fill of whatever immediate pleasures art might offer. With his insatiable ocular greed and through his unwillingness and final virtual inability to make definite qualitative judgements, his achievement was simply to remove any last outside moral or intellectual constraints on the *quantity* of pleasurable experience that might be grasped. His tacit assurance was that *le beau*, if it was nothing else, was simply the highest and most rewarding of legitimate pleasures.

This indeed hardly seems to be an insight to match that of Baudelaire. Yet it is difficult to argue that Gautier made any more specific contribution to contemporary art-critical awareness. He was not even an art historian, in the sense that he made discoveries for himself that would significantly alter the course of public taste; in spite of his immense connoisseurship, and although he did much to disseminate interest in eighteenth-century French, seventeenth-century Spanish, Dutch, and Flemish painting, his achievement is in no sense comparable to that, for example, of Thoré, who, under the Nordic pseudonym William Bürger, thoroughly re-examined and re-attributed the contents of the museums of Holland, and the major result of whose scholarly investigation was the 'discovery' of Vermeer as a single artist with a homogeneous *oeuvre*. Thoré's respect for the sensitivity of Gautier's own observations on Dutch art shines through the footnotes of his *Les Musées de la Hollande*;[41] but Gautier was never to substantiate his impressions with Thoré's time-consuming scholarship. Gautier may seem to have more in

common with the painter, novelist, and critic Eugène
Fromentin, who may indeed be counted among his
inheritors; both men were subjective and pragmatic in their
approach, and they shared a wide connoisseurship and
knowledge of studio technique. Yet Fromentin's *Les Maîtres
d'autrefois* of 1876 was more an original art-historical assessment of Dutch and Flemish art than the prose celebration
Gautier might have written: compare this guidebook by
Fromentin with Gautier's *Guide de l'amateur au Musée du
Louvre*. In Fromentin the concerns of the careful historian
and biographer were allowed free interplay with the perceptions and responses of the practising painter and writer. Even
Arsène Houssaye and the Goncourt brothers have more claim
than Gautier to be pioneers in the history of taste, questions
of historical precedence apart; as publicists of the eighteenth
century, their importance lies above all in the fact that unlike
Gautier, they published their observations in book form.
Their books were reviewed in the press,[42] and their views
were always available, unlike those of the newspaper
journalist, for lengthy perusal, reference, and assimilation.

'The modern reader may feel frustrated and disappointed at
the lack both of Baudelaire's qualities and of those of an art
historian in Gautier, and Baudelaire's observations on the
shortcomings of the kind of approach that Gautier adopted
cannot be ignored. Yet at the same time, if we are to benefit
from him at all, we must be careful not to judge Gautier in
terms of what he was not nor ever pretended to be. If he was a
poet, like Baudelaire, and a dedicated connoisseur, like
Thoré, he was above all a working journalist; he operated
under circumstances which made demands on him that
Baudelaire, the Goncourts, and even Thoré were never
obliged to meet. Unlike these critics, Gautier spent his whole
professional career writing for mass-circulation newspapers;
La Presse, indeed, was the first successful, mass-circulation
newspaper in France. He was incontestably the most prolific
and accessible art critic of the age; he pioneered and
established standards for a kind of criticism which was new to
the nineteenth century, a criticism to appeal to an un-
precedentedly large reading public.

His much remarked upon reserves of generosity, admiration and empathy are not to be passed over simply as endearing personal qualities; they constituted his tremendous value as a working critic, to the extent that they enabled him to be of the greatest possible immediate use both to his public and to artists. Among artists, from Ingres and Courbet to Puvis de Chavannes, he commanded wide respect;[43] he was well aware of the persuasiveness and potential influence of published criticism, and his desire to celebrate and encourage indeed allowed him to do the least possible damage, and to 'leave room for admiration' even where he felt the strongest antipathy. On one level, this desire, with the abdication of judgement it could imply, merely reflected his place in a developing consumer culture; it was also a conscious strategem, in response to what Gautier saw as the nature of his task. As a poet with the common touch, and a *littérateur* whose favourite haunt was the studio, he brought to journalism an inside view of art as it was actually practised in his age, and did so in terms his public could understand and enjoy.

As well as reflecting its decline as a 'movement', Gautier embodies Romanticism's enduring qualities. He wholeheartedly accepted the challenge of confronting works in their own terms (and has paid the price as tastes have changed); inseparable from this was his insistence on the right of the critic, and thus of the spectator, to respond and elaborate on his own account, to acknowledge and welcome his own responses, and to take from this experience what he could. This is a right which bears restating, in a century whose art has developed in such ways as frequently to be inaccessible to the public at large, and in which this public has, as a result, often felt intimidated into an attitude of scorn or indifference. Gautier can remind us, as he reminded his contemporaries, that art only exists at all as part of a community of experience, within which we ourselves belong.

At the same time, he is rigorous in defence of the artist's inalienable right to pursue excellence in his own way; his fundamental demand is not that artists should merely cater for public sensibilities, but that they should both refine and broaden them. His own love of the formal and sculptural has long been recognized, and has been drawn upon and celebrated ever since the 1850s. Less well acknowledged is what underlay this idealism: his emphasis on instinct, as a means of reaching towards a realization of possibility and a fullness of experience. His message both to artists and spectators was one of self-fulfilment, liberation from the constraints of the merely reasonable; many of those exhortations in which this message was put across may be said to stand as literature in their own right, for they strike the modern reader with all their original impact.

Gautier's faith in the unconscious and irrational was unreserved and imperative: it was above all an urgent response to what he correctly discerned to be an historic imbalance, Western, post-Cartesian man's tendency drastically to underestimate the role of his own physical and intuitive life. As such, this insistence on the power of the instinctual and imaginative required, for Gautier, no qualification, no complementary analytical effort, by means of which it might have been extended into a fuller discussion of contemporary emotional and social needs; but if his view of things was, finally, only partial in itself, the insights out of which it grew remain no less crucial to any such fuller discussion. The whole tone of Gautier's writing was determined by a profound and fundamentally humane recognition: that, given an acceptance of the integrity and the ultimately unquantifiable nature of the experience of the other, communication can take place on levels of understanding which are as precise as they are rich and deep; that man's capacity for creating reality and responding to it is limitless. At its best, the weather of Gautier's world has all the radiance of one of Baudelaire's rare and incomparable 'beaux jours de l'esprit';[44] embodied in the very fabric of his Romantic criticism is a vision of art as activity, through which both artists and spectators may begin to rediscover, with themselves and with what is tangible outside, a dynamism and wholeness of relationship. His own determined subjectiveness, his demands for creative participation, and his refusal to pass judgements in the absence of a positive, lived viewpoint of his own, were personal affirmations of faith in the possibility of just such a wholeness.

Appendix I

Gautier's Collection

Collection de Théophile Gautier. Catalogue des tableaux, aquarelles, dessins, gravures, eaux-fortes, lithographies, photographies etc. . . . bronzes et objets d'art. Vente à Paris, hôtel Drouot . . . les 14, 15 & 16 janvier 1873.

The catalogue lists pictures in Gautier's collection by, among others, Baudry, Bellel, Chassériau, Delacroix, Diaz, Fromentin, Gérôme, Hébert, Huet, Ingres, Leleux frères, Muller, Palizzi, Penguilly l'Haridon, Puvis de Chavannes, Riesener, Rioult, Robert-Fleury, Rousseau (Ph. and Th.), Schreyer, Verdier (M.), and Ziegler; drawings, pastels, or water-colours by Aligny, Cabat, Chassériau, Decamps, Delacroix, Doré, Lehmann, Roqueplan, Troyon; bronzes by Barye, Rosa Bonheur, and Préault; lithographs by Delacroix, Flandrin (H.), Hugo, Gavarni, and Nanteuil.

Appendix II

Passages in the original French

1. Ch. II, n. 8

'Notre critique différera de celle des autres journaux, nos frères en Dieu ou en diable (car il n'est pas encore décidé si le journal est chose divine ou diabolique), en ce que, loin de s'étendre longuement sur les défauts et de les mettre curieusement en relief, elle s'attachera plutôt à faire ressortir les beautés. Nous ne comprenons guère la critique autrement. La critique est une espèce de cicérone, qui vous prend par la main et vous guide à travers un pays que vous ne connaissez pas encore. Que diriez-vous d'un cicérone qui vous ferait passer par les rues les plus boueuses et les plus mal bâties de la ville pour vous amener à quelque masure insignifiante, au lieu de vous faire arrêter devant les beaux palais et les vieilles églises? . . . d'un propriétaire qui vous conduirait d'abord aux latrines . . . ?'

2. Ch. II, n. 11, n. 12, n. 15, n. 16

'. . . quel monde immense que celui de l'art! N'est-ce pas toute la nature visible, avec l'émotion de l'homme en plus? N'est-ce pas le rêve prenant pour s'exprimer les formes de la réalité? . . .
. . . L'Écriture parle quelque part de la concupiscence des yeux, concupiscientia oculorum;—ce péché est notre péché, et nous espérons que Dieu nous le pardonnera.—Jamais oeil fut plus avide que le nôtre, et le bohémien de Béranger n'a pas mis en pratique plus consciencieusement que nous la devise: voir, c'est avoir . . .
Quant à nos principes, nous aimons à croire . . . qu'ils sont suffisament connus; nous croyons à l'autonomie de l'Art; l'Art pour nous n'est pas le moyen mais le but;—tout artiste qui se propose autre chose que le beau n'est pas un artiste à nos yeux; nous n'avons jamais pu comprendre la séparation de l'idée de la forme, pas plus que nous ne comprendrions le corps sans

l'âme, du moins dans notre sphère de manifestation—une belle forme est une belle idée, car que serait-ce qu'une forme qui n'exprimerait rien? . . .
On nous a souvent accusé d'indulgence; c'est un reproche que nous ne déclinons pas. La critique, selon nous, doit être plutôt le commentaire des beautés que la recherche des fautes . . . ; nous sommes un poète et non un magister. Étudier une oeuvre, la comprendre, l'exprimer avec les moyens de notre art, voilà quel a été toujours notre but. Nous aimons à mettre à côté d'un tableau une page où le thème du peintre est repris par l'écrivain. Nous admettons chacun au point de vue de son idéal particulier; coloriste avec Delacroix, dessinateur avec Ingres, nous ne leur demandons que ce qu'ils proposent . . . nous épousons momentanément les goûts et les antipathies de ces natures si opposées; nous jugeons leur peinture comme si nous possédions leur âme. Sans doute nous avons aussi nos sympathies secrètes, mais pourquoi se circonscrire, se diminuer, ne pas jouir largement de tout? Pourquoi se priver du plaisir délicieux d'être pour quelque temps un autre, d'habiter sa cervelle, de voir la nature à travers ses yeux comme à travers un prisme nouveau? Le ciel, pour toute richesse, et nous l'en remercions, nous a fait le don de comprendre et admirer, et comme dit le poète persan: si nous ne sommes pas la rose, nous avons vécu près de la rose.'

3. Ch. III, n. 11

'. . . mais il est d'autres génies plus inquiets, plus fantasques pour qui la nature est le point de départ et non pas le but, et dont l'aile ouverte à tous les vents du caprice fouette impétueusement les vitres de l'atelier et les brise; ils voient autrement et autre chose;—à leurs yeux les lignes tremblent comme des flammes ou se tordent comme des serpens, les moindres détails prennent des formes singulières; le rouge s'empourpre, le bleu verdit, le jaune devient fauve, le noir se veloute comme les zébrures d'une peau de tigre; l'eau jette du fond de l'ombre de mystérieuses étincelles, et le ciel regarde à travers le feuillage avec des prunelles d'un azur étrange.'

4. Ch. III, n. 15

'Goethe dit quelque part que tout artiste doit porter en lui le *microcosme*, c'est à dire un petit monde complet d'où il tire la pensée et la forme de ses oeuvres;—c'est dans ce microcosme qu'habitent   les   blanches   héroïnes   et   les   brunes

madones . . . Les artistes qui ont le microcosme, lorsqu'ils
veulent produire, regardent en eux-mêmes et non au dehors;
ils peuvent très bien faire une maison d'après un canard, et un
singe d'après un arbre.—Ce sont les vrais poètes, dans le sens
grec du mot, ceux qui créent, ceux qui font: les autres ne sont
que des imitateurs et des copistes . . .'

5. Ch. III, n. 43

'. . . rien ne meurt, tout existe toujours; nulle force ne peut
anéantir ce qui fut une fois. Toute action, toute parole, toute
forme, toute pensée tombée dans l'océan universel des choses y
produit des cercles qui vont s'élargissant jusqu'aux confins de
l'éternité. La figuration matérielle ne disparaît que pour les
regards vulgaires, et les spectres qui s'en détachent peuplent
l'infini. Pâris continue d'enlever Hélène dans une region
inconnue de l'espace. La galère de Cléopâtre gonfle ses voiles
de soie sur l'azur d'un Cydnus idéal. Quelques esprits
passionnés et puissants ont pu amener à eux des siècles écoulés
en apparence, et faire revivre des personnages morts pour tous.
Faust a eu pour maîtresse la fille de Tyndare, et l'a conduite à
son château gothique, du fond des abîmes mystérieux de
l'Hadès . . .'

6. Ch. III, n. 46

'. . . abandonnons l'embryologie psychique aux philosophes,
ces anatomistes de l'âme; livrons-nous à l'amour, à
l'admiration, à l'enthousiasme, au travail et au loisir, à la
pensée et au rêve, à toutes les ivresses de l'intelligence, à tous
les épanouissements de la vie; étincelons comme des flots,
vibrons comme des lyres; soyons traversés, comme des
prismes, par les rayons des soleils et les effluves des univers!
Laissons les verbes parler par nos lèvres; confions-nous à
l'inconnu . . .'

7. Ch. IV, n. 17

'Essayez d'isoler une figure de M. Delacroix ou de la mettre en
pensée dans un autre milieu, elle vous paraîtra bizarre ou
impossible, car elle est entourée d'une atmosphère qui lui est
propre et respirable seulement pour elle. La couleur, à bon
droit si vantée, de l'artiste est dans les mêmes conditions: elle
ne se recommande pas par des rouges, des verts ou des bleus
d'une grande vivacité, mais par des gammes de nuances qui se

font valoir les unes les autres; ses tons si riches ne sont pas beaux en eux-mêmes, leur éclat résulte de leur juxtaposition et de leur contraste . . .'

8. Ch. IV, n. 33

' . . . il a le don, si rare en peinture, du mouvement: ses personnages remuent, gesticulent, courent, se précipitent; la toile semble les contenir avec peine . . . ils ont sur leurs contours comme un flamboiement perpétuel, comme un tremblement lumineux d'atmosphère; une ligne inflexible ne les attache pas à leurs fonds; ils sont peints aussi de l'autre côté et pourraient se retourner s'ils le voulaient; sans se soucier d'être jolis ou beaux, ils sont tout à leur affaire et ne se distraient pas de l'action pour faire leur torse ou leur tête dans un coin, à l'adresse du spectateur: comme les acteurs anglais, ils tournent souvent le dos au public et ne regardent que leur interlocuteur, au mépris des conventions du théâtre.'

9. Ch. IV, n. 39

'La mer est courte, opaque et clapoteuse, comme après une longue tempête. Le ciel est couvert de nuages bas, gros de pluies et d'éclairs, qui ne jettent que des reflets plombés sur la triste scène qu'ils recouvrent. Au milieu de cette double immensité flotte à l'aventure une petite barque chargée outre mesure. Dans ce frêle esquif sont entassés une trentaine de misérables, hâves, décharnés, livides . . . la famine fait luire devant leurs yeux ses feux rouges et ses éblouissements.'

10. Ch. IV, n. 40

'Ne pensez plus à don Juan, qu'il serait difficile de reconnaître parmi ces visages hâves, creusés, amaigris, convulsés par d'exécrables convoitises . . .—Comme on sent frétiller les requins à triples rangs de dents, sous ces vagues d'un vert glauque, balançant leur crête de mousse blanche! comme le vent et le tonnerre grondent sourdement derrière ces nuages bas, gros d'orage et de pluie!'

11. Ch. IV, n. 50

' . . . Là flottaient toutes les images de la nature, non pas copiées, mais conçues et transformées, et servant comme des mots à exprimer des idées, et surtout des passions. Dans la moindre ébauche comme dans le tableau le plus important, le ciel, le terrain, les arbres, la mer, les fabriques participent à la scène qu'ils entourent; ils sont orageux ou clairs, unis ou tourmentés, sans feuilles ou verdoyants, calmes ou convulsifs, ruinés ou magnifiques, mais toujours ils semblent épouser les colères, les haines, les douleurs et les tristesses des personnages. Il serait impossible de les en détacher . . . Tout se tient, tout est lié et forme un ensemble magique dont aucune partie ne saurait être retranchée ou transposée sans faire s'écrouler l'édifice. En art, nous ne connaissons que Rembrandt qui ait cette unité profonde et indissoluble . . . Rembrandt, comme Delacroix, a son architecture, son vestiaire, son arsenal, son musée d'antiques, ses types et ses formes, sa lumière et sa nuit, ses gammes de tons qui n'existent pas ailleurs et dont il sait tirer des effets merveilleux, rendant le fantastique plus vrai que la réalité.'

12. Ch. V, n. 32

'. . . c'est une traduction de la nature beaucoup plus mot à mot: son dessin serre la forme de plus près; et le caractère de son style est l'exagération dans un principe vrai des détails extérieurs, car M. Ingres soigne principalement la silhouette linéaire de ses personnages, et dessine plus sur le bord que dans le milieu: procédé qui, ôtant beaucoup de relief, a pour résultat un aspect large et simple tout à fait magistral, et qui ferait distinguer au premier coup d'oeil le tableau entre mille.'

13. Ch. VI; 2, n. 74

'Les figures de Léonard de Vinci semblent savoir ce que les hommes ignorent, on dirait qu'ils ont habité, avant de venir se mirer dans la toile, des zones supérieures et inconnues . . . il semble que l'arc de ces lèvres (those of the Mona Lisa) va décocher quelque sarcasme divin, quelque ironie céleste, quelque moquerie angélique; une joie intérieure et dont le secret nous échappe, les fait onduler en courbures inexplicables; . . . sous la forme *exprimée*, on sent une pensée vague, infinie, *inexprimable*, comme une idée musicale; . . . des images déjà vues vous passent devant les yeux, des voix dont on croit reconnaître le timbre vous chuchotent à l'oreille de langoureuses confidences; des désirs réprimés, des espérances qui désespéraient s'agitent douloureusement dans une ombre mêlée de rayons, et vous découvrez que vos mélancolies viennent de ce que la Joconde accueillit, il y a trois cents ans, l'aveu de votre amour avec ce sourire railleur qu'elle garde encore aujourd'hui.'

14. Ch. VI; 2, n. 81

'Un pauvre lièvre, victime prédestinée, malgré la vitesse inquiète de sa course, malgré l'acuité d'ouïe des ses longues oreilles toujours en éveil, a été surpris par le bond violent et brusque d'un jaguar aplati en embuscade sur une branche ou sur une roche; il est là l'oeil fixe et mort, les naseaux dilatés, essayant un soubresaut suprême dans la gueule du monstre dont les crocs lui cassent les reins. Le jaguar fronce les babines, ferme à demi les yeux; les papilles de sa rude langue hument d'avance le sang et la moelle; il semble enivré par cette vapeur de vie qui s'exhale sous sa morsure; sa proie chaude palpitera encore au fond de ses entrailles. Aussi, comme il a peur de la laisser aller, comme ses muscles d'acier se contractent pour la retenir ou la disputer; tout son corps palpite; des frissons de volupté courent le long de son échine onduleuse, arrondie comme le dos du chat qu'on caresse: il y a là plus que l'assouvissement de la faim, il y a le triomphe du chasseur heureux et l'atroce plaisir du méchant qui tue sans risque.'

15. Ch. VI; 2, n. 83

'Ah! belle Hérodiade, lascive et perfide danseuse, tu as été bien modeste en ne demandant qu'une seule tête au tyran, une seule, celle d'un pauvre saint basané et barbu; il t'en aurait donné cinquante pour un sourire de plus, mille pour une de ces ondulations de hanches qui font pétiller d'un feu si vif les robes brochées d'or sous les lampes d'orgie. Mais tu n'en voulais qu'une, capricieuse! pour que les peintres te représentassent éternellement superbe et triomphante, avec ta grâce scélérate, tes regards d'une innocence diabolique, et ton sourire vermeil comme du sang, tenant, par une antithèse pleine de charme et d'horreur, dans l'aiguière d'argent souillée d'épais caillots, la tête livide et convulsée, aux yeux renversés par le spasme suprême, à la bouche tordue, et dont le col d'un sombre pourpre laisse paraître, comme des taches blanches, les vertèbres rompues et les canaux des artères tranchées.'

16. Ch. VI; 3, n. 101

'"Olympia", dont le titre réveille le souvenir de cette grande courtisane romaine dont raffola la Renaissance, ne s'explique à aucun point de vue, même en la prenant pour ce qu'elle est, un chétif modèle étendu sur un drap. Le ton des chairs est sale, le modelé nul. Les ombres s'indiquent par des raies de cirage plus ou moins larges. Que dire de la négresse qui apporte un bouquet dans un papier et du chat noir qui laisse l'empreinte de ses pattes crottées sur son lit? Nous excuserions encore la laideur, mais vraie, étudiée, relevée par quelque splendide effet de couleur. La femme la moins jolie a des os, des muscles, une peau, des formes et un coloris quelconque. Ici, il n'y a rien, nous sommes fâché de le dire, que la volonté d'attirer les regards à tout prix.'

17. Ch. VI; 4, n. 131

'Les gens qui ne voient que l'écorce des choses et qui pleurent d'attendrissement aux sentimentalités romanesques, ont parfois accusé Paul Véronèse d'être froid, de manquer de coeur, de n'avoir pas de passion, d'être sans idée et sans but, et de se complaire uniquement aux merveilles d'une exécution prodigieuse. Jamais peintre n'eut un plus haut idéal. Cette fête éternelle de ses tableaux a un sens profond; ses festins sont tous symboliques, car l'on y mange à peine; et ce n'est pas le feu de l'ivresse qui anime les yeux bruns de ces beaux groupes d'hommes et de femmes, mais un sentiment de joie universelle et d'harmonie générale.'

18. Ch. VI; 4, n. 133

'. . . les hommes retrouvent aisément des félicités plus enivrantes que celles du couple solitaire de l'antique Eden. N'ont-ils pas les femmes, les fleurs, les parfums, l'or, le marbre, la soie, le vin, la musique, la poésie, l'art, cette fleur de la pensée; l'échange de l'idée ou du sentiment avec un être pareil à soi, et pourtant dissemblable; la variété dans l'harmonie; l'admiration, cet amour de l'esprit; l'amour, cette admiration du coeur qui vous élève et vous prosterne; la conscience de faire partie de cet homme perpétuel et collectif avec qui Dieu cause, dans le silence de la création, pour se désennuyer de l'éternité!

Gloire donc à Paul Véronèse, qui fait briller à nos yeux les éléments de bonheur que la bienveillance divine a mis à notre disposition! Une terre où il y a plus de vingt mille espèces de fleurs ou plantes de pur ornement, où la décoration des couchers de soleil est changée tous les soirs, où la forme superbe est si splendidement habillée par la couleur, ne peut pas être une vallée de misère. Oui, si on le voulait, l'eau des "Noces de Cana" pourrait se changer perpétuellement en vin, et les parfums de la courtisane en arômes célestes!'

19. Ch. VII; 2, n. 91

'Ne méprisez pas tant, jeune peintre, votre propre génie. Pourquoi tant de travail et d'inquiétude? Vous avez l'oeil et la main, vous savez et vous pouvez. Donnez plus au hasard et moins à la volonté, ne vous surveillez pas si rigoureusement, laissez quelquefois prendre les pinceaux à cet inconnu qui vient visiter les grands artistes et travaille à leur place sans qu'ils s'en aperçoivent. Cet inconnu a fait les plus belles choses du monde, Homère lui-même n'était que son secrétaire, et Raphaël que son tailleur de crayons.'

20. Ch. VII; 3, n. 147

'Chacun se dit: "Suis-je vraiment une ganache, une perruque, un être momifié, un fossile antédiluvien ne comprenant plus rien à son siècle . . . ?" . . . et l'on pense à l'antipathie, à l'horreur qu'inspiraient, il y a une trentaine d'années, à des gens qui ne manquaient ni d'esprit, ni de talent, ni de goût, ni de largeur d'idées, les premières peintures de Delacroix, de Decamps, de Boulanger, de Scheffer, de Corot, de Rousseau, si longtemps exilés du Salon . . . Et pourtant ces artistes si honnis, si conspués, si persécutés sont devenus des maîtres illustres, reconnus de tous, et ils avaient alors autant de talent qu'ils en eurent jamais, peut-être même davantage, car ils donnaient la fleur de leur génie. Les scrupuleux se demandent, en face de ces exemples frappants et encore tous voisins de nous, si vraiment l'on ne peut comprendre autre chose en art que les oeuvres de la génération dont on est contemporain, c'est à dire avec laquelle on a eu vingt ans. Il est probable que les tableaux de Courbet, Manet, Monet et tutti quanti renferment des beautés qui nous échappent à nous autres anciennes chevelures romantiques déjà mêlées de fils d'argent, et qui sont particulièrement sensibles aux jeunes gens à vestons courts et à chapeaux éscrimés. Pour notre part, nous avons fait en conscience tous nos efforts pour nous accoutumer à cette peinture, et quand nous avons eu l'honneur de faire partie du jury, nous ne l'avons pas repoussée. Nous avons tâché d'être juste envers ce qui nous répugnait . . .'

Notes

INTRODUCTION (pp. 1–8)

1 E. and J. de Goncourt, *Journal des Goncourt – mémoires de la vie littéraire*, 4 vols., Fasquelle et Flammarion, Paris, 1956, 3 Jan. 1857.
2 *J des G*, 3 Jan. 1857.
3 Ibid.
4 'Anyone who is stuck for words when faced with an idea, subtle and unexpected as it may seem, is no writer. The inexpressible does not exist,' Baudelaire reports him as saying, in his article on Gautier first published in *L'Artiste*, 13 May 1859. C. Baudelaire, *L'Art romantique*, Collection Littéraire Julliard, Paris, 1964, XVIII, pp. 151–80.
5 *L'Artiste*, 28 Dec. 1856.
6 *J des G*, 1 May 1857. The *Oxford English Dictionary* defines a 'pschent' as 'The double crown of ancient Egypt, combining the white crown of upper Egypt with the red crown of Lower Egypt'.
7 Cf. Baudelaire's 'N'importe où hors du monde'. C. Baudelaire, *Petits Poèmes en prose*, Librairie José Corti, Paris, 1969, XLVIII, pp. 139–40.
8 First published in *Le Mercure de France au XIXᵉ siècle*, 22 Oct. 1831. R. Jasinski (ed.), *Poésies complètes de Théophile Gautier*, 3 vols., A. G. Nizet, Paris, 1970, vol. III, pp. 133–9.
9 *J des G*, 1 May 1857.
10 *Poésies complètes*, vol. II, pp. 73 & 75.
11 T. Gautier, *Le Roman de la momie*, Garnier-Flammarion, Paris, 1966, pp. 55–7.

I BIOGRAPHY (pp. 9–43)

1 *L'Artiste*, 7 June 1857.
2 *Le Moniteur universel*, 14 Aug. 1863.
3 T. Gautier, *Histoire du romantisme. Notices romantiques . . .* , Charpentier, Paris, 1874, p. 98.
4 *L'Illustration*, 9 Mar. 1867: 'Sommités contemporaines'.
5 E. Bergerat, *Théophile Gautier. Entretiens, souvenirs, et correspondance*, Charpentier, Paris, 1879, p. 28.
6 J. Richardson, *Théophile Gautier. His Life and Times*, Max Reinhardt, London, 1958, p. 17.
7 *L'Illustration*, 9 Mar. 1867.

8 Ibid.
9 Ibid.
10 Ibid.
11 *J des G*, 9 May 1864.
12 *L'Illustration*, 9 Mar. 1867.
13 See *J des G*, 5 Dec. 1857.
14 Ibid., 24 Oct. 1872.
15 *Poésies complètes*, vol. II, p. 144. First published in *La Presse*, 14 Feb. 1837.
16 *H du r*, p. 82.
17 H. Rosenberg, 'The American Action Painters', *Art News*, Sept. 1952.
18 *J des G*, 5 Mar. 1857.
19 *H du r*, pp. 1–2.
20 Ibid., p. 11.
21 Ibid., p. 3.
22 *L'Illustration*, 9 Mar. 1867.
23 R. Jasinski, *Les Années romantiques de Théophile Gautier*, Librairie Vuibert, Paris, 1929, p. 99.
24 The catalogue for the sale of Gautier's collection in 1873 confirms that he owned these paintings. (See Appendix I.)
25 *Poésies complètes*, vol. I, pp. 65–8.
26 *H du r*, p. 2.
27 He continued to draw and paint intermittently throughout his life; other examples of his work are reproduced in Joanna Richardson's biography. Bergerat catalogues works by Gautier in *Théophile Gautier. Entretiens, souvenirs* . . . , pp. 261–72. Bergerat's opinion of Gautier's painting was that it was 'notoriously academic'; as a man of letters and an amateur painter he handled 'the pen like Veronese and the brush like Chênedollé' (ibid., p. 257). The somewhat insipid and amorphous ink drawing of a semi-nude bather reproduced here appears in volume one of Houssaye's *Confessions*; it is possibly after a painting by Rioult. A. Houssaye, *Les Confessions. Souvenirs d'un demi-siècle 1830–1880*, 4 vols., E. Dentu, Paris, 1885, vol. I, p. xxiv.
28 *H du r*, p. 2.
29 Ibid., p. 4.
30 Ibid., p. 5.
31 *L'Illustration*, 9 Mar. 1867.
32 'Gautier, scoffing, rather vulgar', corroborated the diarist Antoine Fontaney in 1831. A. Fontaney, *Journal intime*, Les Presses Françaises, Paris, 1925, p. 34.
33 *H du r*, pp. 91–8.
34 Ibid., p. 97.
35 Ibid., p. 93.
36 Jasinski, *Les Années romantiques* . . . , pp. 65–6.
37 Ibid., pp. 73–4.
38 Ibid., p. 76.
39 *H du r*, p. 30.
40 Ibid., p. 16.

41 Ibid., p. 20.
42 Ibid., pp. 21-2.
43 Ibid., p. 24.
44 Ibid., p. 22.
45 *Mon*, 13 Feb. 1865, repr. in *H du r*, p. 219.
46 *H du r*, pp. 52-61.
47 Jasinski, *Les Années romantiques* . . . , p. 76.
48 *Poésies complètes*, vol. I, p. 83.
49 Jasinski, *Les Années romantiques* . . . , p. 133.
50 Arsène Houssaye, future director of *L'Artiste* and of the Comédie Française, and Gautier's lifelong friend, has this to say on Théophile in 1833: 'Théophile protested against bourgeois painting with his flowing locks and his frock-coat trimmed with brandenburgs. His larger-than-life, Capitaine Fracasse-style swagger was above all a way of hiding his timidity and meekness. When he spoke of philistines he would assume ferocious expressions . . .', and caused the blasé and dandified Nestor Roqueplan to raise an eyebrow at his naïvety. 'Théo was as gentle as a lamb', Houssaye continues, and concludes his account of their first meeting (at the Salon of 1833) with a transcription of a typically mannered Jeune-France conversation: 'When we parted company, Théo said to me: I superinvite you to come and dine improbably tomorrow with the authors of my days.—Where do you hang out?—In that fallacious monument known as the bumpkins' tollgate, for my father is the reverend leader of the publicans . . .' (Houssaye, *Les Confessions*, vol. I, pp. 292-4). As Jasinski points out, the Jeune-France life did not estrange Gautier from home. The debauches of the Petit Cénacle, he suggests, had been poverty-stricken and innocent; Théophile himself did not yet smoke and scarcely drank more than watered-down milk (Jasinski, *Les Années romantiques* . ., pp. 78, 82-3).
51 Jasinski, *Les Années romantiques* . . . , p. 128.
52 *Les Jeunes-France*, p. 189.
53 *La Revue des Deux Mondes*, 1 July 1848.
54 Jasinski, *Les Années romantiques* . . . , p. 115.
55 *Ariel*, 30 Apr. 1836.
56 *H du r*, p. 18.
57 Richardson, p. 35.
58 *La Presse*, 26 Aug. 1836.
59 Ibid., 30 Aug. 1836.
60 E. Feydeau, *Théophile Gautier. Souvenirs intimes*, E. Plon, Paris, 1874, pp. 11-20.
61 T. Silvestre, *Les Artistes français*, vol. I, *Romantiques*, Bibliothèque Dionysienne, Paris, 1926, p. 158; trans. in M. Easton, *Artists and Writers in Paris. The Bohemian Idea, 1803-1867*, Edward Arnold, London, 1964, p. 61.
62 Feydeau, p. 55.
63 *L'Illustration*, 9 Mar. 1867.
64 Bergerat, p. 126. 'I am a Russian in Russia, a Turk in Turkey, a

Spaniard in Spain', he wrote in 1867. *L'Illustration*, 9 Mar. 1867.

65 Feydeau, pp. 142-3.
66 Ibid., p. 139.
67 *La Presse*, 20 Jan. 1845; Richardson, p. 47.
68 Feydeau, p. 74.
69 *La Presse*, 31 Mar. 1846.
70 Richardson, p. 82.
71 M. Du Camp, *Souvenirs littéraires*, 2 vols., Hachette, Paris, 1882 and 1883, vol. I, p. 417.
72 *La Revue des Deux Mondes*, 1 July 1848.
73 *La Presse*, 21-2 Apr. 1848.
74 As 'A. M. Théodore de Banville, Réponse à son Odelette', *L'Artiste*, 13 Sept. 1857.
75 *L'Illustration*, 9 Mar. 1867.
76 Feydeau, pp. 101-3 and 110.
77 Richardson, p. 163, and see M. C. Spencer, *The Art Criticism of Théophile Gautier*, Librairie Droz, Geneva, 1969, pp. 5-7, for an account of Estelle Gautier and Adolphe Bazin's collaboration with the critic on the *Salon of 1870*.
78 Eugène Devéria, for instance, ended his days as keeper of the museum in Pau, and his brother Achille in the Print Department of the Bibliothèque Nationale. Louis Boulanger was appointed director of the museum and École des Beaux-Arts at Dijon in 1860; Célestin Nanteuil accepted this post on Boulanger's death (Easton, pp. 49-50, and 54).
79 M. Du Camp, *Théophile Gautier*, Hachette, Paris, 1890, p. 80.
80 Feydeau, p. 68.
81 *J des G*, 2 Jan. 1867. Comte Alexandre Walewski (1810-68) was a bastard son of Napoleon I and a Minister of State under Napoleon III; he also wrote plays himself. In 1867, he was the president of the Corps législatif. Charles-Camille Doucet was a successful playwright and one of *Le Moniteur*'s theatre critics; he too filled official positions under the Second Empire.
82 Ibid., 20 Jan. 1857.
83 Ibid., 3 May 1862.
84 Richardson, p. 160.
85 Ibid., p. 186.
86 Feydeau, p. 196.
87 Ibid., p. 170. For a taste of Gautier's *esprit* Feydeau recommends his own novel *Sylvie* (*Sylvie. Étude*, E. Dentu, Paris, 1861) which, he says, was inspired by the eccentricities uttered at Mme Sabatier's soirées (Feydeau, p. 164). More accessible is Robert Baldick's superbly entertaining *Dinner at Magny's*, Gollancz, London, 1971.
88 Feydeau, p. 155.
89 Bergerat, p. 85.
90 *J des G*, 14 Feb. 1868.
91 Bergerat, p. 120.

92 Feydeau, pp. 228–9.
93 Ibid., p. 218.
94 E. Montégut, *Nos morts contemporains*, vol. 2, Hachette, Paris, 1884, p. 42; quoted in Richardson, pp. 192–3.

11 THE CRITIC (pp. 44–53)

1 *La France littéraire*, Mar.–Apr. 1833.
2 T. Gautier, *Mademoiselle de Maupin*, Garnier-Flammarion, Paris, 1966, preface, p. 45.
3 Ibid., p. 46.
4 Ibid.
5 Ibid.
6 Ibid., p. 52.
7 *Ariel*, 5 Mar. 1836.
8 *La France industrielle*, Apr. 1834. (See Appendix II, 1.)
9 *Le Cabinet de lecture*, 19 Mar. 1836.
10 *Ariel*, 2 Mar. 1836.
11 *L'Artiste*, 14 Dec. 1856.
12 Ibid. (See Appendix II, 2.)
13 Ibid., 14 Feb. 1858.
14 *L'Illustration*, 8 June 1872.
15 *L'Artiste*, 14 Dec. 1856.
16 Ibid.
17 Ibid.
18 Flaubert's phrase; *J des G*, 3 May 1857.
19 T. Gautier, *Voyage en Espagne-Tra los montes*, Bibliothèque Charpentier, Fasquelle, Paris, 1933, p. 367.
20 *J des G*, Aug. 1861.
21   Je suis comme l'hippopotame;
        De ma conviction couvert,
        Forte armure que rien n'entame,
        Je vais sans peur dans le désert.

('I am like the hippopotamus; clothed in the strong armour of my conviction, which nothing can penetrate, I move fearlessly through the desert.')

Thus Gautier expressed it for himself in a poem entitled 'L'Hippopotame' (which first appeared in *Poésies diverses, 1833–1838*), to be maliciously quoted by Sainte-Beuve, who was not a man to let even the hint of a psychological insight slip by undetected (C. A. Sainte-Beuve, *Les Grands écrivains français. Études des lundis . . . XIXᵉ siècle. Les Poètes*, vol. II, Librairie Garnier Frères, Paris, 1926, p. 185). Reciprocal to this poetically stated conviction was Gautier's almost passionate dislike of cows. 'Cows inspire in us a particular distaste, which would prevent us from being just towards Paulus Potter', he wrote for instance in *L'Artiste* of 19 April 1857; it

was as if he saw reflected in cows the threat of his own incipient
lethargy. 'Gautier's books lack what the man lacks' the Goncourts
decided in 1863 (*J des G*, 10 Nov.), 'nerves, a nervous system. What
comes across as all his own is a deep, cow-like vacancy.' ('Ce qu'il tient
de lui, c'est *vache*.')

22 *L'Artiste*, 14 Dec. 1856.
23 Ibid., 14 Feb. 1858.
24 e.g. *Mon*, 20 July 1859.
25 *L'Artiste*, 14 Feb. 1858.

III THE ARTIST (pp. 54–69)

1 *La Charte de 1830*, 16 Jan. 1837, repr. in T. Gautier, *Fusains et eaux-
   fortes*, Charpentier, Paris, 1880.
2 *La Presse*, 27 Mar. 1839. Compare this characterization with the
   following statement by Préault, which similarly stresses the indifference and sang-froid of the typical Romantic artist: 'There are
   certain select people ('des gens d'élite') who look at great things with
   eagle's eyes, unflinchingly; others who can only blink when they
   confront them' (Silvestre, p. 158).
3 *La Charte de 1830*, 16 Jan. 1837.
4 *La Presse*, 4 Apr. 1839.
5 Ibid., 27 Mar. 1839.
6 *L'Artiste*, 14 Dec. 1856.
7 *L'Événement*, 4 May 1866. E. Zola, *Mon Salon. Manet. Écrits sur l'art*,
   Garnier-Flammarion, Paris, 1970, p. 60.
8 e.g. *La Presse*, 21 July 1853.
9 *L'Artiste*, 20 Sept. 1857 (the poem 'L'Art' had appeared on 13 Sept.).
10 *La Revue de Paris*, 27 Feb. 1842.
11 *La Presse*, 4 Apr. 1839. (See Appendix II, 3.)
12 Jasinski, *Les Années romantiques . . .* , p. 76.
13 *La Presse*, 4 Apr. 1839.
14 D. Parmée (ed.), *Selected Critical Studies of Baudelaire*, Cambridge at
   the University Press, Cambridge, 1949, 'L'œuvre et la vie d'Eugène
   Delacroix', p. 206; and Baudelaire, *L'Art romantique*, XVIII,
   'Théophile Gautier', p. 156.
15 *La Presse*, 4 Apr. 1839. (See Appendix II, 4.)
16 *L'Artiste*, 14 Dec. 1856.
17 Spencer, pp. 109–13.
18 This was the Platonism that was after all inherited by Christianity,
   with its parallel conception of an after-life, and its programme of
   bodily mortification and spiritual contemplation. Gautier, it must not
   be forgotten, had a solidly Catholic family upbringing, to which he
   continued to give at least lip-service, probably until his early twenties
   (see Jasinski, *Les Années romantiques . . .* , p. 81, on the Gautier
   family's adherence to a strong legitimist-Catholic tradition).
19 Bergerat, p. 166.

20 J. Gautier, 'Le Second rang du collier', VIII, *La Revue de Paris*, 1 June 1903, p. 580; P. -G. Castex, *Le Conte fantastique en France de Nodier à Maupassant*, Librairie José Corti, Paris, 1951, p. 216; R. Benesch, *Le Regard de Théophile Gautier*, Juris Druck & Verlag, Zurich, 1969, p. 46, note 12.

21 A. Boschot, *Théophile Gautier*, Desclée et de Brouwer, Paris, 1933, p. 179.

22 *H du r*, pp. 57-8.

23 T. Gautier, *Salon de 1847*, Hetzel, Warnod, Paris, 1847, VIII.

24 *La Presse*, 7 May 1848.

25 Ibid., 1 Mar. 1851.

26 Ibid., 24 June 1853.

27 *Mon*, 15 May 1866.

28 *J off*, 18 June 1869.

29 *La Presse*, 18 Apr. 1853.

30 Ibid., 13 Feb. 1848.

31 Pelagius was a fifth-century British monk and the founder of a heresy; this is a typically *recherché* reference on Gautier's part.

32 *La Revue des Deux Mondes*, 1 July 1848.

33 *La Presse*, 18 Apr. 1853.

34 *L'Illustration*, 19 Jan. 1867, repr. in T. Gautier, *Portraits contemporains: littérateurs, peintres, sculpteurs, artistes dramatiques*, Bibliothèque Charpentier, Paris, n.d.

35 *L'Artiste*, 20 June 1858.

36 *La Presse*, 18 Dec. 1843.

37 Boschot, p. 352.

38 *La Revue de Paris*, 18 Apr. 1841.

39 Preface to *Albertus. Poésies complètes*, vol. I, p. 83.

40 *J des G*, 1 May 1857.

41 Benesch, p. 28, from T. Gautier, *Voyage en Italie (Italia)*, Charpentier, Paris, 1876, p. 338.

42 J. Gautier, p. 580.

43 T. Gautier, *Romans et Contes*, Bibliothèque Charpentier, Fasquelle, Paris, n.d., p. 308, and Benesch, p. 86. (See Appendix II, 5.)

44 Boschot, pp. 118-9.

45 *Mon*, 6 Feb. 1860.

46 *La Revue des Deux Mondes*, 1 Sept. 1847, repr. in T. Gautier, *L'Art moderne*, Michel Lévy Frères, Paris, 1856. (See Appendix II, 6.)

IV DELACROIX (pp. 70-88)

1 *La France industrielle*, Apr. 1834.

2 *La France littéraire*, Mar. 1833.

3 *La France industrielle*, Apr. 1834.

4 For an important example of similarity in the thinking of Gautier and Delacroix, see Delacroix, *Journal* . . . , 3 vols., Librairie Plon, Paris, 1950; vol. II, p. 374 (11 Sept. 1855), where the painter reflects on '*that*

little world which man carries within himself'. See also Spencer, pp. 95–6: Gautier's possible influence on Delacroix here is impossible to ascertain, for such ideas were, we have seen, common currency.

5 To Thiers's support of Delacroix Gautier gave all due credit, as he did to that of Goethe; *H du r*, pp. 206–10.

6 Boschot, pp. 344–5. Delacroix indeed had serious reservations about the value of Gautier's criticism in general. 'He takes a picture, describes it after his own particular fashion, and makes a charming picture himself, but he has not produced a piece of real criticism,' Delacroix wrote of the critic in his diary in June 1855 (*Journal*, vol. II, p. 341); 'provided he has a pretext for coining sparkling, dazzling, macaronic expressions, which he turns up with an obvious pleasure that is sometimes infectious, provided he can cite Spain and Turkey, the Alhambra and the Atmeïdan of Constantinople, he is happy, he has fulfilled his aim as a curious writer, and I do not believe he sees beyond that. When he gets to the French, he will do for each one of them what he has done for the English. Such criticism can contain neither instruction nor philosophy.' There is justice in these remarks, although to what extent Gautier's criticism succeeds or fails in terms of 'instruction' and 'philosophy' remains to be seen; Delacroix's observations were prompted by Gautier's articles on the English painting at the Exposition Universelle of 1855. Yet Gautier's articles on Delacroix's own contribution to the exhibition met with a more favourable response from the painter; Delacroix invited Gautier to dinner along with other 'kind men who have been obliging to me over my exhibition', and recorded in his diary that it was a 'Bonne soirée' (*Journal*, 14 May 1855, vol. II, p. 327). See also a letter of 22 July 1855 (Delacroix, *Correspondance générale . . .*, 5 vols., Librairie Plon, Paris, 1935–8, vol. III, pp. 279–80): 'I thank you . . . from the bottom of my heart, beyond what I can express to you in words. Yes, you must feel some satisfaction on seeing that all those follies, for which, in the past, you stood up almost alone, today seem quite natural . . .' Other favourable comments on Gautier appear in the *Journal*, for instance, vol. I, p. 241 (on his article on Töpffer, *La Revue des Deux Mondes*, 1 Sept. 1847), vol. II, pp. 54, 231–2, 408, and 432. In this last entry Delacroix copied a letter he had written to Gautier complimenting him on his obituary notice of Heinrich Heine; the letter ends: 'I send you this little homage less on account of my other obligations to you than for the sad and sweet pleasure of reading your article.' This is indicative of the good relations that existed between the two men. Delacroix frequently wrote to Gautier in order to enlist his support or to thank him for recent articles; see the *Correspondance générale*, vol. II, pp. 148 and 334–5; vol. III, pp. 61, 189, 279–80, 319, and 368; vol. IV, pp. 152–3, 174–5, 255, and 263.

In volume III, p. 372, it is recorded that Delacroix gave Gautier a *Saint Jérôme*; this was probably in or around 1843. The catalogue of the sale of Gautier's collection in 1873 reveals that the painting, a sketch for a pendentive, was still in Gautier's possession at his death; it also confirms that he owned a *Lady Macbeth* and a *Combat au Giaour*, as Bergerat recalled, although this last picture was, according to the catalogue, painted in collaboration with Poterlet (lots 23, 24, and 25 in the sale). Gautier also possessed two water-colours by Delacroix, an 'Étude de fleurs' and an 'Étude de femme; Tanger' (lots 127 and 128), a Hamlet lithograph and lithographs which comprised 'two series covering the painter's entire *œuvre*'.

7 *Ariel*, 13 Apr. 1836.
8 *L'Artiste*, 18 Jan. 1857.
9 *Ariel*, 13 Apr. 1836.
10 *Mon*, 18 Nov. 1864, repr. in *H du r*, pp. 200-17.
11 *La Revue de Paris*, 18 Apr. 1841.
12 T. Gautier, *Les Beaux-Arts en Europe*, 2 vols., Michel Lévy Frères, Paris, 1855 and 1856, vol. I, p. 172.
13 *La Presse*, 26 Aug. 1836.
14 e.g. *Salon de 1847*, IV.
15 *BA en E*, vol. I, p. 170.
16 *La Revue de Paris*, 18 Apr. 1841.
17 *BA en E*, vol. I, p. 171. (See Appendix II, 7.)
18 *La Presse*, 26 Aug. 1836.
19 *J off*, 14 Feb. 1870.
20 *Poésies complètes*, III, p. 77.
21 Feydeau, pp. 58 and 60.
22 *La Presse*, 13 Mar. 1840.
23 For a similar statement, see *Mon*, 6 Feb. 1860.
24 Zola, p. 87 (*Salon de 1866*, *L'Événement*, 20 May 1866).
25 *Mon*, 21 May 1859.
26 Ibid., 18 Nov. 1864.
27 Anonymous article in *Le Vert-Vert*, 15 Dec. 1835; quoted in Bibliothèque Nationale, *Théophile Gautier*, catalogue of exhibition, Paris, 1961.
28 Although he was fascinated too, especially during the 1830s, by a Hoffmannesque invisible world made visible. Castex, *Le Conte fantastique . . .* , pp. 214-47.
29 *La Revue de Paris*, 18 Apr. 1841.
30 *Mon*, 21 May 1859.
31 *BA en E*, vol. I, pp. 180-1.
32 *Mon*, 21 May 1859.
33 *BA en E*, vol. I, pp. 171-2. (See Appendix II, 8.)
34 *La Presse*, 9 Mar. 1837.
35 Ibid., 26 Aug. 1836.
36 *Mon*, 21 May 1859.
37 *La Presse*, 22 Mar. 1838.
38 *BA en E*, vol. I, p. 177.
39 *La Revue de Paris*, 18 Apr. 1841. (See Appendix II, 9.)
40 *BA en E*, vol. I, pp. 187-8. (See Appendix II, 10.)
41 *Mon*, 3 Aug. 1861.
42 Whatever reservations Delacroix had about Gautier's approach to

criticism, the painter certainly did not feel that his work was misrepresented by Gautier's prose. 'A thousand thanks for your poetic and so very sympathetic article' he wrote to the critic on 4 August 1861 (*Correspondance générale*, vol. IV, p. 263); the article in question was that which had appeared in the *Moniteur* of the previous day and which contained Gautier's evocation of the scene of Jacob wrestling with the angel. Delacroix's letter continues: 'You have spoiled me so often that I'm almost beginning to believe everything your friendship prompts you to write about me; I too easily forget how much your imagination adds to my inventions and your style puts a final varnish on them. So I thank you most sincerely and shake you by the hand.'

43 Delacroix's 'personnages', it has been seen, are compared to English actors, without doubt to those Shakespearian players who, like Macready's company, were responsible for the great Shakespearian vogue in France in the 1820s; the head of *Médée furieuse* reminded Gautier in 1855 of 'that viperine expression that Mademoiselle Rachel can adopt'. (*BA en E*, vol. I, p. 189.)

44 Spencer, p. 101.

45 *L'Artiste*, 14 Dec. 1856.

46 See for instance, *Ariel*, 30 Apr. 1836 and *La Presse*, 27 Apr. 1839, in which Gautier's Salon articles are literally poems.

47 C. Baudelaire, *Écrits sur l'Art*, 2 vols., Le Livre de Poche, Paris, 1971, vol. I, p. 143 (*Salon de 1846*).

48 *BA en E*, vol. I, p. 188.

49 *Mon*, 18 Nov. 1864. *H du r*, pp. 200–17.

50 Ibid., (See Appendix II, 11.)

51 Jasinski, *Les Années romantiques* . . . , p. 78.

V INGRES (pp. 89–110)

1 *BA en E*, vol. I, p. 169.

2 Ibid., pp. 168–9.

3 Ibid., p. 142.

4 Ibid.

5 *Lettre inédite* . . . *écrite à M. Ingres, pendant le voyage en Russie. 7 février, 1859*, pamphlet in Bibliothèque Municipale de Tarbes, Htes. Pyrénées, n.d.

6 Ingres responded to Gautier's devotion by presenting him with an oil study (46 cm × 16 cm) for the *Plafond d'Homère*: 'Les trois grands poètes tragiques grecs (Eschyle, Sophocle et Euripide)'. It was signed on the left-hand side, and inscribed on the back (no. 44 in the Gautier sale catalogue).

7 *La Presse*, 27 June 1847.

8 Ibid., 16 Mar. 1838.

9 *Mon*, 10 Apr. 1862.

10 *La France industrielle*, Apr. 1834.

11 *BA en E*, vol. I, p. 145.

12 Ibid., p. 147.
13 Ibid., p. 152.
14 Ibid., pp. 163-4.
15 Ibid., p. 166.
16 Ibid., p. 145.
17 Ibid., p. 150.
18 Ibid., pp. 149-50.
19 *L'Artiste*, 14 Dec. 1856.
20 Ibid., 14 Feb. 1858.
21 *BA en E*, vol. I, pp. 142-3.
22 *Mon*, 23 Jan. 1867.
23 Ibid.
24 *Aurélia, ou le rêve et la vie*, p. 135, in Nerval, *Promenades et souvenirs. Lettres à Jenny. Pandora. Aurélia*, Garnier-Flammarion, Paris, 1972. Balzac, *Le Lys dans la vallée*, Le Livre de Poche, Paris, 1965, pp. 18-19 and 106.
25 *BA en E*, vol. I, p. 143.
26 Ibid., p. 163.
27 Ibid.
28 Ibid., p. 144.
29 *Mon*, 23 Jan. 1867.
30 *La France littéraire*, Mar. 1833.
31 Feydeau, p. 59.
32 *La France industrielle*, Apr. 1834. (See Appendix II, 12.)
33 *BA en E*, vol. I, pp. 143-4.
34 *Mon*, 10 Apr. 1862.
35 *BA en E*, vol. I, p. 155.
36 *La France littéraire*, Mar. 1833.
37 *BA en E*, vol. I, p. 164.
38 Ibid., p. 154.
39 *Mon*, 4 Feb. 1854.
40 *H du r*, p. 2.
41 *Le Roman de la momie*, p. 84.
42 L. Cerf, *Souvenirs de David d'Angers*, Renaissance du Livre, Paris, 1928, p. 180, and E. Peyrouzet, *Gérard de Nerval inconnu*, Librairie Jose Corti, Paris, 1965, pp. 255-6.
43 *Mon*, 10 Apr. 1862.
44 *L'Événement*, 2 Aug. 1848, repr. in T. Gautier, *Fusains et eaux-fortes*, Charpentier, Paris, 1880.
45 Cerf, p. 180.
46 *La Presse*, 4 Apr. 1839.
47 *BA en E*, vol. I, pp. 152-3.
48 Ibid., pp. 159-60.
49 This is the 1839 *Odalisque à l'esclave* in the Fogg Art Museum, Cambridge, Mass.; the 1842 version in the Baltimore Museum of Art has a landscape background with a large corner of blue sky.
50 *BA en E*, vol. I, pp. 157-9.
51 *L'Artiste*, 1 Feb. 1857.

52 *BA en E*, vol. I, p. 165.
53 T. Gautier, *Œuvres érotiques. Poésies libertines. Lettres à la Présidente*, Arcanes, Paris, 1953.
54 See T. Gautier, *Abécédaire du Salon de 1861*, E. Dentu, Paris, 1861, for Gautier's own account of Boulanger's picture, and Musée des Arts Décoratifs, *Équivoques. Peintures françaises du XIXᵉ siècle*, catalogue of exhibition, Paris, 1973, under Boulanger, where his account is reprinted.

VI NINETEENTH-CENTURY PAGAN (pp. 111–147)

1 *Le Cabinet de lecture*, 9 Apr. 1836.
2 *L'Artiste*, 26 Apr. 1857.
3 *Mon*, 23 June 1859.
4 *La Presse*, 26 Aug. 1836, in Gautier's very first article for the newspaper. See also *La Presse*, 22 Nov. 1836, where, in another manifesto-like feuilleton, entitled 'De la Composition en Peinture', he makes similar general propositions. Delacroix was no doubt the major inspiration for Gautier's programme, having already largely fulfilled it; Eugène Devéria's *Naissance de Henri IV*, the great Romantic success of the Salon of 1827, was also probably instrumental in helping Gautier formulate his views. The picture was just such a fundamentally conservative synthesis, Romantic in the grand style, as Gautier was to propound; it gave rise to unfulfilled hopes, as he wrote in Devéria's obituary (*Mon*, 13 Feb. 1865), that France had found her Veronese. Pontus Grate makes the point that the painting marked a temporary suspension of critical hostilities, satisfying both the supporters of Romanticism and the upholders of the Classical tradition, like Delécluze. P. Grate, *Deux critiques d'art à l'époque romantique. Gustave Planche et Théophile Thoré*, Almquist & Wiksell, Stockholm, 1959, p. 44.
5 *Mon*, 23 June 1859.
6 *Le Cabinet de lecture*, 9 Apr. 1836.
7 *BA en E*, vol. I, p. 177.
8 *Mon*, 29 July 1859.
9 *ABC du Salon de 1861*.
10 *Mon*, 1 Oct. 1863.
11 *BA en E*, vol. I, pp. 118–19.
12 *La Presse*, 2 May 1851.
13 *ABC du Salon de 1861*.
14 *H du r*, p. 29.
15 *Mon*, 21 May 1868.
16 *La France littéraire*, Mar.–Apr. 1833.
17 *La Revue de Paris*, 18 Apr. 1841.
18 *L'Artiste*, 22 Nov. 1857.

19 *La Presse*, 27 Apr. 1837.
20 *BA en E*, vol. I, p. 118.
21 *Salon de 1847*, XI.
22 So token indeed that it only appears in the title.
23 *ABC du Salon de 1861.*
24 *Mon*, 13 June 1863.
25 *La Presse*, 23 Mar. 1838.
26 *Le Cabinet de lecture*, 19 Mar. 1836.
27 *ABC du Salon de 1861.*
28 *Le Cabinet de lecture*, 19 Mar. 1836.
29 *La Presse*, 28 July 1849.
30 *BA en E*, vol. I, p. 117.
31 *La Presse*, 23 Apr. 1848.
32 *Salon de 1847*, XI.
33 *Mon*, 29 July 1859.
34 *Salon de 1847*, XI.
35 *La Presse*, 23 Apr. 1848.
36 *BA en E*, vol. I, pp. 120–1.
37 *Le Cabinet de lecture*, 9 Apr. 1836.
38 Ibid.
39 *La Presse*, 8 Apr. 1837.
40 Ibid., 2 May 1851.
41 *Le Cabinet de lecture*, 9 Apr. 1836.
42 *L'Événement*, 8 Aug. 1848: 'Du Beau antique et du Beau moderne', repr. in T. Gautier, *Souvenirs de théâtre, d'art et de critique*, Charpentier, Paris, 1883.
43 *J des G*, 15 Jan. 1866.
44 The amoral cult of form, exclusive worship of *le beau*, received a devastating moral critique from Baudelaire in his article on 'L'école païenne' (*La Semaine théâtrale*, 22 Jan. 1852), a critique, which, we shall see, has its bearing on any final assessment of Gautier's contribution to nineteenth- and twentieth-century sensibilities.
45 *La France littéraire*, Mar.–Apr. 1833.
46 *La Presse*, 4 Apr. 1839.
47 Ibid., 13 Feb. 1849, repr. in T. Gautier, *Tableaux à la plume*, Charpentier, Paris, 1880.
48 *Le Cabinet de lecture*, 19 Mar. 1836.
49 *Mon*, 25 June 1864.
50 Ibid., 8 July 1863.
51 *La Presse*, 28 Mar. 1851. The painters in question were Gendron, Hamon, Voillemot, and Picou.
52 *L'Artiste*, 14 Dec. 1856.
53 *La Presse*, 24 Mar. 1837.
54 *ABC du Salon de 1861*, under Bellel.
55 Ibid., under Belly.
56 *La Presse*, 9 Aug. 1849.
57 *Ariel*, 19 Mar. 1836.

58 Ibid.
59 *Salon de 1847*, X.
60 *BA en E*, vol. I, p. 233.
61 'A Ernest Hébert sur son tableau "La Mal'aria"', first published in *La Revue des Deux Mondes*, 1 Nov. 1925, repr. in *Dernières poésies*. *Poésies complètes*, vol. III, p. 151.
62 *J off*, 25 June 1869.
63 *ABC du Salon de 1861*.
64 *La Gazette des Beaux-Arts*, 1 May 1862, repr. in *Souvenirs de théâtre* . . .
65 *La Presse*, 3 June 1853.
66 *L'Artiste*, 23 Aug. 1857.
67 *Le Cabinet de l'amateur* . . . , Apr. 1842.
68 *La Gazette des Beaux-Arts*, 1 May 1862, repr. in *Souvenirs de théâtre* . . .
69 *Salon de 1847*, VIII.
70 *La Revue de Paris*, Apr. 1841.
71 *La Gazette des Beaux-Arts*, 1 May 1862, repr. in *Souvenirs de théâtre* . . .
72 *La Presse*, 22 Nov. 1836.
73 *Mon*, 13 July 1859.
74 *L'Artiste*, 12 Apr. 1857. (See Appendix II, 13.)
75 W. Pater, *The Renaissance. Studies in Art and Poetry*, Collins, The Fontana Library, London, 1961, pp. 122–3.
76 *Tableaux à la plume*, p. 29.
77 Pater, pp. 122–3.
78 *Salon de 1847*, IX.
79 *La France industrielle*, Apr. 1834.
80 *La Presse*, 1 May 1851.
81 Ibid. (See Appendix II, 14.)
82 *Le Cabinet de lecture*, 19 Mar. 1836.
83 *La Presse*, 29 Apr. 1848. (See Appendix II, 15.)
84 *L'Illustration*, 9 Mar. 1867.
85 *Le Cabinet de lecture*, 9 Apr. 1836.
86 *La Presse*, 20 Mar. 1840.
87 Ibid., 17 Mar. 1837.
88 *L'Artiste*, 14 Feb. 1858.
89 *Mon*, 4 July 1866.
90 *J off*, 28 June 1869.
91 *Mon*, 8 July 1863.
92 Ibid., 1 July 1859, on Muller's *Proscription des jeunes irlandaises catholiques en 1655*.
93 *La Presse*, 15 Feb. 1851.
94 Ibid., 21 July 1853.
95 *Mon*, 7 July 1859.
96 *La Presse*, 1 May 1838.
97 *Mon*, 7 July 1859.
For a fuller account of *Le Lundi*, see Philadelphia Museum of Art,

The Second Empire 1852–1870. Art in France under Napoleon III, 1978, pp. 260–1.

98 *La Presse*, 21 July 1853.
99 *Mon*, 25 June 1864.
100 *J off*, 18 July 1870.
101 *Mon*, 14 June 1865. (See Appendix II, 16.)
102 *L'Artiste*, 14 Dec. 1856.
103 Ibid., 20 Sept. 1857.
104 *Mon*, 24 June 1865.
105 *Salon de 1847*, III.
106 *L'Artiste*, 20 Sept. 1857.
107 *BA en E*, vol. II, p. 45.
108 *Mon*, 23 Apr. 1859.
109 *Mademoiselle de Maupin*, pp. 201–2.
110 *La Presse*, 5 May 1848.
111 Ibid., 6 June 1852.
112 *Mon*, 17 July 1866.
113 Ibid., 11 May 1868.
114 Ibid., 27 June 1868.
115 *La Revue de Paris*, 18 Apr. 1841.
116 *Mon*, 27 June 1868.
117 *ABC du Salon de 1861*.
118 *L'Artiste*, 3 May 1857. Casimir Delavigne (1793–1843) was an extremely successful playwright, who dealt, like Delaroche, with subjects from English and French history. His tragedy *Les Enfants d'Édouard* was inspired by Delaroche's painting of the same name. See C. Gould, *Delaroche and Gautier*, The National Gallery, London, 1975.
119 *La Presse*, 10 Mar. 1837.
120 *La France littéraire*, Mar.–Apr. 1833.
121 *La Presse*, 10 Mar. 1837.
122 *La France industrielle*, Apr. 1834.
123 *La Presse*, 10 Mar. 1837.
124 *J des G*, 5 Mar. 1857.
125 Hence a preference for spectacle, and for ballet in particular; *Giselle* and *La Péri* are after all among Gautier's most lastingly successful creations. The visible world and the visual arts provided inspiration for more than just a descriptive literary style; Bergerat records a project for a ballet directly inspired by a picture. 'The emotion of the critic had awoken the genius of the poet.' Gautier's *Le Mariage à Séville* was to be based on the Spanish painter Fortuny's *Mariage dans la Vicaría de Madrid* (now in the Barcelona Museum) exhibited at Goupil's in Paris in 1870. This 'ballet chanté'—for it was also to serve as a frame for 'all the Spanish song or dance tunes, seguidillas, or boleros, that could be collected'—was an extension of Fortuny's dazzlingly colourful world into one more fully realized in terms of local colour, its complete sensual fulfilment. The project is a supreme example of Gautier's collaborative, creative approach to criticism; it

represents the highest of compliments to Fortuny and demonstrates the power and fertility of Gautier's preoccupation with his visual experience. (Bergerat, p. 208 et seq.)

126 *La Presse*, 10 Mar. 1837.
127 Ibid., 22 Nov. 1836.
128 Ibid., 21 July 1853.
129 D. Piper, *Painting in England, 1500–1880*, Pelican, Harmondsworth, 1965, p. 150.
130 *Mon*, 10 Apr. 1862.
131 'Les Noces de Cana de Paul Véronèse', *Gravure de M.Z. Prévost, Une Brochure*, May 1852, repr. in *Souvenirs de théâtre* . . . (See Appendix II, 17.)
132 In A. Huxley, *Heaven and Hell* (his account of the aesthetic transports and terrors of mescaline hallucination), Chatto and Windus, London, 1956.
133 *La Presse*, 10 Feb. 1849, repr. in *Tableaux à la plume*. (See Appendix II, 18.)

VII JOURNALIST AND CONTEMPORARY (pp. 148–205)

1 *BA en E*, vol. I, p. 145.
2 Ibid., vol. II, p. 208.
3 W. Benjamin, *Charles Baudelaire: A Lyric Poet in the Era of High Capitalism*, NLB, London, 1973, p. 27.
4 *Encyclopaedia Britannica*, article on the Press.
5 C. Ledré, *Histoire de la presse*, Arthème Fayard, Paris, 1958.
6 R. Mazedier, *Histoire de la presse parisienne* . . . *1631–1945*, Pavois, Paris, 1945.
7 *La Presse*, 1 July 1836.
8 R. Manévy, *L'Évolution des formules de présentation de la presse quotidienne*, Éditions Estienne, Paris 1956, p. 29.
9 Mazedier, p. 132.
10 Ledré, p. 254.
11 *La Presse*, 4 Oct. and 21 Dec. 1841, and 14 Mar. 1837. For a fuller discussion of *La Presse*, the feuilleton, and the *physiologie*, see Benjamin, pp. 27–31, 35–38 etc.
12 Ibid., 19 Oct. 1841.
13 Ibid., 3 Oct. 1841.
14 Quoted by Ledré, p. 219.
15 Preface to *Albertus*, *Poésies complètes*, vol. I, p. 81.
16 *Les Jeunes-France*, p. 30.
17 Ibid., p. 28.
18 Ibid., p. 192.
19 Ibid., p. 189.
20 Ibid., p. 190.
21 Ibid., pp. 28–9.
22 His journey to Belgium with Nerval in 1836 only served to confirm his opinions on nature. From the window of his coach Gautier observed a

very well-executed sky, but found the foreground and horizon 'much less successful'. He could not understand how nature could look so unnatural, so like cheap dining-room wall-paper. 'I have quite often had a strange feeling in front of reality; real landscapes have seemed painted to me . . . merely incompetent imitations of Cabat or Ruysdael.' *La Chronique de Paris*, 25 Sept. 1836.

23 *Le Cabinet de l'amateur* . . . ., Apr. 1842.
24 *La Presse*, 1 Mar. 1839.
25 Ibid., 26 Apr. 1848.
26 *La Presse*, 5 July 1838.
27 *La France littéraire*, Mar. 1833.
28 *La France industrielle*, Apr. 1834.
29 *La Presse*, 31 Mar. 1838.
30 Ibid., 16 Apr. 1845.
31 Ibid., 27 Mar. 1839.
32 Ibid., 27 Apr. 1839, and *Poésies complètes*, vol. II, p. 225.
33 Ibid., 23 Feb. 1837.
34 Ibid., 8 Mar. 1837.
35 'Imagine yourself cooped up in a middle-class drawing-room, taking coffee, after dinner, with the *master* of the house, the *lady* of the house and her *young ladies*', wrote Baudelaire in his long article on Gautier in *L'Artiste* of 13 May 1859 (*L'Art romantique*, p. 153). 'Soon the conversation will turn to music, perhaps painting, but literature without fail. Théophile Gautier's turn will come . . . ("How witty he is! Isn't he amusing! How well he writes, and what a *flowing style* he has! . . .") . . . Everyone has read Monday's feuilleton . . .' There was no question about Gautier's fame as a journalist: '. . . there is no doubt that his reviews of the Salons . . . are oracles for all those exiles who cannot judge for themselves and feel with their own eyes . . .' Baudelaire was deploring the fact that outside certain esoteric coteries Gautier the poet nevertheless remained 'un homme *inconnu*'.
36 *La Presse*, 31 Jan. 1837.
37 Ibid., 11 Mar. 1837.
38 Ibid., 27 Mar. 1840.
39 Ibid., 2 June 1845.
40 Ibid., 5 July 1838.
41 Ibid., 30 Aug. 1836.
42 Ibid., 25 Oct. 1836.
43 Ibid., 2 Mar. 1838.
44 Ibid., 20 Mar. 1837.
45 Ibid., 30 Aug. 1836.
46 Ibid., 21 Sept. 1838.
47 *J des G*, 2 Dec. 1868.
48 *Salon de 1847*, VIII.
49 Ibid., VI.
50 *La Presse*, 9 Oct. 1841.
51 *Figaro – Journal-Livre-Revue quotidienne*, 24, 25, and 27 Apr. 1837.
52 A. Hauser, *The Social History of Art*, 2 vols., Routledge and Kegan

Paul, London, 1951, vol. 11, p. 732.
53 *La Presse*, 21 Mar. 1839.
54 Ibid., 11 Mar. 1840.
55 Ibid., 11 Mar. 1845.
56 Baudelaire, *Écrits sur l'art*, vol. I, p. 54.
57 *La Presse*, 31 Mar. 1846 and 30 Mar. 1847.
58 Ibid., 11 Mar. 1840.
59 Ibid., 11 Mar. 1845.
60 Ibid., 20 Mar. 1845.
61 Letter to his father, 6 Apr. 1845. H. Shapiro (ed.), *Ruskin in Italy*, Clarendon Press, Oxford, 1972, p. 8.
62 *La Presse*, 15 Apr. 1845.
63 Ibid., 18 Mar. 1845.
64 Ibid., 15 Apr. 1845.
65 Ibid., 26 Mar. 1844.
66 Ibid., 13 Mar. 1840.
67 *La Revue de Paris*, 18 Apr. 1841.
68 *Salon de 1847*, XI.
69 *La Presse*, 11 Mar. 1845.
70 Ibid., 3 Jan. 1837.
71 Ibid., 13 and 27 Dec. 1836.
72 *La Revue de Paris*, 27 Feb. 1842.
73 *Salon de 1847*, III.
74 Baudelaire, *Écrits sur l'art*, vol. I, p. 146.
75 Ibid., p. 53.
76 Ibid., p. 147.
77 Ibid., pp. 125–6.
78 Ibid., pp. 185–6.
79 Ibid., p. 145.
80 Ibid., p. 126.
81 *Salon de 1847*, III.
82 *La Presse*, 28 Mar. 1844.
83 Ibid.
84 Ibid., 30 Mar. 1844.
85 Ibid., 23 Mar. 1838.
86 Ibid., 24 Mar. 1840.
87 Ibid., 19 Apr. 1855.
88 Ibid., 18 May 1839.
89 Ibid., 10 June 1852.
90 *La Revue des Deux Mondes*, 1 Sept. 1847.
91 *La Presse*, 27 Mar. 1840. (See Appendix II, 19.)
92 Ibid., 27 Mar. 1840.
93 Ibid., 19 Mar. 1845.
94 Ibid., 3 May 1848.
95 Ibid., 24 Mar. 1844.
96 H. de Balzac, *Œuvres complètes*, 50 vols., Société des Éditions Littéraires et Artistiques, Paris 1900–13, vol. 37, *La Peau de chagrin*, p. 374.

97 *La Presse*, 26 Mar. 1844.
98 Ibid., 31 Mar. 1846.
99 Ibid., 21–2 Apr. 1848.
100 *J des G*, 12 May 1857.
101 Ibid., 3 Jan. 1857.
102 Ibid.
103 *Mon*, 10 Apr. 1862. See also the poem 'Après le feuilleton', first published in *La Revue nationale et étrangère*, 10 Dec. 1861.
104 *La Presse*, 21–2 Apr. 1848.
105 See ibid., 26 April 1848 for another exercise in the revolutionary manner. Ingres is reprimanded for his absence from the Salon in the style of a revolutionary tribunal: 'We hereby declare him guilty of the crime of high treason against art. The beautiful belongs to all, and no one has the right to hoard it for himself'. It is ironic that on June 25, at the end of the June days and as part of the reaction against that chaotic enthusiasm for change and renewal which was so blandly reflected by Gautier, *La Presse* was among publications suppressed by Cavaignac's provisional government as threatening to public order. The Legitimist Girardin was briefly imprisoned; along with Victor Hugo he was shortly to put his weight as a publicist behind the presidential candidature of Louis-Napoléon.
106 *La Charte de 1830*, 2 Feb. 1837 (repr. in *Fusains et eaux-fortes*).
107 *Le Journal*, 28 July 1848 (repr. in *Fusains et eaux-fortes*).
108 *L'Événement*, 8 Aug. 1848 (repr. in *Souvenirs de théâtre . . .*).
109 *Mon*, 4 May 1862.
110 Yet his intuitions did not fail him in his visions of the architecture of the future. Writing in 1861 on the exhibition of projects for the new Opéra, for instance, he seems to anticipate some Futurist manifesto on town-planning, dreaming of 'a colossal theatre in stone, marble, bronze, iron, and gold, the sparkling heart of a great star-shaped network of railways' (*Mon*, 11 Feb. 1861).
   In 1858 he had made some even more pertinent observations. 'We are at the end of a world . . . but a world which will be reborn more brilliant and radiant. Who can foresee the forms which will be called forth by new inventions, by stupendous scientific discoveries which industry will immediately harness . . . a new style will inevitably and unpredictably emerge, using forms other than the classical and adapted to usages which are not yet established. In 1958 people will no doubt speak of a Napoleon III style just as we speak of Louis XIV.' His real preoccupations remain, however, outside any eager anticipation of this future: 'the beautiful will still be the same; Homer, Ictinus, and Phidias will still be sitting on their golden thrones, their feet on ivory stools!' (*L'Artiste*, 5 Sept. 1858.)
111 *La Presse*, 31 Mar. 1846. See also *La Presse*, 4 Apr. where Gautier speaks of disappearing 'lines of demarcation'.
112 *La Presse*, 26 July 1849.
113 Ibid., 5 Feb. 1851.
114 Ibid., 4 May 1852.

115 Ibid., 4 Mar. 1852.
116 *BA en E*, vol. I, pp. 2–3.
117 Ibid., p. 9.
118 *L'Artiste*, 14 Dec. 1856.
119 See *L'Artiste*, 14 June and 15 Feb. 1857: 'Who gets worked up nowadays for or against a painter, poet, or composer? Those fine furies and passionate admirations no longer exist'. And ibid. 22 Nov. 1857: 'The character of the age is a diffusion of talent and a sort of mediocre perfection which satisfies but does not move you . . . Nowadays what art tries above all to do is to avoid making mistakes, and it succeeds. There was a time when it was less in awe of criticism, and sought beauty at all costs; that was much better'.
120 Ibid., 21 June 1857.
121 Richardson, p. 167. The Goncourts reported on Gautier's daily work on his feuilleton at *Le Moniteur* in 1864: 'The father does the beginning and the end of the article. The son, up to his ears in old books, mugs up the historical material and the dates for the middle'. *J des G*, 21 Feb. 1864.
122 *La Presse*, 4 Mar. 1852.
123 *Mon*, 18 May 1864.
124 *J des G*, 5 Mar. 1857.
125 *L'Artiste*, 21 Dec. 1856.
126 *H du r*, p. 82.
127 Thus even Huysmans's Des Esseintes began to weary of Gautier's descriptions: '. . . his admiration for the incomparable painter of word pictures that Gautier was had recently been diminishing day by day, so that now he was more astonished than delighted by his almost apathetic descriptions. Outside objects had made a lasting impression on his remarkably perceptive eye, but that impression had become localised, had failed to penetrate any further into brain or body . . .' (J.-K. Huysmans, *A Rebours*, Charpentier, Paris, 1895, p. 251, trans. R. Baldick, *Against Nature*, Penguin, Harmondsworth, 1959, p. 189.) Gautier and Des Esseintes had much in common, moreover; where Des Esseintes was able to simulate a visit to London by absorbing himself in the décor of an English-style café, Gautier, with his verbal algebra in which a 'pschent' always equalled a 'pschent', and in which the object often seems to have been by-passed by its verbal notation, was similarly side-stepping real experience, as in evoking Egypt in *Le Roman de la momie* before he had ever been there, or in describing pictures he had never seen, perhaps. Des Esseintes's décor and Gautier's language arguably fulfil the same functions.
128 *L'Artiste*, 7 Nov. 1857.
129 *Mon*, 16 July 1864.
130 It is possible that Gautier's real opinion of some of these painters was more favourable than it might appear; perhaps no irony was intended in his remarks, for he owned not only a painting by Schreyer, called *La Tourmente* (and described in the sale catalogue as *Cheval attaché à la porte d'une chaumière: effect de neige*), but also a Palizzi: *Les Chèvres*

dans les vignes. It is also possible, of course, that these paintings were simply gifts from their grateful authors; or perhaps, on the other hand, Gautier felt obliged to write graciously about the painters *because* of these generous gifts. Such, no doubt, was the banal complexity of the life of a professional critic.

131 *Mon*, 25 May 1868.
132 Ibid., 4 June 1868.
133 *Mon*, 2 June 1868.
134 *L'Artiste*, 16 May 1858.
135 *Mon*, 29 Dec. 1857.
136 Ibid., 16 Aug. 1863.
137 *La Presse*, 9 July 1853.
138 *J off*, 16 May 1869.
139 *ABC du Salon de 1861*.
140 *L'Artiste*, 20 Sept. 1857.
141 *La Presse*, 7 May 1851.
142 Ibid., 6 May 1851.
143 Ibid., 1 Oct. 1853.
144 *L'Artiste*, 21 June 1857.
145 *Mon*, 23 June 1859.
146 *ABC du Salon de 1861*.
147 *Mon*, 11 May 1868. (See Appendix II, 20.)
148 *J off*, 23 June 1869. See also: *L'Illustration*, June (?) 1869, *J off*, 30 Aug. 1869, *J off*, 17 June 1870, *J off*, 5 Sept. 1870, etc.; *Tableaux de siège*, Charpentier, Paris, 1871, and, on Gautier's enthusiasm for Regnault and Fortuny, Bergerat, p. 208. Regnault reminded Zola of Delacroix, but of Delacroix 'revised and corrected by Gérôme'. Zola found the *Exécution sans jugement* 'coarse and violent'. *Le Messager de l'Europe*, June 1878; Zola, p. 291.
149 *Le Bien public de Paris*, 28 May 1872. See also the poem 'Affinités secrètes. Madrigal panthéiste', first published in *La Revue des Deux Mondes*, 15 Jan. 1849.
150 *Mon*, 13 Oct. 1856, reprinted, along with many similar examples, in *Portraits contemporains*.
151 *Salon de 1847*, VIII.
152 e.g. *La Presse*, 21 July 1853.

CONCLUSION (pp. 206–223)

1 *Mon*, 7 Jan. 1854. See also Spencer, pp. 93–5.
2 'Théophile Gautier', *L'Artiste*, 13 May 1859, and 'Réflexions sur quelques-uns de mes contemporains', IV, 'Théophile Gautier,' (1861–2); reprinted in Baudelaire, *L'Art romantique*, XVIII, pp. 151–80 and XXI, pp. 250–4.
3 Ibid., p. 167.
4 *Mon*, 26 Nov. 1861.
5 'Gautier was always perhaps the most indulgent of us where

Baudelaire's impertinences were concerned.' By 'us', Feydeau meant the literary and artistic group that would gather for Madame Sabatier's Sunday dinners in her house in the rue Frochot, and which included Sainte-Beuve, Du Camp, the sculptor Préault, and Henri Monnier, among others. Feydeau remarks in passing that he did in fact have to invite himself to these exclusive gatherings; Baudelaire's presence there seems to have aroused his unbridled petulance and irritation, and on the face of it Baudelaire is only mentioned at all in order to demonstrate Gautier's boundless tolerance in action. For 'you really did need the best of characters to swallow all Baudelaire's affronts'. Part of the outburst that follows is worth quoting in full (in all it runs to about seven pages): 'The author of *Les Fleurs du mal* was constantly racking his brains for ways of making himself absolutely insufferable, and he succeeded. Baudelaire had managed to insinuate his way into the little literary phalanx to which I had the honour of belonging, thanks to his genuine talent as a poet; but he got on the nerves of all of us, let's face it, he *stunned* us with his insufferable vanity, his mania for *posing*, the imperturbable coolness with which he uttered the first and least amusing stupidities that came into his head. The mad, unremitting fear of bearing the slightest resemblance to that *bête noire* of artists, which in their circles they call the *bourgeois*, had rapidly dragged the poor boy below the level even of Joseph Prudhomme himself.

'The most amusing thing was, Baudelaire didn't even suspect this. Since his brain was disordered, he naturally abhorred good sense, yet he believed himself to be a superior man in every respect . . .' One day he went just too far for Feydeau. 'I was in no mood. I took offence. I can sometimes be rather sharp. Baudelaire wanted to make some concessions; but it was too late. I told him what I thought of him.'

Such was Baudelaire's effect on Feydeau; Gautier no doubt found Baudelaire's presence more flattering than maddening. Gautier was after all an acknowledged master of the monstrous paradox himself, and one can begin to understand the social relationship of the two poets by envisaging the dinner-table scenes Feydeau recalls. Gautier and Flaubert exercise their wit: 'He and Flaubert would often amuse themselves with witty verbal rallies, and the ingenuous Baudelaire of course took everything they said at face value.' Feydeau, pp. 153–65.

6 Baudelaire, *Petits poëmes en prose*, XLVIII, pp. 139–40.
7 *Mon*, 11 June 1859.
8 '. . . the best account of a picture might be a sonnet or an elegy', Baudelaire wrote in 1846 (*Écrits sur l'art*, vol. I, p. 143), perhaps taking his cue from Gautier. The art criticism of both can be read as a programme for self-fulfilment.
9 *Les Jeunes-France*, preface, pp. 28–9.
10 Parmée, pp. 130–4.
11 *Notices romantiques*, p. 219.
12 Quoted in Grate, p. 129.
13 When Gautier's feelings were blocked, when he found nothing to

engage him in a work of art, he reverted to a similar critical method; he too admitted a concept of that which was 'outside the sphere of art'. See for instance the traditional terms within which he sought to rationalize his antipathy for Courbet's *Enterrement à Ornans*. Every admiration added to the store of Gautier's pleasure; every failure to identify and admire was a personal failure. It is symptomatic of his reluctance to remain uninvolved and unmoved that where he hardly feels obliged to place his pleasurable responses within a larger critical hierarchy, he must always try to justify and temper his dislikes within just such an art-historical or philosophical framework. For Gautier, a traditional, reasoning approach was thus a last resort. As such, it reflects his increasing need for a sense of belonging in the world, and his corresponding desire to experience to the full.

14 Grate, p. 152.
15 Ibid., p. 153. Yet the following year an article by Thoré on 'L'Art des parfums' was published in Gautier's *Ariel* (13 Apr. 1836), the short-lived, deliberately unpolitical organ of *l'art pour l'art*. Thoré's article itself reflects the preoccupations of an aesthete (or of a Gautier) rather than those of a social thinker: '...perfumes, like music, awaken the intuition of things...Does not each fraction of the finite reflect infinity?...'
16 For instance in the preface to his *Salon de 1845*, Alliance des Arts, Paris, 1845, p. XVII, and in *Les Musées de la Hollande*, 2 vols., Renouard, Paris, 1858 and 1860, vol. I, p. 326.
17 Thoré, *Les Musées de la Hollande*, vol. I, conclusion, and vol. II, introduction.
18 *H du r*, p. 18.
19 *J des G*, 26 Dec. 1895.
20 Ibid., 1 May 1857.
21 Ibid., 8 June 1884.
22 Feydeau, p. 115.
23 'No new idea brought forward, no human truth of any depth, no sense of the unfolding pattern of history; nothing but symphonies executed in the commonplaces current in our studios and artists' dens since 1830. The whole written or spoken output of this poet has been an astonishing display of gymnastics in the arena of paradox...One has been charmed, perhaps, but not instructed. Hence the absolute emptiness of his work.' Zola, in *Le Messager de l'Europe*, July 1879. Quoted in P. E. Tennant, *Théophile Gautier*, University of London Press, The Athlone Press, London, 1975, p. 120.
24 Henry James, *French Poets and Novelists*, Macmillan, London, 1878, quoted in Tennant, p. 120.
25 J. L. Sweeney (ed.), *Henry James. The Painter's Eye*, Rupert Hart-Davis, London, 1956, p. 177.
26 Ibid., p. 35.
27 Ibid., p. 184.
28 *Mon*, 6 July 1859.
29 Sweeney, p. 184.

30 Ibid., p. 261.

31 From a letter to Henry Adams, quoted in L. Edel, introduction to Henry James, *The Tragic Muse*, Harper Torchbooks, New York, 1960, p. xvii.

32 'L'Ecole païenne', in *La Semaine théâtrale*, 22 Jan. 1852, repr. in Baudelaire, *L'Art romantique*, X, p. 69.

33 Ibid., p. 70.

34 *Journaux intimes—Mon cœur mis à nu*, LXIX, in Baudelaire, *L'Art romantique*, p. 429.

35 Baudelaire, *L'Art romantique*, X, p. 70.

36 Baudelaire, *Écrits sur l'art*, vol. I, p. 126.

37 Parmée, pp. 107–39.

38 Baudelaire, *L'Art romantique*, XXI, p. 253.

39 *La Presse*, 2 May 1851.

40 Grate, p. 45.

41 For instance, volume I, p. 201, note 1, on Rembrandt the realist against Rembrandt the visionary; p. 212, note 1, on their mutual misgivings in front of Paulus Potter's bull in the Mauritshuis, The Hague; p. 273, note 1, on Vermeer. In June 1858, according to Thoré, after volume I of *Les Musées de la Hollande* had gone to press but before its publication, Gautier had produced a series of articles on the seventeenth-century Dutch school for *Le Moniteur*; it is to these that Thoré claims to refer in the above footnotes, although the nearest traceable article by Gautier on seventeenth-century Dutch painting is to be found in *L'Artiste*, 19 Apr. 1857.

42 They were reviewed favourably and at length by Gautier himself; see for instance an article in *Le Moniteur* of 7 January 1854, which covers the fifth edition of Houssaye's *Galerie des portraits du 18ᵉ siècle*, and *Le Moniteur*, 1 April 1862, on *L'Art au dix-huitième siècle* by Edmond and Jules de Goncourt. If Gautier's contribution to the nineteenth century's taste for the eighteenth cannot be pinned down to any single art-critical or art-historical publication, he remains an early promoter of this taste, as his poetry attests (see, for instance, *Poésies complètes*, vol. II, pp. 73–5. Seymour O. Simches fully explores the vogue of the eighteenth century in *Le Romantisme et le goût esthétique du XVIIIᵉ siècle*, PUF, Paris, 1964). The same argument stands for Gautier and Spanish art, which, again, he approached in the spirit of a traveller and poet, rather than as an art historian bent on discovery and assessment. See also Spencer, pp. 79–87.

43 See Richardson, pp. 140, 142, 278, 286; and Du Camp, *Théophile Gautier*, p. 80, in which a solicitous letter from Courbet is reprinted. 'If I make art,' writes the painter, 'it is firstly to try to earn a living from it, and then to be worthy of the criticism of a few men such as yourself, who will rejoice in my progress all the more for the trouble they have taken in curing me of my vices.'

44 Baudelaire, on Delacroix, in 'L'Exposition Universelle de 1855', *Écrits sur l'art*, vol. I, p. 405.

Selected Bibliography

Baldick, Robert, *Dinner at Magny's*, Victor Gollancz, London, 1971.

Balzac, Honoré de, *Le Lys dans la vallée*, Le Livre de Poche, Paris, 1965.
> *La Peau de chagrin*, (*Oeuvres complètes*, vol. 37,) Société des Editions Littéraires et Artistiques, Paris, 1900–1913.

Baudelaire, Charles, *L'Art romantique, suivi de Fusées, Mon cœur mis à nu, et Pauvre Belgique*, présentation d'Hervé Falcon, Collection Littéraire Julliard, Paris, 1964.
> *Écrits sur l'art*, édition établie, présentée, et annotée par Yves Florenne, 2 vols., Le Livre de Poche, Paris, 1971.
> *Les Fleurs du mal et autres poèmes*, chronologie et préface par Henri Lemaître, Garnier-Flammarion, Paris, 1964.
> *Petits poèmes en prose*, édition critique par Robert Kopp, Librairie José Corti, Paris, 1969,
> and see Parmée.

Benesch, Rita, *Le Regard de Théophile Gautier*, thèse présentée à la Faculté de Lettres de l'Université de Zurich, Juris Druck & Verlag, Zurich, 1969.

Benjamin, Walter, *Charles Baudelaire: A Lyric Poet in the Era of High Capitalism*, trans. Harry Zohn, New Left Books, London, 1973.

Bergerat, Émile, *Théophile Gautier. Entretiens, souvenirs et correspondance*, avec une préface de Edmond de Goncourt et une eau-forte de Félix Braquemond, Charpentier, Paris, 1879.

Bibliothèque Nationale, *Théophile Gautier*, catalogue de l'exposition, 1961–2, Bibliothèque Nationale, Paris, 1961.

Boime, Albert, *The Academy and French Painting in the Nineteenth Century*, Phaidon, London, 1971.

Boschot, Adolphe, *Théophile Gautier*, (Temps et Visages,) Desclée et de Brouwer, Paris, 1933.

Brookner, Anita, *The Genius of the Future. Studies in French Art Criticism. Diderot, Stendhal, Baudelaire, Zola, the Brothers Goncourt, Huysmans*, Phaidon, London, 1971.

Bürger, William, see Thoré.

Castex, Pierre-Georges, *Le Conte fantastique en France de Nodier à Maupassant*, Librairie José Corti, Paris, 1951.
    La Critique d'art en France au XIXe siècle, vols. I and II, Centre de Documentation Universitaire, Paris, 1958.

Cerf, Léon, *Souvenirs de David d'Angers*, Renaissance du Livre, Paris, 1928.

Clark, Timothy J., *The Absolute Bourgeois: artists and politics in France, 1848–1852*, Thames and Hudson, London, 1973.

Cobban, Alfred, *A History of Modern France*, vol. II, *1799–1871*, Penguin, Harmondsworth, 1963.

Delacroix, Eugène, *Correspondance générale d'Eugène Delacroix*, publiée par André Joubin, 5 vols., Librairie Plon, Paris, 1935–8.
    Journal d'Eugène Delacroix, publiée par André Joubin, 3 vols., Librairie Plon, Paris, 1950.

Du Camp, Maxime, *Souvenirs littéraires*, 2 vols., Hachette, Paris, 1882 and 1883.
    Théophile Gautier, (Les Grands Écrivains Français,) Hachette, Paris, 1890.

Easton, Malcolm, *Artists and Writers in Paris. The Bohemian Idea, 1803–1867*, Edward Arnold, London, 1964.

Edel, Leon, Introduction to James, Henry, *The Tragic Muse*, Harper Torchbooks, New York, 1960.

Feydeau, Ernest, *Théophile Gautier. Souvenirs intimes*, E. Plon, Paris, 1874.

Fontaney, Antoine, *Journal intime*, Les Presses Françaises, Paris, 1925.

Fromentin, Eugène, *Les Maîtres d'autrefois. Belgique–Hollande*, Librairie Plon, Paris, 1890.

Gautier, Judith, 'Le Second rang du collier', VIII, *La Revue de Paris*, 1 June 1903.

Gautier, Théophile, *Abécédaire du Salon de 1861*, E. Dentu, Paris, 1861.

L'Art moderne, Michel Lévy Frères, Paris, 1856.

Les Beaux-Arts en Europe, 2 vols., Michel Lévy Frères, Paris, 1855 and 1856.

Le Capitaine Fracasse, préface, chronologie, et notes par Antoine Adam, Gallimard, Paris, 1972.

Caprices et zigzags, Victor Lecou, Paris, 1852.

Fusains et eaux-fortes, Charpentier, Paris, 1880.

Guide de l'amateur au Musée du Louvre, suivi de la vie et les œuvres de quelques peintres, Charpentier, Paris, 1882.

Histoire du romantisme. Notices romantiques. Les progrès de la poésie française depuis 1830, Charpentier, Paris, 1874.

Les Jeunes-France. Romans goguenards, introduction et notes par René Jasinski, Nouvelle Bibliothèque Romantique, Flammarion, Paris, 1974.

Mademoiselle de Maupin, introduction par Geneviève van den Bogaert, Garnier-Flammarion, Paris, 1966.

Ménagerie intime, Lemerre, Paris, 1869.

Œuvres érotiques. Poésies libertines. Lettres à la Présidente, Arcanes, Paris, 1953.

Poésies complètes de Théophile Gautier, publiées par René Jasinski, 3 vols., A. G. Nizet, Paris, 1970.

Portraits contemporains: littérateurs, peintres, sculpteurs, artistes dramatiques, Bibliothèque Charpentier, Fasquelle, Paris, n.d.

Le Roman de la momie, préface par Geneviève van den Bogaert, Garnier-Flammarion, Paris, 1966.

Romans et Contes, Bibliothèque Charpentier, Fasquelle, Paris, n.d.

Salon de 1847, Hetzel, Warnod, Paris, 1847.

Souvenirs de théâtre, d'art et de critique, Charpentier, Paris, 1883.

Tableaux à la plume, Charpentier, Paris, 1880.

Tableaux de siège. Paris, 1870–1871, Charpentier, Paris, 1871.

Trésors de l'art de la Russie ancienne et moderne, Gide, Paris, 1861–1862.

Un Trio de romans, Charpentier, Paris, 1888.

Voyage en Espagne—Tra los montes, Bibliothèque Charpentier, Paris, 1933.

Voyage en Italie (Italia), Charpentier, Paris, 1876.

Goncourt, Edmond et Jules de, *Journal des Goncourt—mémoires de la vie littéraire*, édité et annoté par Robert Ricatte, 4 vols., Fasquelle et Flammarion, Paris, 1956.

   L'Art au dix-huitième siècle, 3 vols., E. Dentu, Paris, 1856–1865.

Gould, Cecil, *Delaroche and Gautier*. *Gautier's views on the 'Execution of Lady Jane Grey' and other compositions by Delaroche*, The National Gallery, London, 1975.

Grate, Pontus, *Deux critiques d'art à l'époque romantique. Gustave Planche et Théophile Thoré*, Almquist & Wiksell, Stockholm, 1959.

Guthrie, W. K. C., *The Greek Philosophers from Thales to Aristotle*, University Paperbacks, Methuen, London, 1967.

Hauser, Arnold, *The Social History of Art*, 2 vols., Routledge and Kegan Paul, London, 1951.

Hemmings, Frederick W. J., *Culture and Society in France, 1848–1898: dissidents and philistines*, (Studies in Cultural History,) Batsford, London, 1971.

Houssaye, Arsène, *Les Confessions. Souvenirs d'un demi-siècle 1830–1880*, E. Dentu, Paris, 1885.

   Galerie de portraits par A. H. Le dix-huitième siècle. Les Poètes et les Philosophes. La Cour et le Théâtre. La Peinture, Charpentier, Paris, 1845.

Hugo, Victor, *Les Feuilles d'automne*, ed. Laurence Bisson, Blackwell, Oxford, 1944.

   Préface de Cromwell, ed. Edmond Wahl, Clarendon Press, Oxford, 1909.

Huysmans, Joris-Karl, *A Rebours*, Bibliothèque Charpentier, Paris, 1895.

James, Henry, see Edel and Sweeney.

Jasinski, René, *Les Années romantiques de Théophile Gautier*, Librairie Vuibert, Paris, 1929.

   (ed.), *Poésies complètes de Théophile Gautier*, 3 vols., A. G. Nizet, Paris, 1970.

Ledré, Charles, *Histoire de la presse*, (Les Temps et les Destins,) Librairie Arthème Fayard, Paris, 1958.

Lovenjoul, Vicomte Spoelberch de, *Histoire des œuvres de Théophile Gautier*, 2 vols., Charpentier, Paris, 1880.

Manévy, Raymond, *L'Évolution des formules de présentation de la presse quotidienne*, Éditions Estienne, Paris, 1956.

Mazedier, René, *Histoire de la presse parisienne de Théophraste Renaudot à la IVᵉ République. 1631–1945*, Éditions du Pavois, Paris, 1945.

Montégut, Émile, *Nos morts contemporains*, vol. II, Hachette, Paris, 1884.

Musée Des Arts Décoratifs, *Équivoques. Peintures françaises du XIXᵉ siècle*, catalogue compilé et presenté par Olivier Lépine, Musée des Arts Décoratifs, Paris, 1973.

Nerval, Gérard de, *Promenades et Souvenirs. Lettres à Jenny. Pandora. Aurélia*, chronologie et préface par Léon Cellier, Garnier-Flammarion, Paris, 1972.

Parmée, D. (ed.), *Selected Critical Studies of Baudelaire*, Cambridge at the University Press, Cambridge, 1949.

Pater, Walter, *The Renaissance. Studies in Art and Poetry*, introduction and notes by Sir Kenneth Clark, Collins, The Fontana Library, London, 1961.

Perouzet, Édouard, *Gérard de Nerval inconnu*, Librairie José Corti, Paris, 1965.

Philadelphia Museum of Art, *The Second Empire 1852–1870. Art in France under Napoleon III*, Philadelphia Museum of Art, Philadelphia, 1978.

Regard, Maurice, *Gustave Planche, 1808–1857. Correspondance—bibliographie—iconographie*, Nouvelles Éditions Latines, Paris, 1954.

Richardson, Joanna, *Théophile Gautier. His Life and Times*, Max Reinhardt, London, 1958.

Ruskin, John, see Shapiro.

Sainte-Beuve, Charles-Augustin, *Les Grands écrivains français*. *Études des lundis et des portraits*, classées selon un ordre nouveau et annotées par Maurice Allem, *XIXe siècle: Les Poètes*, vol. II, Librairie Garnier Frères, Paris, 1926.

Shapiro, Harold I. (ed.), *Ruskin in Italy. Letters to his parents 1845*, Clarendon Press, Oxford, 1972.

Silvestre, Théophile, *Les Artistes français*, vol. I, *Romantiques*, Bibliothèque Dionysienne, Paris, 1926.

Spencer, Michael Clifford, *The Art Criticism of Théophile Gautier*, Librairie Droz, Geneva, 1969.

Sweeney, John L. (ed.), *Henry James. The Painter's Eye. Notes and Essays on the Pictorial Arts*, Rupert Hart-Davis, London, 1956.

Tennant, P. E., *Théophile Gautier*, University of London Press, The Athlone Press, London, 1975.

Thoré, Théophile, *Le Salon de 1845*, Alliance des Arts, Paris, 1845 (Bürger, William,) *Les Musées de la Hollande*, vol. I, *Amsterdam et la Haye. Études sur l'école hollandaise*, vol. II, *Musée van der Hoop, à Amsterdam et Musée de Rotterdam*, Renouard, Paris, 1858 & 1860.

Zola, Émile, *Mon Salon. Manet. Écrits sur l'art*, préface par Antoinette Ehrard, Garnier-Flammarion, Paris, 1970.

Newspapers and Periodicals Consulted

Ariel, journal du monde elégant (1836)

L'Artiste (1856-9)

Le Bien public (1872)

Le Cabinet de l'amateur et de l'antiquaire (1842-3)

Le Cabinet de lecture (1832 & 1836)

L'Événement (1848)

Figaro (1836-7)

La France industrielle (1834)

La France littéraire (1832-1833)

La Gazette des Beaux-Arts (1860 & 1862)

L'Illustration (1866-1867, 1869-1870, & 1872)

Le Journal des Débats (1824)

Le Mercure de France au dix-neuvième siècle (1831)

Le Moniteur universel, continued as *Le Journal officiel de l'empire français* and then as *Le Journal officiel de la république française* (1854-1870)

La Presse (1836-1854), and supplement of June 1848: *Documents pour servir à l'histoire. Révolution française de 1848, liberté de la presse*

La Revue des Deux Mondes (1841, 1847-8)

La Revue de Paris (1841-2)

Index

Numbers in italics refer to plates

Rubens 20, 30, 82, 137
Ruskin, John 172, 176, 178

Saal, Georges 201
Sabatier, Apollonie-Aglaé ('La Présidente') 42, 116, 253–4 n. 5
Sainte-Beuve, Charles-Augustin 37, 42, 175, 237 n. 21, 253–4 n. 5
Saint-Victor, Paul, comte de 39, 51, 167
Scheffer, Ary 64, 165, 166, 173
Schreyer, Adolphe App. I, 252–3, n. 130
—*Chevaux de cosaques irréguliers* 201
Scott, Sir Walter 18, 182
Scribe, Eugène 37, 155
sculpture 114–20, 130–1, 174
—Greek versus medieval 133
Shakespeare, William 18, 75, 242 n. 43
Simart, Pierre-Charles 9, 167
Sorr, Charlotte de 155–6
Soufflot, Jacques-Germain 166
Spoelberch de Lovenjoul, Charles, vicomte de 2
Steen, Jan 137
Stendhal (Henri-Marie Beyle) 4, 45–6, 85, 152–3, 177, 208, 213, 215, 220
superstitions and myths, Gautier's use of 60–9 *passim*, 168
—the avatar, 61–3, 65, 67–8, 94, 97, 202
—the *jettatura* 60–1, 66, 167–8
—the microcosm 58–60, 62, 65–8 *passim*, 72, 76–7, 87–8, App. II 4 and 11, 239–40 n. 4
—*See also* correspondences
Symbolist movement 214

Taine, Hippolyte 215
Teniers, David 28–9
Thackeray, William Makepeace 148
Thiers, Adolphe 72, 240 n. 5
Thoré, Théophile ('William Bür-

ger') 209–11, 220, 255 n. 15, 256 n.41
Titian 24, 52, 82, 120, 129, 182
Tom, Napoléon (Napoléon Thomas) 22
Töpffer, Rodolphe 68
Troyon, Constant App. I
Turner, Joseph Mallord William 30

Velazquez 22–3
Verdier, Marcel App. I
Vermeer 220, 256 n. 41
Verne, Jules 200
Vernet, Émile-Jean-Horace 37, 159
—*Judith* 179
—*La Prise de la Smala* 172
Veronese 82, 146–7
—*The Marriage at Cana* 146–7, App. II 17 and 18, *12*
Vetter, Hégésippe-Jean 62
Vigny, Alfred de 64, 156
Villon, François 17, 46
violence, scenes of 129–32, 179
Viollet-le-Duc, Eugène-Emmanuel 37, 39
Vitet, Louis 215
Voillemot, André-Charles 245 n. 51
Voltaire (François-Marie Arouet) 20

Walewski, Alexandre, comte de 40, 236 n. 81
Watteau, Jean-Antoine 7, 56, 62, 89, 212
Wattier, Émile 62
Whistler, James Abbott McNeill, *La Princesse du pays de la porcelaine* 139
Wilde, Oscar 158
Winckelmann, Johann Joachim 113–14, 146
Winterhalter, Franz-Xavier 160, 165

Ziegler, Jules-Claude 91, 176–7, 179, 190, App. I
Zola, Émile 55–6, 79, 139, 211, 213–14, 217, 253 n. 148, 255 n. 23